.5%
JFMAMJJASONDJFMAMJJASONDJFMAMJJASON
EW YORK STOCK EXCHAN

# Artificial Neural Networks: Forecasting Time Series

*V. Rao Vemuri*
*Robert D. Rogers*

IEEE Computer Society Press
Los Alamitos, California

Washington • Brussels • Tokyo

**Library of Congress Cataloging-in-Publication Data**

Vemuri, V.
    Artificial Neural Networks: Forecasting Time Series / V. Rao Vemuri, Robert D. Rogers.
        p. cm.
    Includes bibliographical references.
    ISBN 0-8186-5120-2 (pbk.) — ISBN 0-8186-5121-0 (microfiche)
    1.  Neural networks (Computer science) I.  Rogers, Robert D.
    II. Title.
    QA76.87.V47  1994
    003'.85'01136 — dc20

93-37174
CIP


Published by the
IEEE Computer Society Press
10662 Los Vaqueros Circle
P.O. Box 3014
Los Alamitos, CA  90720-1264




IEEE Computer Society Press Order Number 5120-05
Library of Congress Number 93-37174
IEEE Catalog Number EH0382-2
ISBN 0-8186-5120-2 (paper)
ISBN 0-8186-5121-0 (microfiche)

Additional copies can be ordered from

IEEE Computer Society Press
Customer Service Center
10662 Los Vaqueros Circle
P.O. Box 3014
Los Alamitos, CA  90720-1264
Tel:  (714) 821-8380
FAX: (714) 821-4641
E-mail: cs.books@computer.org

IEEE Service Center
445 Hoes Lane
P.O. Box 1331
Piscataway, NJ  08855-1331
Tel:  (908) 981-1393
FAX: (908) 981-9667

IEEE Computer Society
13, avenue de l'Aquilon
B-1200 Brussels
BELGIUM
Tel:   +32-2-770-2198
FAX: +32-2-770-8505

IEEE Computer Society
Ooshima Building
2-19-1 Minami-Aoyama
Minato-ku, Tokyo 107
JAPAN
Tel:   +81-3-3408-3118
FAX: +81-3-3408-3553

Technical Editor: Jon Butler
Production Editor: Lisa O'Conner
Cover art: Joe Daigle
Printed in the United States of America by KNI, Incorporated

THE INSTITUTE OF ELECTRICAL AND ELECTRONICS ENGINEERS, INC.

# Table of Contents

# Introduction

# Time Series and the Forecasting Problem

Predictability is fundamental to the modern scientific view of nature. When we write down Newton's laws to calculate the motion of a projectile or a planet, we are implicitly assuming that the motion of such a system is predictable. It is the expectation that we can make meaningful predictions that drives us to seek underlying principles to explain the behavior of systems we observe. In control engineering, for example, the goal is often to combine measurements on a system with some set of fundamental rules to predict and control the system's behavior. In the time series problem we would like to use a series of measurements of a single observable as a function of time to predict what values future measurements will yield.

Many examples of time series are important in engineering and science. One of the best-studied time series is electric power demand, as discussed in "Electric Load Forecasting Using an Artificial Neural Network" by Park et al. in chapter 2. The ability to predict the demand placed on an electric power supply enables a system manager to make effective decisions about consumption of resources. Meteorologists have spent years studying various techniques for forecasting the weather, and although the full problem is inherently three-dimensional, some weather phenomena can be usefully studied as one-dimensional time series. The ability to predict the activity of stocks and other financial instruments carries with it major implications for how investing and securities trading are carried out. In this age of computerized trading, fast, effective analysis and forecasting strategies are highly sought after in the financial markets. Chemical engineers have studied the chaotic behavior of some chemical reactions as a time series problem in order to improve control over the rates at which these processes proceed (see "Nonlinear Signal Processing and System Identification: Application to Time Series from Electrochemical Reactions" by Hudson et al. in chapter 2.) There are many important time series in medicine. For example, the white blood cell count of a cancer patient must be monitored and controlled. Decisions regarding drug dosages for such a patient can be greatly aided by predictions of the white blood cell count time series. Many other chemical relationships in the body, such as the blood glucose and insulin concentrations, can also be studied as time series. In addition, the EEG and ECG time series are of great interest.

Time series themselves exhibit reasonably well-understood behaviors. Often, as is the case for the price of a stock, a time series is composed of a long-term trend plus various periodic and random components. Some periodic components, such as a cyclic variation in the price of grain, are related to the seasons of the year, or they can be related to some other periodic phenomenon, such as a limit cycle. Linear and periodic components are usually easy to model and remove from the time series. One is then left with a series that appears to be random. The prediction of this random component is often the focus of the time series forecasting problem.

The apparently random component of a time series usually falls into one of two categories. In the first case, the apparently random component is truly random; that is, the measurements are drawn from some underlying probability distribution. In this case, the random component can be characterized by a statistical distribution function or by the statistical moments of the data: mean, variance, skew, kurtosis, and so on. To a large extent, short-time-scale variations of stock prices are of this nature, as is the count rate in a Geiger counter placed near a radioactive isotope. In this category of time series, the simple statistical description of the system might be improved if the time series data are correlated on the time scale of interest. The level of water in a river can exhibit such behavior. The water level may fluctuate on short time scales, but measurements made within a single day will cluster around some mean that varies from day to day. Such correlations allow more precise predictions of future values and the expected deviations from these predictions.

The second class of apparently random behavior in time series is not random at all, but rather, chaotic. A chaotic time series is characterized by values that appear to be randomly distributed and non periodic but are actually the result of a completely deterministic process. The deterministic behavior in a chaotic time series is usually due to underlying nonlinear dynamics.

The behavior of a dynamical system can be described in terms of its trajectory in phase space. For a system whose dynamics are a function of only one variable ($x$), the phase space is the $\dot{x}$ - $x$ plane, often called the phase plane. The set of all values of $\dot{x}$ and $x$ taken by the system form a non-self-intersecting trajectory in this plane. Figure 1 shows the phase space trajectory for the one-dimensional nonlinear oscillator governed by the equation

$$\ddot{x} = -x - \frac{1}{2}(\dot{x})^2 \ . \tag{1}$$

The trajectories of nonlinear systems in phase space are generally constrained to move on surfaces that have significantly fewer dimensions than the full phase space of the system. A two-dimensional dynamical system (for example, one that can move in the two dimensions $x$ and $y$) would have a four-dimensional phase space, but might actually only move on the surface of a sphere inscribed in the four-dimensional phase space. Constraints such as this are the result of conservation laws that severely limit the types of behavior the system can exhibit. For instance, the total energy of an isolated dynamical system can never increase, since energy is a conserved quantity. In a dynamical system without dissipation, the trajectories of the system in phase space are a set of nested closed curves. In a dissipative nonlinear system, all initial conditions lead to trajectories that either lie on a single surface or converge to individual points in phase space. The set of these surfaces and points in phase space, to which all possible trajectories of the system converge, is called the attractor of the system. The attractor of a chaotic system has nonintegral, or fractal, dimension and is called a strange attractor.

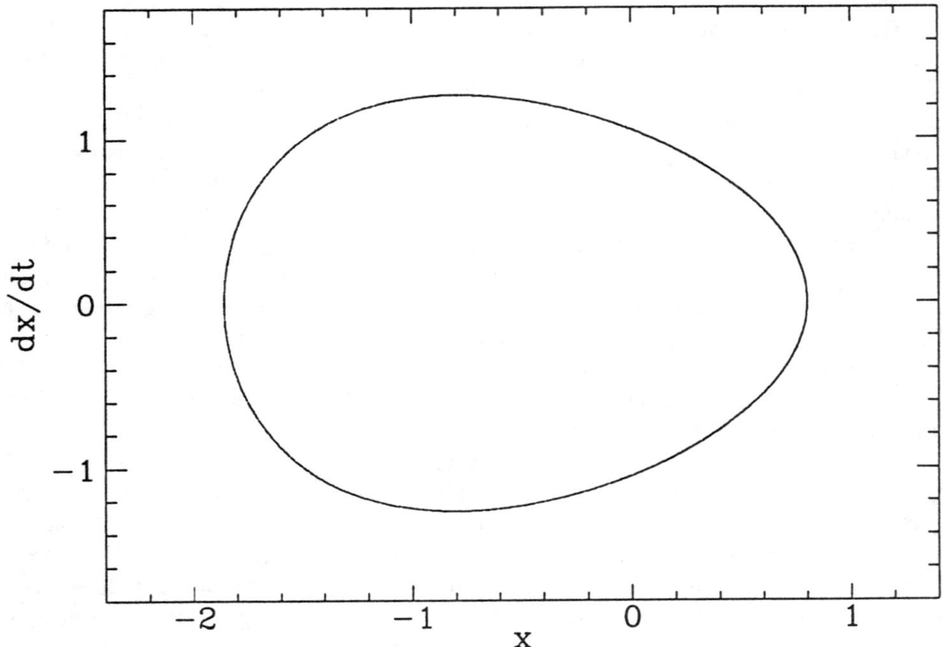

**Figure 1. Trajectory in the phase plane of nonlinear oscillator described by equation (1).**

The importance of the strange attractor to the forecasting of a chaotic time series is twofold. First, its structure determines a theoretical limit to how far into the future the time series can be predicted. On the strange attractor surface, nearby trajectories diverge exponentially from one another, implying that any small error in a prediction of a chaotic time series will grow exponentially. The result is that long-term predictions are impossible. There is a natural time scale associated with this exponential growth of errors, which is specific to the type of chaotic system under consideration. This divergence is quantified by a

Liapunov exponent of the system. Since chaotic time series are deterministic, short-term predictions of them can be made, as long as the length of the prediction is shorter than this error growth time. Second, as we shall see later, the shape of the strange attractor determines how an artificial neural network predicts a chaotic time series.

Now that the desirability of modeling time series has been demonstrated, one might ask, "How do we go about making predictions of time series?" Ideally, we would like to use past data to construct a set of basic rules, like Newton's laws, that can be used to make predictions under very general circumstances. Unfortunately, this approach cannot always be carried out in practice. In some cases, the underlying principles are not known or are poorly understood because the system of interest is very complicated. This is the case with the stock market, in which relationships between various parameters are not known, and some of the relevant parameters, such as public opinion and world events, may not be accessible to us or quantifiable. Another problem with this approach is that often, even when the basic laws are known, direct solution of the equations is not possible without detailed information about initial values and boundary conditions. Fluid flow is an example of this situation because the hydrodynamic laws are known but their exact solution requires us to specify the initial conditions throughout the volume of interest as well as the boundary conditions along the entire surface, which may be quite complex. In practice, even barring the possibility of turbulence in the system, it is often impossible to make enough measurements to specify the system sufficiently.

In a second approach to time series analysis one avoids these problems by making the assumption that a well-defined relationship exists between the past and future values of a single observable. In this phenomenological approach one seeks an approximate functional relationship between past values and the future value one wants to calculate. There are various ways to model this relationship. One can make a recursive prescription for extrapolating the most recent data points based on the success of previous extrapolations. One can also parameterize the time dependences of the various statistical moments and time derivatives of the time series of interest. Alternatively, one can try to find a single function that gives a future value of the observable as its output when some set of past observables is supplied as its input. This last model is implemented by artificial neural networks (ANNs), as will be explained below. The main thrust of this volume is to present an exposition of how ANNs carry out this procedure and to describe the research that has resulted from exploring this viewpoint.

An artificial neural network is essentially a group of interconnected computing elements, or neurons. Typically, a neuron computes the sum of its inputs (which are either the outputs of other neurons or external inputs to the system) and passes this sum through a nonlinear function, such as a sigmoid or hard threshold. Each neuron has only one output, but this output is multiplied by a weighting factor if it is to be used as the input to another neuron. The result is that there is a separate, adjustable weight parameter for each connection between neurons.

Neural networks typically exhibit two types of behavior. If no feedback loops connect neurons, the signal produced by an external input moves in only one direction and the output of the network is just the output of the last group of neurons in the network. In this case the network behaves mathematically like a nonlinear function of the inputs. This feedforward type of network is most often used in time series forecasting, with past time series values as the inputs and the desired future value as the output. The second type of network behavior is observed when there are feedback loops in the neuron connections. In this case the network behaves like a dynamical system, so the outputs of the neurons vary with time. The neuron outputs can then oscillate, or settle down into steady state values, or, since the threshold function introduces nonlinearity into the system, they can become chaotic.

Since neural networks are inherently nonlinear and often exhibit chaotic behavior, a great deal of research is being done on their dynamical behavior, especially behavior that mimics real-world chaotic systems. A companion volume to this book, *Artificial Neural Networks: Oscillations, Chaos and Temporal Sequences,* by Lipo Wang and Daniel L. Alkon, (IEEE CS Press, Los Alamitos, Calif., 1993) addresses this exciting field of research and discusses many of the current applications. Such applications include modeling of chaotic processes in the brain and using chaotic dynamics to encode and decode speech signals for automated speech recognition.

In this introductory treatment of how ANNs predict time series, the specifics of the training process will not be discussed. For a review of how feedforward networks are trained, see the article "Learning Representations by Back-Propagating Errors" by Rumelhart, Hinton, and Williams. A more general discussion of the different types of ANNs available and how they are trained can be found in the books listed in the bibliography. For the purposes of time series analysis, an ANN can be thought of as a general nonlinear mapping between some subset of the past time series values and a future time series value. The specific mapping performed by the network depends on the architecture of the network (number of neurons, number of hidden layers, the manner in which neurons are connected, and so on) and the values of the connection weights between neurons. For a specific network architecture, training can then be thought of as the process of adjusting the weight parameters to achieve a mapping that approximates the underlying relationship between past and future time series values. The output error of a network is defined to be the r.m.s. sum of the differences between the network outputs and the actual time series values they are supposed to predict. In this light, training a neural network can be viewed as an optimization problem: the minimization of the output error with respect to the weights. Optimization is a well-studied field, and many excellent optimization techniques are available for training neural networks in addition to the classical back-propagation algorithm. In fact, it is important to recognize that back-propagation is an algorithm for calculating the derivatives of the error with respect to the network weights. These derivatives can then be used in an optimization algorithm such as the generalized delta rule (method of steepest descent) and the conjugate gradient algorithm. Other algorithms, such as simulated annealing, might not use the local derivatives at all, but can still train a neural network efficiently.

In practice one usually subdivides the available time series data into two time segments: the training data set and the test data set. The data from the first segment are used to train the network. The network that results from the training process is then checked against the data from the test data set to determine whether the mapping performed by the network is a good representation of the time series and can therefore be expected to make reasonable predictions. This step can be accomplished in two ways. To test for short-term prediction accuracy, the network is given actual time series values from the test data set as its input and the resulting output is compared with the next time series point. This is done for every point in the test data set, and an error statistic is calculated. This error estimates the accuracy of short-term predictions by the network.

The ability of the network to make longer-term predictions can also be tested. To do this, the network is given an input vector from near the beginning of the test data set. The output of the network, which is the predicted future time series value, is then used as part of the next input vector. The output from the second prediction is likewise used as part of the third input vector. Continuing the process in this way, the network recursively propagates the time series forward in time to make a prediction many time steps ahead. The divergence of the prediction from the actual time series as a function of the number of time steps indicates how far into the future the network predictions can be used. Often the short- and long-term prediction properties of ANNs are very different, so this is a useful test to perform before making predictions longer than one time step into the future.

Another practical issue in time series prediction is the size of the network. As in most ANN research, no rule determines how many input and hidden-layer neurons to use. There are a few practical guidelines, however. In order for the network to be a completely general mapping, there must be at least one hidden layer. This is a well-known result of ANN research (see, for example, the books by Rumelhart and McClelland that are listed in the Annotated Bibliography). The smallest network that can learn the training data is usually desirable, because it is more likely to be generalizable to new time series data than a larger network. A network that is too large will tend to overfit the data points from the training data set without finding any underlying relationship between them. Such a network cannot predict the behavior of the time series for input vectors it hasn't seen before. A small network, with fewer free parameters, is forced to find an underlying relationship between inputs and output, and this mapping is more likely to be generalizable to future time series behavior. On the other hand, a network that is too small may not have enough free parameters to learn the training data. In practice one often starts with a very small network and increases the number of hidden-layer neurons until the desired prediction performance is obtained.

Similar considerations apply to the number of inputs to the network. The network must be given enough past data in each input vector to span the phase space of the time series, but too many inputs simply slow down convergence of the training process and increase the number of possible undesirable mappings. Again, unless something is known about the dynamics generating the time series, experimentation is required to determine the optimum number of inputs. Performance on the test data set is usually the best guide available.

We have seen that the training process results in a neural network that maps the past values of a time series into a future value of that time series. The formation of this mapping is an interpolation process, which ANNs are particularly good at. In the training process the network effectively interpolates a surface between the input and output vectors. When the time series is a dissipative dynamical system, the interpolation surface is generally an approximation to the attractor of the system or, in the case of a chaotic system, the strange attractor. As an example, consider the iterative map generated by the rule

$$x_{i+1} = ax_i (1 - x_i) \tag{2}$$

which is chaotic when $a \geq 3.5699$. As discussed by Lowe and Webb in chapter 2 of this volume, when trained with data from this map, the network interpolates the parabolic shape of the locus of allowed points in the $x_{i+1} - x_i$ plane and *not* the time series itself. This is an important point: neural networks generally interpolate an underlying dynamical relationship, not the explicit time dependence of the time series. Many questions regarding exactly how ANNs do this remain unanswered. For instance, no quantitative criteria exist for how complicated a dynamical system a particular ANN can learn or for how many past data are required to achieve some desired prediction accuracy. Hopefully this book will stimulate future work in these areas.

## Organization of this volume

In choosing the papers for this volume from the many works in the field, we have tried to bring together representative papers from as many different points of view as possible. The resulting collection of papers does represent a broad array of approaches in time series forecasting with ANNs and also points out an important aspect of the current literature in this rapidly changing field. The majority of the work reflects the state of the art, which is still in an exploratory phase. One goal of this collection was to combine many of these efforts into a single volume so that newcomers to the field can quickly see what has been done and what needs to be worked on in the future. Another implication of this approach is that some papers have been included because they represent a unique perspective on the problem, even though they may be flawed in some other way.

This volume is logically organized into four sections. The first section is an introduction to time series forecasting with ANNs, which begins with this introductory chapter. As part of our introductory material we have included the paper "Learning Representations by Back-Propagating Errors" by Rumelhart, Hinton, and Williams, which discusses the back-propagation method for feedforward neural networks, the most commonly used architecture in time series analysis. We included this paper because it describes neural networks and the basic concepts of network training. However, it is important to note that training is an optimization problem. As such, many optimization techniques are available that are more efficient than the classical back-propagation algorithm. At the end of this book we have included a review of some of the resources available in neural computing. This list includes information about ANN bulletin boards, public domain software, commercial neural network software and hardware, and other resources that might be helpful to both the experienced and the novice neural network user.

The second section of this volume contains articles on the basic principles of the time series problem and the application of ANNs to it. The first article, by Lowe and Webb, explores the relationships between dynamical systems, functional interpolation, and ANNs. Although it does not give much detail on the neural networks used in the analysis, this paper is one of only a few that elucidate the relationships between time series forecasting with ANNs and dynamical systems theory. The paper by Tang et al. makes a quantitative comparison between ANN and classical time series forecasting methods and serves to introduce some of these methods, including the Box-Jenkins technique. The reader should note that the authors of this paper do not quote the statistical significance of their results, which we feel is necessary for comparisons between techniques. The paper by Weigend et al. presents a method for eliminating superfluous network weights (pruning) based on information-theoretic ideas and then applies the resulting system to predict sunspot activity and currency exchange rates. (There are many other pruning techniques with such picturesque names as "optimal brain damage" and "optimal brain surgeon," and the reader is encouraged to explore the literature on this topic.) The papers by Hudson et al. and Park et al. demonstrate the application of ANNs to the forecasting of electrochemical reactions and the loads on electric power systems, respectively. An important component of the Hudson et al. paper is its discussion of the behavior of the time series in the phase plane. The final paper in this section, by Chakraborty et al., studies the use of ANNs in multivariate time series forecasting and compares the results of neural networks and classical methods for forecasting futures prices.

Articles in the third section of this volume focus on chaotic time series and discuss work in predicting them with ANNs. The article by Farmer and Sidorowich discusses the basic principles of, and theoretical limitations on, predicting chaotic time series. The other paper in this section, by Deppisch et al., presents a hierarchical neural network model in which successive network modules are trained to improve performance and speed up the training process. The resulting system is applied to the problem of forecasting chaotic time series.

The final section of this book is a collection of papers that present the results of some experiments using neural networks other than the simple feedforward network. This section, which begins with the article by Sanger on a network whose architecture is modified during training, is intended to give the reader a flavor of the various approaches available to the engineer interested in studying time series with ANNs. The Sanger paper describes some of the important relationships between function approximation and time series forecasting that make ANNs appropriate for prediction problems. The paper by Zaknich et al. describes a modification of the probabilistic neural network (PNN) that makes it suitable for time series forecasting. Mead et al. discuss the connectionist normalized local spline (CNLS) network and demonstrate its effectiveness in predicting the chaotic Mackey-Glass equation, a benchmark time series problem. Ensley and Nelson test the forecasting performance of the cascade correlation network, another network whose architecture evolves during training. These authors also discuss an alternative error statistic that is useful in comparing the forecasting accuracies of different methods. This section is concluded with a partially annotated bibliography of other important articles in the field of time series forecasting that did not appear in this volume because of space limitations.

While assembling this collection of papers, we were impressed by the wide range of fields in which ANN techniques have been used to forecast the behavior of time series. ANN methods are often simpler to implement and can yield better predictions than classical time series forecasting methods. We hope that this collection of papers will help make this interesting and powerful technique available to more people whose work can benefit by it and that it encourages further development of some of the techniques and ideas found within these pages.

# Learning representations
# by back-propagating errors

David E. Rumelhart*, Geoffrey E. Hinton†
& Ronald J. Williams*

* Institute for Cognitive Science, C-015, University of California,
San Diego, La Jolla, California 92093, USA
† Department of Computer Science, Carnegie-Mellon University,
Pittsburgh, Philadelphia 15213, USA

---

**We describe a new learning procedure, back-propagation, for networks of neurone-like units. The procedure repeatedly adjusts the weights of the connections in the network so as to minimize a measure of the difference between the actual output vector of the net and the desired output vector. As a result of the weight adjustments, internal 'hidden' units which are not part of the input or output come to represent important features of the task domain, and the regularities in the task are captured by the interactions of these units. The ability to create useful new features distinguishes back-propagation from earlier, simpler methods such as the perceptron-convergence procedure[1].**

There have been many attempts to design self-organizing neural networks. The aim is to find a powerful synaptic modification rule that will allow an arbitrarily connected neural network to develop an internal structure that is appropriate for a particular task domain. The task is specified by giving the desired state vector of the output units for each state vector of the input units. If the input units are directly connected to the output units, it is relatively easy to find learning rules that iteratively adjust the relative strengths of the connections so as to progressively reduce the difference between the actual and desired output vectors[2]. Learning becomes more interesting but

more difficult when we introduce hidden units whose actual or desired states are not specified by the task. (In perceptrons, there are 'feature analysers' between the input and output that are not true hidden units because their input connections are fixed by hand, so their states are completely determined by the input vector: they do not learn representations.) The learning procedure must decide under what circumstances the hidden units should be active in order to help achieve the desired input–output behaviour. This amounts to deciding what these units should represent. We demonstrate that a general purpose and relatively simple procedure is powerful enough to construct appropriate internal representations.

The simplest form of the learning procedure is for layered networks which have a layer of input units at the bottom; any number of intermediate layers; and a layer of output units at the top. Connections within a layer or from higher to lower layers are forbidden, but connections can skip intermediate layers. An input vector is presented to the network by setting the states of the input units. Then the states of the units in each layer are determined by applying equations (1) and (2) to the connections coming from lower layers. All units within a layer have their states set in parallel, but different layers have their states set sequentially, starting at the bottom and working upwards until the states of the output units are determined.

The total input, $x_j$, to unit $j$ is a linear function of the outputs, $y_i$, of the units that are connected to $j$ and of the weights, $w_{ji}$, on these connections

$$x_j = \sum_i y_i w_{ji} \tag{1}$$

Units can be given biases by introducing an extra input to each unit which always has a value of 1. The weight on this extra input is called the bias and is equivalent to a threshold of the opposite sign. It can be treated just like the other weights.

A unit has a real-valued output, $y_j$, which is a non-linear function of its total input

$$y_j = \frac{1}{1 + e^{-x_j}} \tag{2}$$

Reprinted by permission from *Nature*, Vol. 323, October 9, 1986, pp. 533-536. Copyright © 1986 Macmillan Magazines Ltd.

---

† To whom correspondence should be addressed

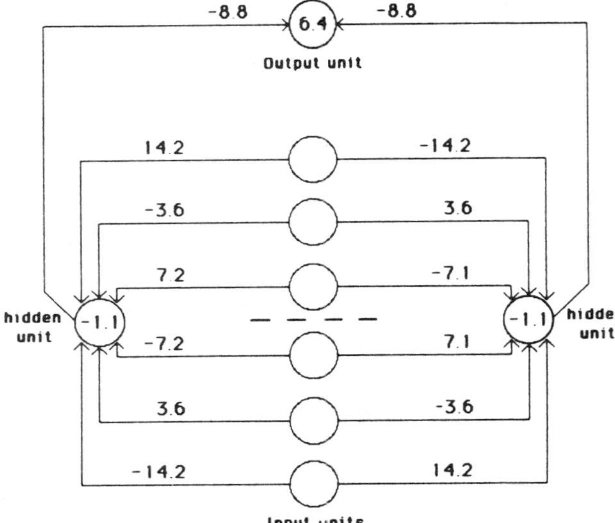


**Fig. 1** A network that has learned to detect mirror symmetry in the input vector. The numbers on the arcs are weights and the numbers inside the nodes are biases. The learning required 1,425 sweeps through the set of 64 possible input vectors, with the weights being adjusted on the basis of the accumulated gradient after each sweep. The values of the parameters in equation (9) were $\varepsilon = 0.1$ and $\alpha = 0.9$. The initial weights were random and were uniformly distributed between $-0.3$ and $0.3$. The key property of this solution is that for a given hidden unit, weights that are symmetric about the middle of the input vector are equal in magnitude and opposite in sign. So if a symmetrical pattern is presented, both hidden units will receive a net input of 0 from the input units, and, because the hidden units have a negative bias, both will be off. In this case the output unit, having a positive bias, will be on. Note that the weights on each side of the midpoint are in the ratio $1:2:4$. This ensures that each of the eight patterns that can occur above the midpoint sends a unique activation sum to each hidden unit, so the only pattern below the midpoint that can exactly balance this sum is the symmetrical one. For all non-symmetrical patterns, both hidden units will receive non-zero activations from the input units. The two hidden units have identical patterns of weights but with opposite signs, so for every non-symmetric pattern one hidden unit will come on and suppress the output unit.

It is not necessary to use exactly the functions given in equations (1) and (2). Any input–output function which has a bounded derivative will do. However, the use of a linear function for combining the inputs to a unit before applying the nonlinearity greatly simplifies the learning procedure.

The aim is to find a set of weights that ensure that for each input vector the output vector produced by the network is the same as (or sufficiently close to) the desired output vector. If there is a fixed, finite set of input–output cases, the total error in the performance of the network with a particular set of weights can be computed by comparing the actual and desired output vectors for every case. The total error, $E$, is defined as

$$E = \tfrac{1}{2} \sum_c \sum_j (y_{j,c} - d_{j,c})^2 \qquad (3)$$

where $c$ is an index over cases (input–output pairs), $j$ is an index over output units, $y$ is the actual state of an output unit and $d$ is its desired state. To minimize $E$ by gradient descent it is necessary to compute the partial derivative of $E$ with respect to each weight in the network. This is simply the sum of the partial derivatives for each of the input–output cases. For a given case, the partial derivatives of the error with respect to each weight are computed in two passes. We have already described the forward pass in which the units in each layer have their states determined by the input they receive from units in lower layers using equations (1) and (2). The backward pass which propagates derivatives from the top layer back to the bottom one is more complicated.

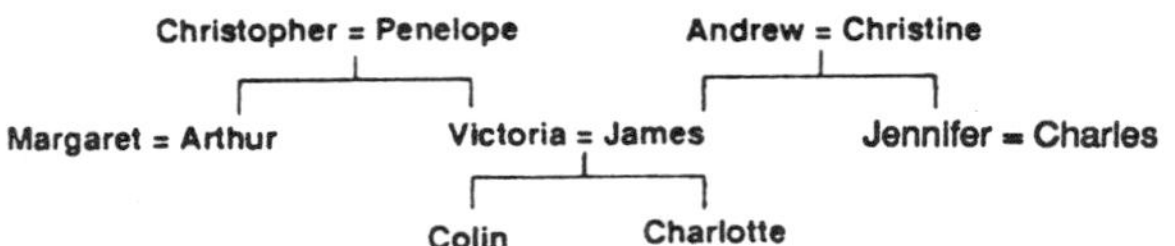


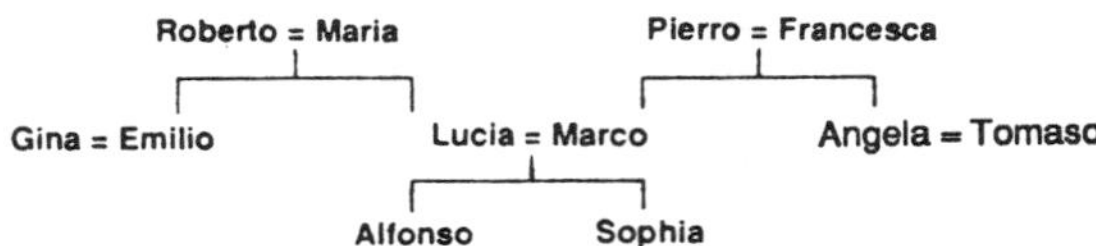


**Fig. 2** Two isomorphic family trees. The information can be expressed as a set of triples of the form ⟨person 1⟩⟨relationship⟩⟨person 2⟩, where the possible relationships are {father, mother, husband, wife, son, daughter, uncle, aunt, brother, sister, nephew, niece}. A layered net can be said to 'know' these triples if it can produce the third term of each triple when given the first two. The first two terms are encoded by activating two of the input units, and the network must then complete the proposition by activating the output unit that represents the third term.

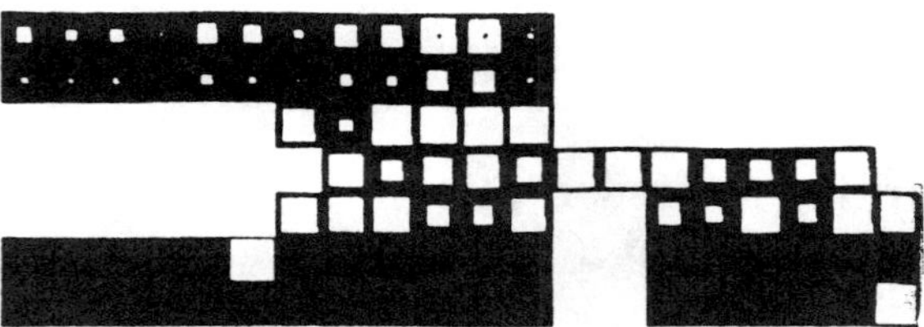

**Fig. 3** Activity levels in a five-layer network after it has learned. The bottom layer has 24 input units on the left for representing ⟨person 1⟩ and 12 input units on the right for representing the relationship. The white squares inside these two groups show the activity levels of the units. There is one active unit in the first group representing Colin and one in the second group representing the relationship 'has aunt'. Each of the two input groups is totally connected to its own group of 6 units in the second layer. These groups learn to encode people and relationships as distributed patterns of activity. The second layer is totally connected to the central layer of 12 units, and these are connected to the penultimate layer of 6 units. The activity in the penultimate layer must activate the correct output units, each of which stands for a particular ⟨person 2⟩. In this case, there are two correct answers (marked by black dots) because Colin has two aunts. Both the input units and the output units are laid out spatially with the English people in one row and the isomorphic Italians immediately below.

The backward pass starts by computing $\partial E / \partial y$ for each of the output units. Differentiating equation (3) for a particular case, $c$, and suppressing the index $c$ gives

$$\partial E / \partial y_j = y_j - d_j \qquad (4)$$

We can then apply the chain rule to compute $\partial E / \partial x_j$

$$\partial E / \partial x_j = \partial E / \partial y_j \cdot dy_j / dx_j$$

Differentiating equation (2) to get the value of $dy_j / dx_j$ and substituting gives

$$\partial E / \partial x_j = \partial E / \partial y_j \cdot y_j (1 - y_j) \qquad (5)$$

This means that we know how a change in the total input $x$ to an output unit will affect the error. But this total input is just a linear function of the states of the lower level units and it is also a linear function of the weights on the connections, so it is easy to compute how the error will be affected by changing these states and weights. For a weight $w_{ji}$, from $i$ to $j$ the derivative is

$$\partial E / \partial w_{ji} = \partial E / \partial x_j \cdot \partial x_j / \partial w_{ji}$$
$$= \partial E / \partial x_j \cdot y_i \qquad (6)$$

and for the output of the $i^{\text{th}}$ unit the contribution to $\partial E / \partial y_i$

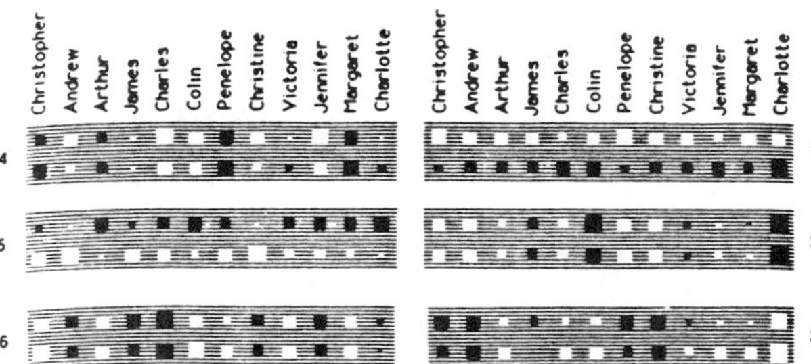

**Fig. 4** The weights from the 24 input units that represent people to the 6 units in the second layer that learn distributed representations of people. White rectangles, excitatory weights; black rectangles, inhibitory weights; area of the rectangle encodes the magnitude of the weight. The weights from the 12 English people are in the top row of each unit. Unit 1 is primarily concerned with the distinction between English and Italian and most of the other units ignore this distinction. This means that the representation of an English person is very similar to the representation of their Italian equivalent. The network is making use of the isomorphism between the two family trees to allow it to share structure and it will therefore tend to generalize sensibly from one tree to the other. Unit 2 encodes which generation a person belongs to, and unit 6 encodes which branch of the family they come from. The features captured by the hidden units are not at all explicit in the input and output encodings, since these use a separate unit for each person. Because the hidden features capture the underlying structure of the task domain, the network generalizes correctly to the four triples on which it was not trained. We trained the network for 1500 sweeps, using $\varepsilon = 0.005$ and $\alpha = 0.5$ for the first 20 sweeps and $\varepsilon = 0.01$ and $\alpha = 0.9$ for the remaining sweeps. To make it easier to interpret the weights we introduced 'weight-decay' by decrementing every weight by 0.2% after each weight change. After prolonged learning, the decay was balanced by $\partial E/\partial w$, so the final magnitude of each weight indicates its usefulness in reducing the error. To prevent the network needing large weights to drive the outputs to 1 or 0, the error was considered to be zero if output units that should be on had activities above 0.8 and output units that should be off had activities below 0.2.

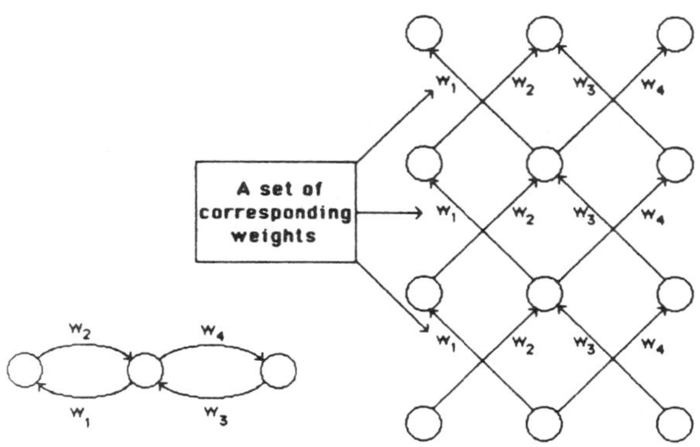

**Fig. 5** A synchronous iterative net that is run for three iterations and the equivalent layered net. Each time-step in the recurrent net corresponds to a layer in the layered net. The learning procedure for layered nets can be mapped into a learning procedure for iterative nets. Two complications arise in performing this mapping: first, in a layered net the output levels of the units in the intermediate layers during the forward pass are required for performing the backward pass (see equations (5) and (6)). So in an iterative net it is necessary to store the history of output states of each unit. Second, for a layered net to be equivalent to an iterative net, corresponding weights between different layers must have the same value. To preserve this property, we average $\partial E/\partial w$ for all the weights in each set of corresponding weights and then change each weight in the set by an amount proportional to this average gradient. With these two provisos, the learning procedure can be applied directly to iterative nets. These nets can then either learn to perform iterative searches or learn sequential structures[4].

resulting from the effect of $i$ on $j$ is simply

$$\partial E/\partial x_j \cdot \partial x_j/\partial y_i = \partial E/\partial x_j \cdot w_{ji}$$

so taking into account all the connections emanating from unit $i$ we have

$$\partial E/\partial y_i = \sum_j \partial E/\partial x_j \cdot w_{ji} \tag{7}$$

We have now seen how to compute $\partial E/\partial y$ for any unit in the penultimate layer when given $\partial E/\partial y$ for all units in the last layer. We can therefore repeat this procedure to compute this term for successively earlier layers, computing $\partial E/\partial w$ for the weights as we go.

One way of using $\partial E/\partial w$ is to change the weights after every input–output case. This has the advantage that no separate memory is required for the derivatives. An alternative scheme, which we used in the research reported here, is to accumulate $\partial E/\partial w$ over all the input–output cases before changing the weights. The simplest version of gradient descent is to change each weight by an amount proportional to the accumulated $\partial E/\partial w$

$$\Delta w = -\varepsilon \partial E/\partial w \tag{8}$$

This method does not converge as rapidly as methods which make use of the second derivatives, but it is much simpler and can easily be implemented by local computations in parallel hardware. It can be significantly improved, without sacrificing the simplicity and locality, by using an acceleration method in which the current gradient is used to modify the velocity of the point in weight space instead of its position

$$\Delta w(t) = -\varepsilon \partial E/\partial w(t) + \alpha \Delta w(t-1) \tag{9}$$

where $t$ is incremented by 1 for each sweep through the whole set of input–output cases, and $\alpha$ is an exponential decay factor between 0 and 1 that determines the relative contribution of the current gradient and earlier gradients to the weight change.

To break symmetry we start with small random weights. Variants on the learning procedure have been discovered independently by David Parker (personal communication) and by Yann Le Cun[3].

One simple task that cannot be done by just connecting the input units to the output units is the detection of symmetry. To detect whether the binary activity levels of a one-dimensional array of input units are symmetrical about the centre point, it is essential to use an intermediate layer because the activity in an individual input unit, considered alone, provides no evidence about the symmetry or non-symmetry of the whole input vector, so simply adding up the evidence from the individual input units is insufficient. (A more formal proof that intermediate units are required is given in ref. 2.) The learning procedure discovered an elegant solution using just two intermediate units, as shown in Fig. 1.

Another interesting task is to store the information in the two family trees (Fig. 2). Figure 3 shows the network we used, and Fig. 4 shows the 'receptive fields' of some of the hidden units after the network was trained on 100 of the 104 possible triples.

So far, we have only dealt with layered, feed-forward networks. The equivalence between layered networks and recurrent networks that are run iteratively is shown in Fig. 5.

The most obvious drawback of the learning procedure is that the error-surface may contain local minima so that gradient descent is not guaranteed to find a global minimum. However, experience with many tasks shows that the network very rarely gets stuck in poor local minima that are significantly worse than the global minimum. We have only encountered this undesirable behaviour in networks that have just enough connections to perform the task. Adding a few more connections creates extra dimensions in weight-space and these dimensions provide paths around the barriers that create poor local minima in the lower dimensional subspaces.

The learning procedure, in its current form, is not a plausible model of learning in brains. However, applying the procedure to various tasks shows that interesting internal representations can be constructed by gradient descent in weight-space, and this suggests that it is worth looking for more biologically plausible ways of doing gradient descent in neural networks.

We thank the System Development Foundation and the Office of Naval Research for financial support.

Received 1 May; accepted 31 July 1986.


1. Rosenblatt, F. *Principles of Neurodynamics* (Spartan, Washington, DC, 1961).
2. Minsky, M. L. & Papert, S. *Perceptrons* (MIT, Cambridge, 1969).
3. Le Cun, Y. *Proc. Cognitiva* **85,** 599–604 (1985).
4. Rumelhart, D. E., Hinton, G. E. & Williams, R. J. in *Parallel Distributed Processing: Explorations in the Microstructure of Cognition.* Vol. 1: *Foundations* (eds Rumelhart, D. E. & McClelland, J. L.) 318–362 (MIT, Cambridge, 1986).

# Time Series Forecasting with Feedforward Networks

# Time series prediction by adaptive networks: a dynamical systems perspective

D. Lowe
A.R. Webb

"Time Series Prediction by Adaptive Networks: A Dynamical Systems Perspective" by D. Lowe and A.R. Webb from *IEE Proceedings-F*, Vol. 128, No. 1, Feb. 1991, pp. 17-24. Copyright © 1991 by the Institution of Elecrical Engineers, reprinted with permission.

*Indexing terms: Nonlinear time series prediction, Neural networks, Dynamical systems, Iterated maps*

**Abstract:** The links between adaptive layered networks, functional interpolation and dynamical systems are considered and applied to the nonlinear predictive analysis of time series. The ability of networks to produce interpolation surfaces to generators of data (i.e. differential equations, iterative maps) is used to analyse a variety of time series. If a network may be trained to approximate a (static) generator of data, the network may be iterated on its own output to produce a time series with the same characteristics as the training waveform. However, since iterated networks are one example of nonlinear dynamical systems, this raises problems of sensitive dependence upon initial conditions leading ultimately to deterministic chaos. An introduction to the relevant concepts is presented and illustrations are provided from simple chaotic maps, nonlinear differential equations, and stock-market prediction. The latter example is included to illustrate the problems which often occur in real-world data due to noise, undersampling, high dimensionality and insufficient data.

## 1 Introduction

One of the central rôles of science in the study of naturally occuring phenomena is in forecasting: given knowledge about a system and its past behaviour, what predictions can be made regarding its future evolution. The two basic methods by which such predictions are made may be classified into a model-based approach and a statistical approach. The first approach assumes that there is sufficient a priori information (for instance in the form of physical conservation laws) that a first-principles derivation may be made to construct an accurate model of the mechanism which is generating the observed processes. There are two difficulties with this approach. One is that it is not often possible to generate an accurate model since the underlying 'laws' may not be fully understood, as in stock-market forecasting. Secondly, even if an accurate model can be constructed, the specification of the current state from which the model can predict, may require much more information than is practically obtainable. In weather forecasting the model takes the form of a set of partial differential equations whose initial state requires functions to be continuously specified in three dimensions, whereas in practice one may have a spatially nonuniform sparse sample of observations to specify the initial state.

The second approach attempts to analyse the sequence of observations produced by the underlying mechanism directly. From the statistics or dynamics obtained from the observation sequence one hopes to be able to infer some knowledge about the future evolution of the observation sequence. The problem with this latter approach is that nature tends to produce very complicated, often irregular, chaotic behaviour which is apparently the result of a self interaction of a system with a large (possibly infinite) number of degrees of freedom. Consistent with this viewpoint, contemporary forecasting theory has developed to assume that the observation sequence may be considered to be one specific realisation of a random process, where the randomness arises from the many independent degrees of freedom interacting linearly. However, the emerging view in dynamical systems theory is that apparently random behaviour may be generated by deterministic systems with only a small number of degrees of freedom, but which interact *nonlinearly* to produce deterministic chaos. This reflects one of the difficulties in attempting to construct a model of the underlying *generator* of the observation sequence, since most of contemporary physics and engineering relies on the superposition principle — an inherent assumption concerning a system's linearity.

Of course, certain classes of artificial 'neural' networks (particularly multilayer perceptron-like networks) may be considered as flexible nonlinear parameterised models where the parameters may be adapted according to the available data. Indeed, adaptive network techniques have been used recently [1–3] with some success to predict the behaviour of chaotic time series — deterministic sequences whose second-order persistent statistics seem to indicate that they are random. This success stems from the ability of adaptive networks to produce an interpolation surface which approximates the actual nonlinear map which generated the data (this will be illustrated in the next Section). Thus, adaptive networks may be applied to time series prediction, as long as the observed time series is generated by an underlying iterative mapping, if the mapping itself is 'smooth' enough to allow an interpolation surface to be constructed.

It is known that current network models perform well when operating as static pattern classifiers, and the reason for their effectiveness in this domain may be explained [4, 5] by exploiting relationships with traditional discriminant analysis. However, such network models do *not* manipulate dynamic information appropriately. The best methods for automatic continuous

Paper 7734F (E5), received 15th March 1990

© Controller HMSO, London, 1990

The authors are with the Royal Signals and Radar Establishment, St. Andrews Road, Great Malvern, Worcs. WR14 3PS, United Kingdom speech recognition are the established hidden Markov models, and not 'neural' networks. The encoding of time by adapative networks, and how such networks should deal with temporal sequences is, perhaps, the major difference between the artificial connectionist models and real neural networks. This paper accepts the limited temporal repertoire of connectionist models, but emphasises a class of problems where, by viewing them as models of dynamical systems, a broad response range is obtainable by a suitable choice of parameter values. Thus, this paper considers the use of adaptive networks as forecasting models for time series prediction by exploiting the links between adaptive networks, dynamical systems theory and functional interpolation.

## 2    Dynamical systems preliminaries

For the purposes of this paper, it is sufficient to consider a dynamical system as specifying the evolution, or 'flow' of the state of a system in its phase space. We are only interested in finite dimensional phase spaces of dimension $d$, which determines the number of *possible* degrees of freedom available to the system. The state of a system at time $t_i$ is given by a vector $x(t_i) \in \mathbb{R}^d$ and the evolution of this vector is determined, generically, by a nonlinear equation of motion, $dx/dt = f(x)$. For deterministic dynamical systems, the evolution trajectories, the solutions of the equation of motion, do not cross in the phase space. Although the system could potentially evolve in the full $d$ dimensional phase space, it is usually the case, due to conservation laws, imposed restrictions or dissipative dynamics, that the flow of a system is asymptotically constrained to evolve on a much lower dimensional non-Euclidean submanifold $\mathcal{M}$ of dimension $m$. This asymptotic hypersurface is called an *attractor*. If an attractor may be characterised by a non-integer dimension (a 'fractal' Hausdorff dimension [6]), then the attractor is a *strange attractor* and evolution on this attractor is chaotic. That is, if two initial conditions are specified which are close together, their subsequent evolution trajectories will diverge exponentially. Thus, unless the initial condition is known to infinite precision, it is impossible to be able to predict the state of the system at a future time. Since evolution on the hypersurface is a reduced-dimension representation the dynamics compared to the potential dimensionality of the original equations of motion, the asymptotic behaviour should be specified by a model system with fewer degrees of freedom. It is usually the case in physical systems that this is an enormous reduction in the degrees of freedom of the system, corresponding to self organisation.

Unfortunately, this submanifold is non-Euclidean (only in a local region may the manifold be characterised by a Euclidean space of dimension $m$), and adaptive networks are only really useful when performing transformations between Euclidean spaces. However, theorems have been developed which allow arbitrary, smooth hypersurfaces to be 'embedded' into spaces which are diffeomorphic (the embedding transformation and its inverse are differentiable) to an equivalent-dimensional Euclidean space. In particular, Whitney [7] showed that a smooth $m$ dimensional manifold may be embedded in a Euclidean space of at most dimension $2m + 1$. This is the basis of phase space reconstruction techniques developed since 1980 when Takens [8] and Packard *et al.* [9] discussed methods where the phase space information equivalent to the underlying dynamical system could be reconstructed from a single time series and derivatives

obtained from the time series. Takens' approach was to effect a reconstruction using time-lagged vectors created from the time series, a technique known as the 'method-of-delays', which was extended into a regularised analysis tool to deal with real data in a series of papers by Broomhead *et al.*[10–12] It is analogous to the window length employed in linear predictive analysis in digital signal processing. According to the method-of-delays, an $n$ dimensional phase portrait can be obtained by constructing the sequence of vectors

$$x_i^T = (x_i, x_{i-1}, \ldots, x_{i-n+1})$$

from the discrete time series $x_1, x_2, x_3, \ldots$. The work of Takens showed that this construction is sufficient (but not necessary) to give an embedding of the underlying $m$ dimensional manifold if $n \geqslant 2m + 1$. From the point of view of networks, the number of input units is given by $n$, the size of the enclosing Euclidean space in which the dynamical system is embedded.

## 3    Functional interpolation preliminaries

One view [2, 13] on the operation of adaptive, feedforward layered networks such as the multilayer perceptron is that they perform well for certain tasks by exploiting their modelling flexibility to create an implicit interpolation surface in a high-dimensional space. Specifically, in mapping a finite set of $P$, $n$ dimensional 'training' patterns to the corresponding $n'$ dimensional 'target' patterns, $s: \mathbb{R}^n \to \mathbb{R}^{n'}$ one may think of this map as being generated by a 'graph' $\Gamma \subset \mathbb{R}^n \otimes \mathbb{R}^{n'}$ (in the same way that an Ordnance Survey contour plot, $s: \mathbb{R}^2 \to \mathbb{R}$ mapping the surface to a height may be viewed as a landscape in three dimensions). The input and target pattern pairs are points on this graph. The learning phase of adaptive network training corresponds to the optimisation of a fitting procedure for $\Gamma$ based on knowledge of the datapoints. This is curve fitting in the generally high dimensional space $\mathbb{R}^n \otimes \mathbb{R}^{n'}$. Thus *generalisation* becomes synonymous with *interpolation* along the constrained surface which is the 'best' fit to $\Gamma$. The radial basis function network [2] was introduced simply to make this point more explicit, but it also applies to networks such as the multilayer perceptron. It is clear that, by analogy with curve fitting in one or two dimensions, one can create an interpolation surface which is guaranteed to pass through every point in a finite training set provided that the model is of a sufficiently high order (e.g. sufficient numbers of hidden units equivalent to a sufficient number of Fourier coefficients). However, this is an incorrect strategy for real data which is confused by extrinsic and intrinsic noise effects and corresponds to overtraining a network. Often a large amount of prior knowledge is required to allow a fitting surface to be produced which is just smooth enough to fit the structure in the data, thus allowing good generalisation performance, without being over-complex to permit the fitting of noise on top of the data.

## 4    Synthetic problems

In this Section, some of the opening remarks will be illustrated by explicit application to problems where the 'ground truth' is firmly established. Specifically we consider the problem of reconstructing the *generator* of data, where the 'data' is a single time series obtained either from an iterated chaotic map (the first example) or from a nonlinear differential equation (the second and third examples). The aim in both cases is to use deterministic networks to attempt a reconstruction of the generator of the data, which may then be used to synthesise data with the characteristics of the true data. Since the time series may be chaotic (although this will not be the case in the differential equation example) using the network to generate data will produce a flow in the phase space which will rapidly diverge from the actual flow from a given starting value. This emphasises the point that networks do not interpolate the time series themselves.

### 4.1 Iterated maps: the quadratic map

Consider perhaps the simplest first-order nonlinear difference equation

$$x_{t+1} = \alpha x_t(1 - x_t) \tag{1}$$

This equation was considered as long ago as 1845 by Verhulst in a study of population growth in a finite habitat in which the population growth increases as the population itself increases, but decreases as the available living area decreases. The remaining living area is, of course, dependent on the total population. The value of the waveform at time $t + 1$ is determined solely from the value of the waveform at time $t$. The parameter $\alpha$ specifies the degree of nonlinearity of the equation. Note that this equation is often known as the Feigenbaum, or the *logistic* map. However, because of the potential confusion with the logistic activation function in networks, we will refer to eqn. 1 generically as the quadratic map.

The behaviour of the time series generated by eqn. 1 depends critically upon the value of $\alpha$. If $\alpha < 1$, the map has a single fixed point at the origin and so, from a random start in the closed interval $[0, 1]$, the time series would quickly collapse to a constant value (zero). For $1 < \alpha < 3$ the fixed point at the origin becomes unstable and a new stable fixed point appears. The iterated waveform tends to a nonzero constant. For $\alpha > 3$ the map generates attractors of period $2^r$ and the iterated waveform becomes periodic, the higher periods occurring as $\alpha$ increases, until $\alpha$ reaches a value of approximately 3.5699 .... Beyond this degree of nonlinearity the map is chaotic. The second-order statistics of the iterated time series appear to indicate that it is random, and yet its future value at any time is deterministically known in terms of its initial condition (if the initial condition is known to infinite precision).

For this experiment we use a value of $\alpha = 4$. A short segment of the time series and its power spectrum are shown in Figs. 1 and 2, respectively. It appears from Fig.

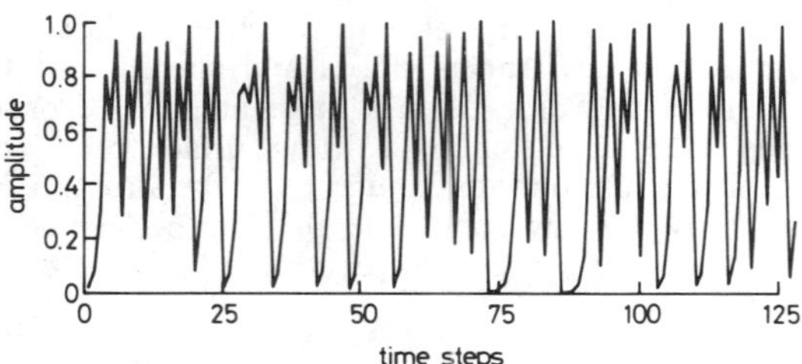

Fig. 1 *Piece of the waveform generated by iterating the quadratic map*

1 that the waveform has no structure, and the power spectrum in Fig. 2 fluctuates around a constant value (apart from the DC term which is not shown), indicating the spectrum of a white noise process. This is consistent with the analysis presented in the appendix of Reference 2 in which it was shown that the autocorrelation function of this waveform is $\delta$-correlated, i.e. $\langle x_{i+j} x_i \rangle \propto \delta_{j,0}$.

The network experiment consisted of training a radial basis function network to predict the $(t + 1)$th waveform sample given only knowledge of the waveform at time $t$

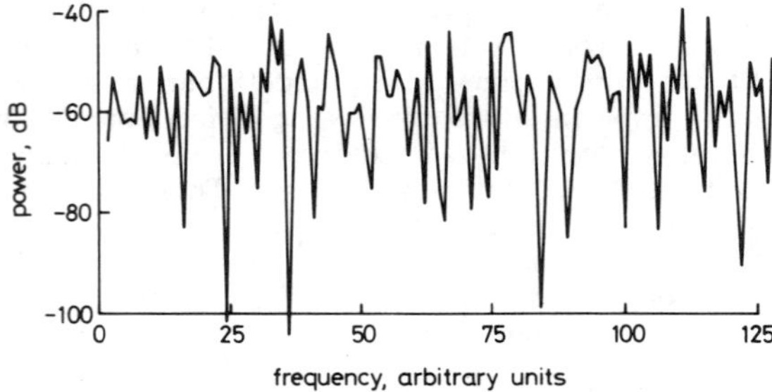

Fig. 2 *Power spectrum computed from the waveform used in Fig. 1*

(using a window length of unity). Thus the actual value $x_{t+1}$ was approximated by a network solution $s_{t+1}$ where

$$s_{t+1} = \lambda_0 + \sum_{j=1}^{n_0} \lambda_j \phi(\|x_t - y_j\|) \tag{2}$$

where $\lambda$ is the vector of adjustable parameters and there are $n_0$ centres or hidden units $y_j$ to be chosen. The training set consisted of 256 consecutive pairs of $(x_t, x_{t+1})$ generated time series values. A further test set of 50 pairs was created by selecting starting values uniformly spaced over the interval $[0, 1]$. The radial basis function network requires the set of centres to be specified and is not adapted in this paper (see Reference 14 for an example of adapting the nonlinearities used in the radial basis function network). For the illustration in Fig. 3, there were

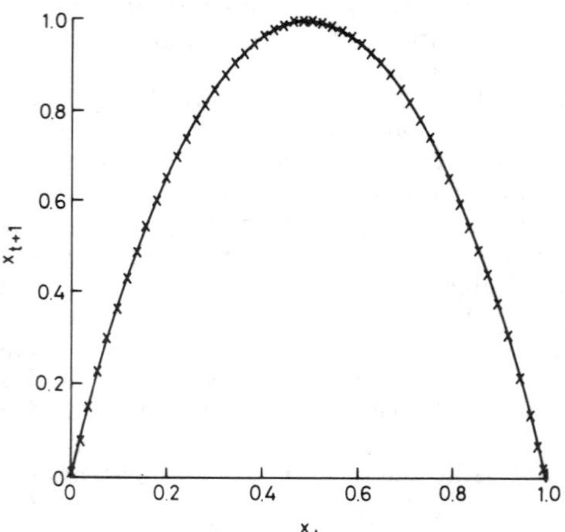

Fig. 3 *Actual quadratic map and network's prediction evaluated on an unseen test set*



ten centres chosen sequentially from the training file and the form of the nonlinearity of the centres was taken to be of the form

$$\phi(z) = z^2 \log_e(z)$$

The number of chosen centres is not the optimal (in the sense of producing the smallest sum square error on the test set) number of centres to use, but was chosen to be illustrative of the behaviour. Neither is the precise form of nonlinearity crucial. The nonlinearity used in eqn. 1 is less likely to produce a singular matrix in the learning phase, and it has been found to produce useful interpolation properties (of course, extrapolation is poor, but this is to be expected as adaptive networks are unable to extrapolate without extra prior knowledge). Once the centres had been fixed, the weights were obtained by a linear pseudo-inverse method. The 'trained' network was then tested on the previously unseen test data: a test set pattern was used as input to the network to predict the next sample value in the time series. Fig. 3 illustrates the predicted and actual values of the test experiment. Clearly, the network has produced an adequate interpolation surface to the map which generated the data (it does not interpolate the waveform itself which is a fruitless exercise as ought to be evident by inspection of the waveform of Fig. 1).

### 4.2  Differential equations

*4.2.1 The van der Pol oscillator:* The van der Pol equation is a second-order nonlinear differential equation which was introduced in 1927 [15] to provide an approximate description of a triode valve oscillator and its response to small signals. It may be expressed as

$$\frac{d^2u}{dt^2} - \mu(1 - u^2)\frac{du}{dt} + u = 0 \tag{3}$$

where $u$ is the charge and $\mu$ is a positive constant indicating the strength of the voltage-dependent resistance term. The flow of charge is periodic and it is the presence of the nonlinear term in the equation which prevents exponential growth, causing the current to be damped if $u > 1$. The equation has an unstable fixed point at the origin and a stable limit cycle.

Time series were generated from the above equation using a fifth-order Runge–Kutta integration routine, waiting until the transient had decayed and motion was on the attractor. The sampling interval was $\pi/50$. This time series was used to create training and test sets for a multilayer perceptron. The input window was taken to be two. We know that this should be sufficient since the differential equation generating the time series is of second order. Multilayer perceptrons, with a variable number of logistic hidden units, were trained on the data for 100 different random starts for the weights, which were chosen from a uniform distribution on $[-1.0, 1.0]$. The optimisation of the first layer weights was performed by a nonlinear gradient optimisation scheme (a Broyden–Fletcher–Goldfarb–Shanno (BFGS) method), and a globally optimum pseudo-inverse technique was used to determine the final layer weights. The final weights corresponding to the solution with lowest training error were then used in a network to generate a time series iteratively. Illustrative results are shown in Fig. 4 which compares the actual phase portrait of the van der Pol oscillator with the phase potrait as generated by iterating the trained network which had four hidden units. Several distinct starting positions were used in the phase space, giving rise to the distinct trajectories in Fig. 4. Derivative information has been estimated from the waveform by calculating differences.

Fig. 5 illustrates a typical iterated waveform generated by the network solution started in the region of the attractor which is virtually indistinguishable from the actual waveform. In particular, the network has managed to capture the periodicity of the training data. An analysis of the network weights used to generate this waveform shows that the map

$$u_{t+1} = F(u_t, u_{t-1}; \lambda, \mu) \tag{4}$$

(where $\lambda$, $\mu$ are the adjustable final and first layer weights, respectively) has a *stable* fixed point at $u = 0.0689$ surrounded by an unstable limit cycle of small radius. This differs from the differential equation which has an *unstable* fixed point at the origin.

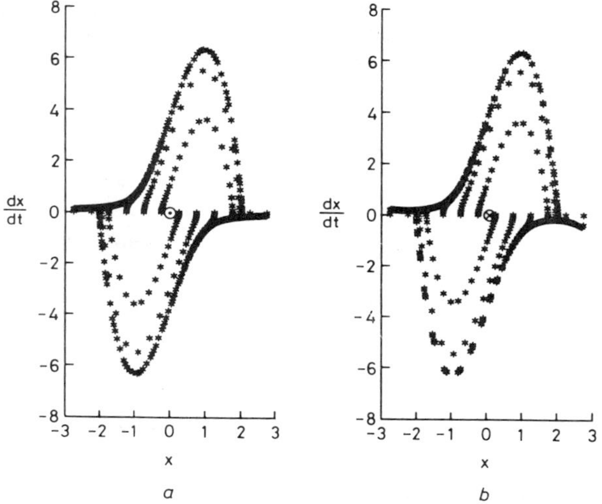

**Fig. 4**  *Comparison of the phase portraits of the actual van der Pol oscillator and the phase portrait generated by the iterated network (a 2-4-1 multilayer perceptron)*

⊙ unstable fixed points;   ⊗ stable fixed points
*a* Actual phase portrait
*b* Iterated phase portrait

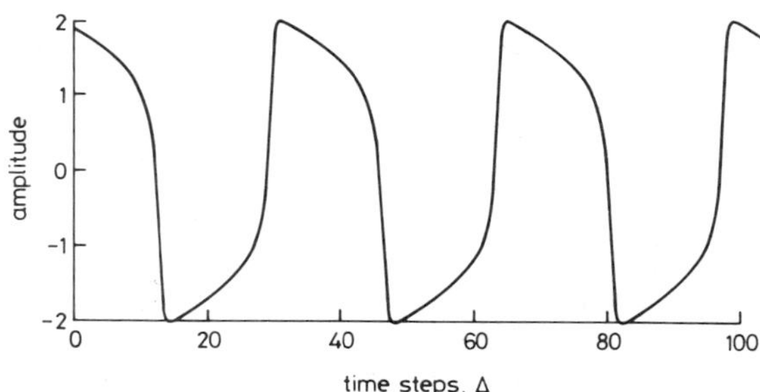

**Fig. 5**  *Example of the iterated waveform generated by the trained network for the van der Pol oscillator*

Training a network on data which lies on a limit cycle implies that the network can only capture reliably, if at all, the structure of the map which generates the data in the region of the limit cycle itself. An attractor is an example of low-dimensional, self-organising behaviour which many distinct systems could potentially exhibit. Therefore, it would be surprising if the network also captured relevant structure off the limit cycle without imposing prior knowledge of how the network should extrapolate. Indeed we find that, for a starting value for the network well away from the limit cycle, the resulting iterated waveform is a poor approximation to the transient behaviour.

To capture transient behaviour we could choose to generate a better approximation to the underlying map by using the differential equation 3 directly as a basis for generating the training data for the network over the entire phase plane of interest, rather than the time series on the limit cycle. Of course, in the analysis of experimental time series in general, the differential equation giving rise to the time series under consideration is usually unavailable to us. Alternatively, one should train the network on time series initialised from many different starting points in the phase plane.

A further illustration of how the network manages to produce an interpolation surface to the map which generated the data is to approximate the differential equation as a map and compare with the generated network solution. Specifically, if we approximate the derivatives in eqn. 3 by finite differences, then $u_{t+1}$ may be expressed as a function of $u_t$ and $u_{t-1}$ as

$$u_{t+1} = \frac{4\left(1 - \frac{\Delta^2}{2}\right)u_t - (2 + \mu\Delta(1 - u_t^2))u_{t-1}}{2 - \mu\Delta(1 - u_t^2)} \quad (5)$$

where $\Delta$ is a small time interval. Expanding this map around the origin for a value of $\Delta = \pi/50$ and $\mu = 4.0$ gives the approximate map

$$u_{t+1} = 2.2829u_t - 1.2874u_{t-1}$$
$$- 0.3281u_t^3 + 0.3288u_t^2 u_{t-1} + \mathcal{O}(u^4) \quad (6)$$

Expanding the network solution which generated Fig. 5 around the origin gives the approximate map

$$u_{t+1} = 0.0004 + 2.2758u_t - 1.2823u_{t-1}$$
$$- 0.0042u_t^2 + 0.0059u_t u_{t-1} - 0.0031u_{t-1}^2$$
$$- 0.3291u_t^3 + 0.3403u_t^2 u_{t-1} - 0.0380u_t u_{t-1}^2$$
$$+ 0.0284u_{t-1}^3 + \mathcal{O}(u^4) \quad (7)$$

The power series for the iterated map approximates the power series of the approximation to the differential equation up to terms of order three and thus the network is approximating the generator of the data again. In this sense, from knowledge of the time series alone, the network is being employed to recover equations of motion which are consistent with the observed time series.


*4.2.2 The thalamic neuron:* This Section considers a more complicated example, which has interesting links to real neural networks. Amongst some of the dynamic features exhibited in the nervous system, of particular interest are intrinsically excitable or oscillatory processes exhibited by single cells as well as assemblies of neurons. In particular, such systems are capable of exhibiting a range of behaviour, from pacemaking, generators of single pulses, beating oscillators, plateauing cells or showing a periodic 'bursting' effect. Whichever mode these systems operate in depends upon the state that the neurons are in at the instant they are excited by external influences. They are not 'black box' systems which can be characterised by correlating output to input since the state of the box itself governs the response.

The particular model we consider is one discussed by Rose and Hindmarsh [16] which approximates the oscillatory behaviour of a particular type of cell found in the thalamic region of the brain. If this thalamic neuron is in its resting state, the application of a short subthreshold depolarising current pulse elicits a passive response (the depolarisation decays back to the resting level). If the thalamic neuron is in a depolarised state, the application of the same current pulse can trigger a tonic firing activity of the cell with a frequency proportional to the current. However, if the cell is in a hyperpolarised state, this current pulse elicits a 'bursting' response. To describe this range of behaviour, Rose and Hindmarsh considered

the three coupled first-order differential equations

$$\frac{dx}{dt} = f(x) - y - z + I$$

$$\frac{dy}{dt} = g(x) - y \quad (8)$$

$$\frac{dz}{dt} = \tau \times (h(x) - z)$$

where $x$ has the significance of the membrane potential, $y$ is a recovery variable and $z$ relates to the adaptation current, which has a time constant $\tau$. $I$ is the externally applied current and the nonlinearities have the explicitly chosen forms

$$f(x) = \begin{cases} x^3 - 3x^2 & \text{for } x \notin [0, 2k] \\ ax^3 + bx^2 + cx + d & \text{for } x \in [0, 2k] \end{cases}$$

$$g(x) = 1 - 5x^2 \quad (9)$$

$$h(x) = K\frac{\mu^{(x+1+k)-1}}{\mu^{(1+2k)-1}}$$

where $k$ was chosen to satisfy $k^2 = 1 - k$ and $a$, $b$, $c$, $d$ were chosen to ensure that $f(x)$ is continuous and satisfies $f(k) = 5k - 4$. $K$ and $\mu$ are constants, and $h(x)$ is chosen to reflect the exponential dependence on the membrane potential of the steady-state calcium-activated potassium conductance.

Integrating these equations for special choices of the constants exhibits the wide range of behaviour discussed (see Reference 16 for a discussion on the behaviour of these equations), depending upon the state of the system (the initial conditions). Fig. 6 shows an example of bursting behaviour obtained by integrating eqns. 8.

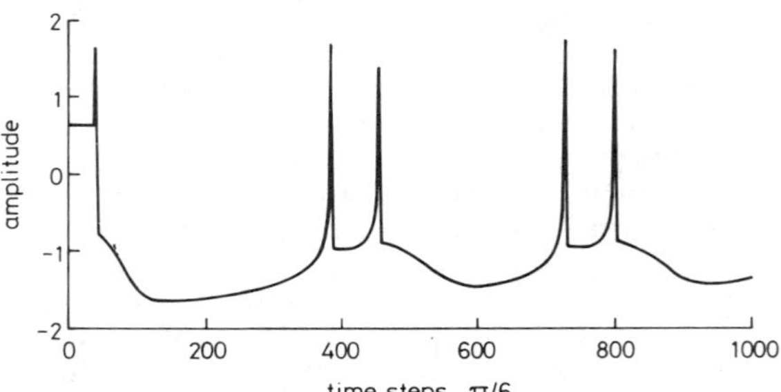


**Fig. 6** *Example of the bursting waveform (including the initial resting state prior to excitation) generated by the equations of Rose and Hindmarsh*

Thus, just using the time series shown in Fig. 6, is it possible to use the interpolating predictive power of adaptive networks to construct an approximation to the generator of the data? The perversity of using a 'neural' network model to model a model of a neuron is incidental. Training and test sets of patterns to perform a three-step prediction (exploiting the prior knowledge that the 'order' of the problem is three) were generated from the time series of Fig. 6, which lies on the stable limit cycle of eqns. 9. Both train and test sets contained 1024 patterns. A multilayer perceptron, with one hidden layer with a varying number of units with logistic nonlinearity, and a linear output layer was trained using the BFGS optimisation strategy to minimise the output error. For each hidden layer size, ten random weights starts were performed, and the weights corresponding to the lowest error over the ten starts used in an iterative network. A network with nine hidden units was selected as the one which gave smallest error on the training set *and* a correspondingly small error on the test set (which for these purposes may be regarded as an evaluation set).

Fig. 7 depicts an iterated waveform obtained from the trained multilayer perceptron with nine hidden units. It is

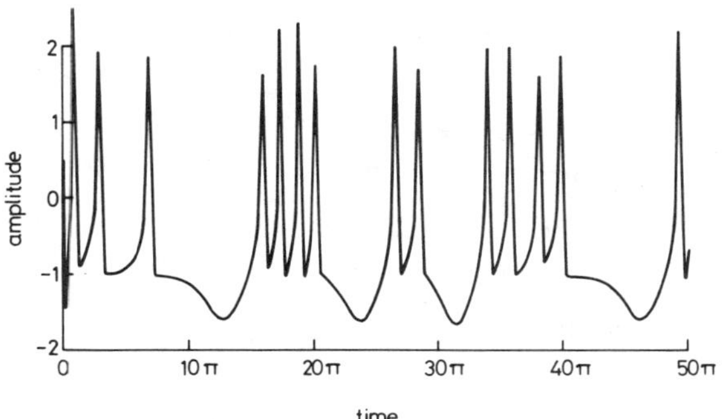

**Fig. 7** *Example of the iterated waveform produced by the trained network. Although evidence of bursting is clear, the rate is much faster than the training waveform*

clear that, although essential features of the original time series have been captured (the fast bursting spikes superimposed on the peaks of a much slower background oscillation) the actual period of the iterated data is much more rapid than the original data. The dynamical system generated by the network is much more sensitive to uncertainties than the original model. Even though upon inspection the short term prediction errors are good, continually iterating upon the network output produces this increased frequency behaviour. Uncertainties are magnified so as to produce an apparently faster evolution. Whether it is the exponential nonlinearity in the original model which produces a more difficult surface to interpolate is not clear.

## 5  Real problems

The illustrative examples considered so far have been 'ideal' in the sense that we have had control over the time series. In particular, it was not necessary to consider effects due to real background extrinsic noise, intrinsic noise effects in the data (quantisation errors — the data was generated with 32-bit floating-point arithmetic) or sampling effects (we could generate sufficiently oversampled data if it were considered necessary). Additionally we had extra knowledge regarding the 'order' of the problem. In real physical situations we do not have this control. In a previous paper [17] we considered speech waveform prediction where the speech was quantised to $\simeq 14$ bits, had a high signal-to-noise ratio and was oversampled with respect to the vowel sounds. Nevertheless, it was still difficult to obtain adequate network solutions to reproduce the waveforms (although relevant 'features' could be reproduced). The noise has the effect of forcing the actual low dimensional behaviour back into a high dimensional space. This implies that the apparent 'order' of the data is higher than it needs to be, which complicates the task of finding an appropriate window size in which the evolution of the system may be captured. The significant advances in dynamical systems practice have been in devising regularised approaches to deal with noise problems to determine how to project the data into subspaces in which the variance of the noise is minimised (e.g. Reference 10). Currently there are no equivalent regularised schemes to deal with these prob-

lems using adaptive networks and this is an obvious area for future development.

In addition to problems due to limited control over data (such as reducing, but not eliminating noise), one is also often confronted with times series over which there can be no control at all. Typical examples in this category are economic and social forecasting where available prior knowledge for model-building is minimal. Even if a long history of samples is obtainable, it is likely that the generator of the data (if one exists) is not static but evolves on a slower time scale to the local variation of the data. Thus the significance of generated data depends upon its history. In such circumstances one wishes to be able to predict the likely evolution of a system based on a sparse, noisy, nonuniformly sampled set of data points where the reliability of each data point can be different. The final example considered in the paper is one such time series: that of stock-market prediction.

### 5.1  Stock-market prediction

This problem (see Reference 18 for an interesting viewpoint on the use of mathematics in investment) is an example of a 'social' phenomenon producing multidimensional time series where the underlying physical mechanisms governing the system's evolution are poorly understood. Nevertheless, we assume that the observations (stock-market prices and market indicators) are produced by an underlying generator which is a reasonably low dimensional, nonlinear dynamical system and the apparent complexity of the observations is due to the (unknown) nonlinear interaction between a few significant variables. The experiment is to see to what extent an adaptive network can be used to approximate the underlying relationships simply from knowledge of a single time series (see also Reference 19). In a more elaborate experiment one should exploit the knowledge of the multiple simultaneously known time series and market indicators, but this paper is concerned with one-dimensional time series analysis.

Against this strategy is the 'efficient markets hypothesis'. That is, the view that the local fluctuations of a stock, around an expected overall appreciation are totally unpredictable from publically available information. In short, market prices follow a random walk [20–22]. On the face of it, this is an attractive hypothesis, although it does assume a system capable of perfectly responding to change and able to equilibrate instantly. A standard way of testing for the efficient markets hypothesis is by a linear autoregressive model applied to the stock returns. If a suitable fit cannot be found, this could be taken as evidence *for* the hypothesis. Alternatively, it may also be taken as evidence for the existence of a nonlinear relationship amongst the data which the linear autoregressive model is unable to approximate. Adaptive networks can operate as nonlinear filters, and it is sensible, therefore, to apply contemporary network methods to this problem.

The experiment is to discover if adaptive networks can produce short time predictions which are consistently better than standard 'linear' models. The example taken is of the daily closing prices of the British Telecom stock over the time period September 1989 to the end of February 1990, a total of only 113 samples (shown in Fig. 8). Of the 113 samples, the first 90 samples were used for the training set and the remaining 23 samples used to evaluate the models' predictions. There are not sufficient samples to create a test set which would normally be used to decide an appropriate model order. Therefore, the model order has to be decided on the basis of the training set alone. This is a deliberately chosen example which has a minimum of information upon which a decision has to be made. It is clearly undersampled and ambiguous, but is it random or is there an element of short time predictability?

**Fig. 8**   *British Telecom stock over the period September 1989 to March 1990*

Fig. 9 shows typical prediction residuals, comparing a radial basis function network with a linear predictor of the same window size. An input window of five samples

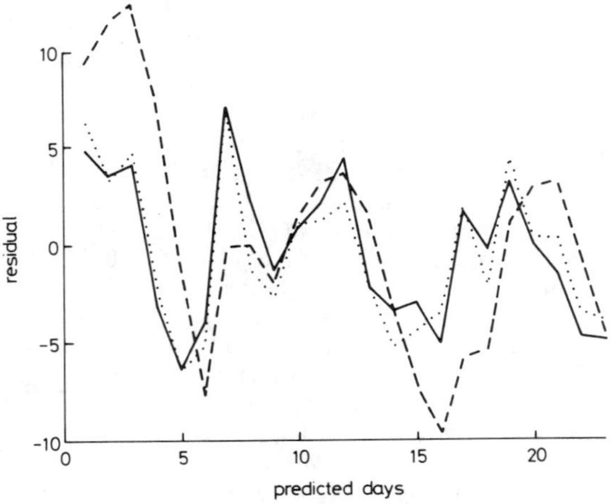



**Fig. 9**   *Actual stock price minus the prediction*

———— radial basis function network
·······  LPC method
– – –  mean prediction

(days) was employed for each method. This input size was chosen on the basis of the normalised error on the training set. The radial basis function used seven centres with a $z \log z$ nonlinearity, which were chosen uniformly randomly from the training set. Also shown for comparison are the results of predicting the next value estimated as the mean of the preceding five samples.

The training error, the mean and the standard deviation of the nonlinear predictor in Fig. 8 are all superior to those of the linear methods. However, no conclusion may be drawn from these results since it is possible to find other linear models which, although they have worse

residual error on the training set, give better performance on the evaluation data. For instance, the prediction method whereby the predicted value on one day is taken to be just the value on the previous day returns a smaller evaluation set error, mean and standard deviation. This latter method, is, of course, incapable of capturing any implicit structure in the generator of the data and so will be unable to predict further into the future. Unfortunately, if the data is chaotic then neither will the nonlinear model. This is because the implicit model of the data generator will be approximate and this is equivalent to adding noise to the data itself (even if the data were 'clean'). Thus, the uncertainties in the network are likely to be exponentially magnified as the prediction time increases. A tradeoff occurs in chaotic time series prediction between the number of prediction time steps which are required to be reliable, and the accuracy to which the parameters of the network need to be determined. Noise on the data itself sets a lower bound to the performance, irrespective of the tradeoff. These are indicative of problems for which the methodology is still developing in the linear models, which indirectly will prevent the consistent application of nonlinear network models to real forecasting.

## 6   Conclusion

This paper has considered time series prediction using adaptive networks to approximate the generator of that data. This has required the introduction of concepts from interpolation and dynamical systems theory.

Several points should be made. In the synthetic problems of chaotic time series prediction and approximating nonlinear differential equations, we had access to the generator of the data itself. Thus, we knew a priori the model order which would work, we could minimise effects due to noise and we could sample the data accordingly. Given these restrictions it was demonstrated that networks were capable of approximating the systems which generated the information. The ability of the approximate implicit models to perform forecasting depended upon whether the data was chaotic or not.

In real-world problems these advantages are lost. Generally, data may be generated by processes for which we are unable to formulate an explicit model, and on the basis of data alone it is necessary to attempt an implicit model construction allowing subsequent data synthesis. If the assumption that the data generator is static is not correct, or the data is unavailable in sufficient quality and quantity, then the nonlinear predictive methods are not likely to be significantly better compared with simple linear methods. In the stock market example, only a single time series was considered, which ought to be sufficient (assuming that there exists an underlying dynamical system driving the evolution of the stock market as a whole) if the sampling interval and window size could be chosen arbitrarily. As the sampling is fixed (and sparse) it is likely that the techniques developed in dynamical systems will have to be extended to incorporate simultaneous observation events: multidimensional time series prediction. This is a problem for the future.

## 7   References

1 CASDAGLI, M.: 'Nonlinear prediction of chaotic time series', *Physica D*, 1989, **35**, pp. 335–356
2 BROOMHEAD, D.S., and LOWE, D.: 'Multi-variable functional interpolation and adaptive networks', *Complex Systems*, 1988, **2**, (3), pp. 269–303

3 DOYNE FARMER, J., and SIDOROWICH, J.J.: 'Predicting chaotic time series', *Phys. Rev. Lett.*, 1987, **59**, (8), pp. 845–848

4 WEBB, A.R., and LOWE, D.: 'The optimised internal representation of multilayer classifier networks performs nonlinear discriminant analysis', *Neural Networks*, 1990, **3**, (4), pp. 367–375

5 LOWE, D., and WEBB, A.R.: 'On networks, optimised feature extraction and the Bayes decision', *Pattern Analysis & Machine Intelligence* (in press), also available as RSRE Memorandum 4342, St. Andrews Rd., Great Malvern, Worcs. WR14 3PS, United Kingdom

6 SHUSTER, H.G.: 'Deterministic chaos' (Physik-Verlag, 1984)

7 WHITNEY, H.: 'The self-intersections of a smooth $N$-manifold in $2N$ space', *Ann. Math.*, 1944, **45**, p. 220

8 TAKENS, F.: 'Detecting strange attractors in turbulence', *in* RAND, D.A., and YOUNG, L.-S. (Eds.): 'Lecture notes in mathematics', **898**, (Springer, Berlin, 1981), p. 366

9 PACKARD, N.H., CRUTCHFIELD, J.P., FARMER, J.D., and SHAW, R.S.: 'Geometry from a time series', *Phys. Rev. Lett.*, 1980, **45**, p. 712

10 BROOMHEAD, D.S., and KING, G.P.: 'Extracting qualitative dynamics from experimental data', *Physica D*, 1986, **20**, pp. 217–236

11 KING, G.P., JONES, R., and BROOMHEAD, D.S.: 'Phase portraits from a time series', *Nucl. Phys. B*, 1987, **2**, pp. 379–390

12 BROOMHEAD, D.S., JONES, R., and KING, G.P.: 'Topological dimension and local coordinates from time series data', *J. Phys. A*, 1987, **20**, pp. L563–L569

13 LAPEDES, A., and FARBER, R.: 'How neural networks work'. Los Alamos report, LA-UR-88-418

14 LOWE, D.: 'Adaptive radial basis function nonlinearities and the problem of generalisation'. Ist IEE Int. Conf. on Artificial neural networks, October 1989, *IEE Conf. Publ. 313*, pp. 171–175

15 VAN DER POL, B.: 'Forced oscillations in a system with nonlinear resistance', *Phil. Mag.*, 1927, **3**, pp. 65–80

16 ROSE, R.M., and HINDMARSH, J.L.: 'A mode of a thalamic neuron', *Proc. R. Soc. Lond. B*, 1985, **225**, pp. 161–193

17 LOWE, D., and WEBB, A.R.: 'Adaptive networks, dynamical systems, and the predictive analysis of time series'. 1st IEE Int. Conf. on Artificial neural networks, October 1989, *IEE Conf. Publ. 313*, pp. 95–99

18 PIKE, E.R.: 'Mathematics and investment', *Inst. Math. & Appl.*, 1984, **20**, (11/12), pp. 162–170

19 WHITE, H.: 'Economic prediction using neural networks: the case of IBM daily stock returns'. IEEE Int. Conf. on neural networks, San Diego, 1988, pp. II-451

20 MALKIEL, B.G.: 'A random walk down Wall Street' (W. Norton & Co., New York, 1973)

21 OSBORNE, M.F.M.: 'Brownian motion in the stock market', *Oper. Res.*, 1959, **1**, pp. 145–173

22 GRANGER, C.W.J., and MORGENSTERN, O.: 'Predictability of stock market prices' (D.C. Heath & Co., Lexington, Massachusetts, 1970)

*SIMULATION* 57:5, 303-310
© 1991, Simulation Councils, Inc.
ISSN 0037-5497/91 $3.00 + .10
Printed in the United States of America

# Time series forecasting using neural networks vs. Box-Jenkins methodology

Zaiyong Tang , Chrys de Almeida *        Paul A. Fishwick **
* Department of Decision & Information Sciences
** Department of Computer & Information Sciences
*University of Florida*
Gainesville, FL 32611

*We discuss the results of a comparative study of the performance of neural networks and conventional methods in forecasting time series. Our work was initially inspired by previously published works that yielded inconsistent results about comparative performance. We have experimented with three time series of different complexity using different feed forward, backpropagation neural network models and the standard Box-Jenkins model. Our experiments demonstrate that for time series with long memory, both methods produced comparable results. However, for series with short memory, neural networks outperformed the Box-Jenkins model. We note that some of the comparable results arise since the neural network and time series model appear to be functionally similar models. We have found that for time series of different complexities there are optimal neural network topologies and parameters that enable them to learn more efficiently. Our initial conclusions are that neural networks are robust and provide good long-term forecasting. They are also parsimonious in their data requirements. Neural networks represent a promising alternative for forecasting, but there are problems determining the optimal topology and parameters for efficient learning.*

## Introduction

Artificial neural networks have been widely studied and applied to a variety of areas. One of these areas is forecasting. Although there have been many encouraging reports, there are, at the same time, several questions remaining unanswered. Many reports fail to compare their neural network performances against those of traditional methods.

Lapedes and Farber (1987) reported that simple neural networks can outperform conventional methods, sometimes by orders of magnitude. Their conclusions are based on two specific time series without noise. Sharda and Patil (1990) conducted a forecasting competition between a neural network model and a traditional forecasting technique (namely t he Box-Jenkins method) using 75 time series of various nature. They concluded that the simple neural network model could forecast about as well as the Box-Jenkins forecasting system. Each of the methods performed better then the other about half of the time. The experiment of Fishwick (1989) shows, however, for a ballistics trajectory function approximation problem, the neural network used offered little competition to the traditional linear regression and surface response model. Surveying those papers leads us to ask why there is such a discrepancy? Can neural networks really compete with conventional methods? Why, or why not?

Experimental results from Sharda and Patil (1990) show that periodicity of time series does not have significant influence on the relative performance of the neural ne tworks and the Box-Jenkins approach. But there are significant performance differences as these two methods are applied to some of their chosen time series. For example, in terms of MAPS (mean absolute percent error), neural networks sometimes outperformed the Box-Jenkins approach by more than 100 percent. In some other cases, the latter proved much better. The authors did not provide any explanations as to when and why one approach is superior to the other. In light of the controversy about neural network applications, we feel it is of both theoretic and practical importance to answer some of these questions.

In this paper, a comparative study is carried out to investigate the forecasting capability of neural networks and Box-Jenkins models which are among those forecasting models most successfully applied in practice. Three typical time series were selected: international airline passenger data, domestic car sale data in the U.S., and foreign car sale data in the U.S.. Box-Jenkins model forecasting was done with the time series analysis package *TIMESLAB* (Newton, 1988). Neural network simulations were performed using the *Back Propagation* (BP) program in the *Parallel Distributed Processing* (PDP) package by McClelland and Rumelhart (1988).

In the following section, we present the experiments of forecasting with Box-Jenkins models and the neural networks. Section 3 focuses on the effects of neural network parameters and structure on training and forecasting performance. Following that, in section 4, we will offer some insights that we gained from our experiments, and discuss the questions we raised above. Finally, in section 5, we present our conclusions and directions for further research.

## Box-Jenkins Model vs. NN Forecasting

### Data

The three time series we selected are shown in Figure 1. Airline Passenger data (Fig. 1a) shows a long memory pattern — there is an apparent increasing trend and seasonal pattern. Domestic car sale (Fig. 1b) and foreign car sale data (Fig. 1c) also show seasonal patterns, though not very clearly. Foreign car sales presents an increasing trend while domestic car sales appears more irregular, and can hence be classified as a short memory time series.

### Box-Jenkins Models

The most popular ARMA-model based forecasting method is the Box-Jenkins approach, which involves the following steps (Newton, 1988):

(1) model identification

(2) parameter estimation

(3) consideration of alternative ARIMA models, if necessary

(4) forecasting based on the chosen models.

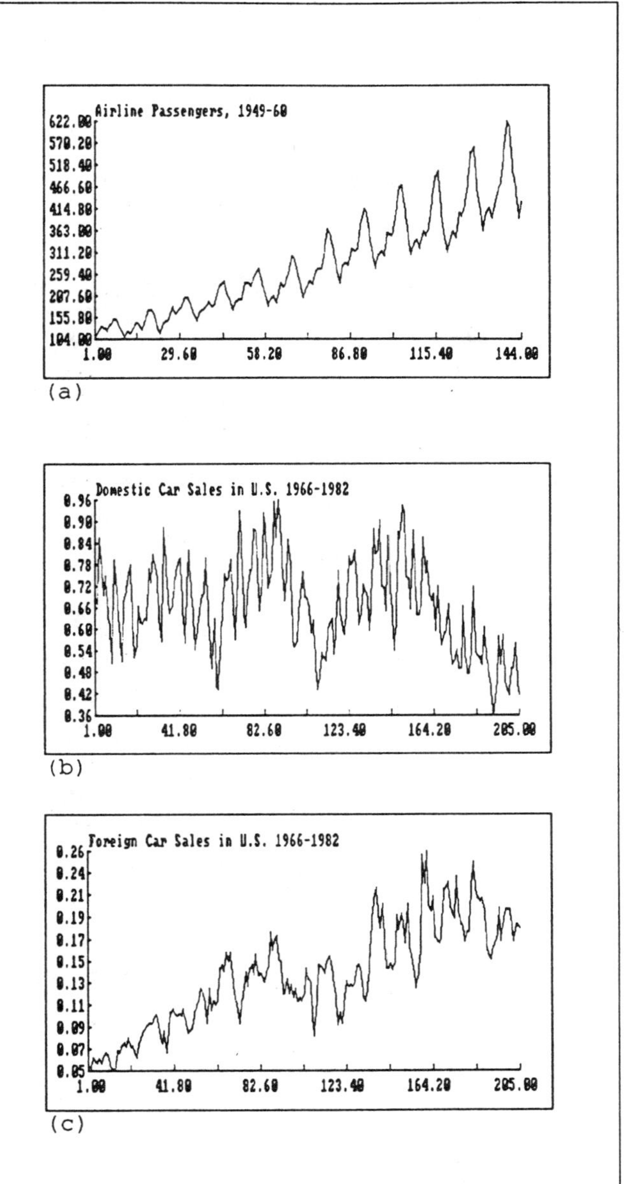



**Figure 1.** Time Series Data

The general Box-Jenkins model has the following form (Bowerman, 1987, P. 120).

$$\phi_p(B)\,\phi_P(B^L)\,(1-B^L)^D\,(1-B)^d y_t = \delta + \theta_q(B)\theta_Q(B^L)a_t \quad (1)$$

where $\phi(B)$ and $\theta(B)$ are autoregressive and moving average operators respectively ; B is the back shift operator; $a_t$ is called white noise with normal distribution $N(0,\sigma^2)$; $\delta$ is a constant, and $y_t$ is the time series data, transformed if necessary.

Using *TIMESLAB*'s model identification macro, we determined the Box-Jenkins model for the airline data to be:

$$(1 - B^{12})\,(1 - B)y_t = (1 - \theta_1 B)\,(1 - \theta_{1,12}B)\,a_t \qquad (2)$$

and the model for the car sales data to be:

$$(1 - \phi_1 B + \phi_2 B^2 + \phi_3 B^3)\,(1 - B_{12})\,(1 - B)\,y_t = (1 - \theta_{1,12}B)a_t \qquad (3)$$

### Neural Network Models

Although there has been some research on the design of optimal neural network structures (Kurg and Hwang, 1988), it is still largely an art to determine the number of hidden layers and number of units in each hidden layer. The effects of neural network structure on the training of and forecasting by the neural network will be discussed in the next section. To ensure an effective comparison, in this section we use one hidden layer for all of the neural networks considered. This configuration is also the choice of Sharda and Patil (1990). The number of units in the hidden layer equals the number of inputs, which are set to be 1, 6, 12 and 24, corresponding to one month, half a year, one year and two year input data respectively. The number of output units are set to be 1, 6, 12 and 24, corresponding to 1, 6, 12 and 24-period- ahead forecasting respectively. Neural network structure is denoted as IxHxO, where I, H, and O represent number of input units, hidden units, and output units respectively.

The training parameters are initially set to be the same for different neural network structures, that is, learning rate = 0.5 and momentum = 0.9. The discussion on how to choose the best combination of the parameters will be left to the next section. In this part of the experiment, instead of using fixed training parameters, we adjusted the parameters during training to facilitate faster convergence. We observed that a training schedule, just like the cooling schedule in simulated annealing, plays an important role in neural network learning.

### Forecasting results

Three cases were investigated in the forecasting performance comparison. (1) the amount of data used; (2) the number of periods for the forecast; and (3) the number of input variables. Of the original time series, the last 24 items were saved to compare with forecasted values. The forecasting results are summarized in the following tables. Note that all real values represent the total sum of square error (tss) for the 24 period forecast.

Table 1 shows that with one-period-ahead and six-period-ahead forecasts, the Box-Jenkins model outperforms the neural network for the selected structures and training methods, while for the 12-period-ahead and 24-period-ahead forecasts the neural network is better. It is not surprising that as the forecast horizon extends, Box-Jenkins model performs less well, since the model is best suited for short term forecast. The relative performance of the neural network improves as the forecast horizon increases. This suggests that the neural network is a

**Table 1.** Airline passenger forecast (tss)

| forecast period | Box-Jenkins model | Neural network |
|---|---|---|
| 1 | 0.0071 | 0.0105 |
| 6 | 0.0168 | 0.0285 |
| 12 | 0.0340 | 0.0336 |
| 24 | 0.1318 | 0.0129 |

**Table 2.** Training error and forecast error (tss with different input pattern)

| input pattern | training error | forecast error |
|---|---|---|
| $1 \times 6 \times 1$ | 0.1008 | 0.0614 |
| $6 \times 6 \times 1$ | 0.0940 | 0.0613 |
| $12 \times 12 \times 1$ | 0.0338 | 0.0113 |
| $24 \times 24 \times 1$ | 0.0221 | 0.0105 |

**Table 3.** Input data amount and forecast error (tss)

| input data | training error | forecast error |
|---|---|---|
| 2 yr. | 0.0044 | 0.1524 |
| 5 yr. | 0.0156 | 0.0208 |
| 10 yr. | 0.0338 | 0.0113 |

**Table 4.** Car Sale Forecast (tss)

| input data | Box-Jenkins model | Neural net (12 inputs) |
|---|---|---|
| domestic car | | |
| 9 yr. | 0.19439 | 0.10130 |
| 15 yr | 0.18156 | 0.10110 |
| foreign car | | |
| 9 yr. | 0.00724 | 0.00590 |
| 15 yr. | 0.00670 | 0.00630 |

better choice for long term forecasting. Note that for the 24-period-ahead forecast, the neural network resulted in much smaller error then the Box-Jenkins model. The fact that the 24- period-ahead forecast is better than the 6-period-ahead and the 12-period-ahead forecast suggest that in the later case, the networks may not have been trained to produce the optimal results.

Examining the forecast errors resulting from the Box-Jenkins model and the neural network, we found that the neural network provides very nice forecasts except for the small bumps at each yearly cycle. The Box-Jenkins model can nicely reproduce the 'details' of the original series, while the neural network we trained

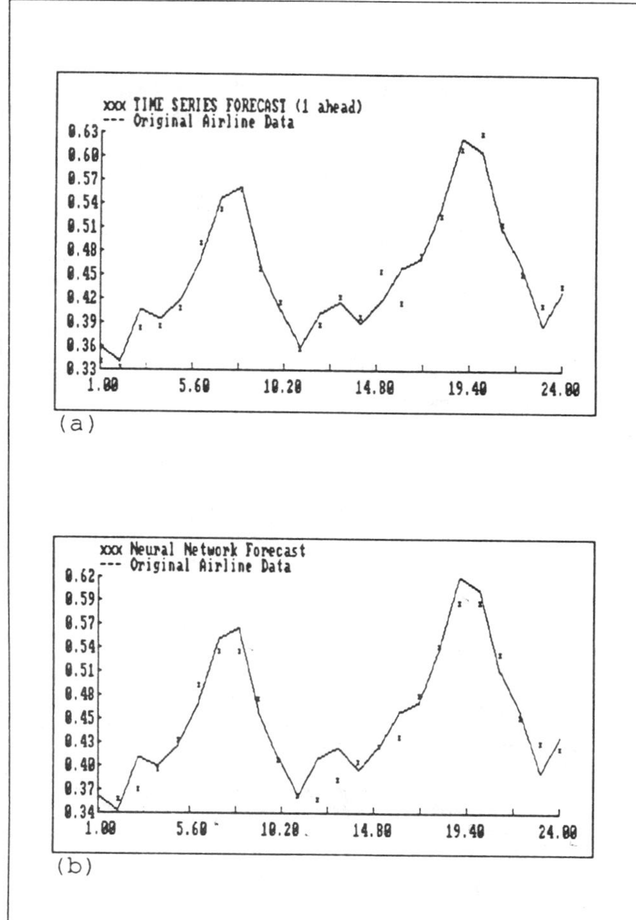

**Figure 2.** Box-Jenkins vs NN Forecasts

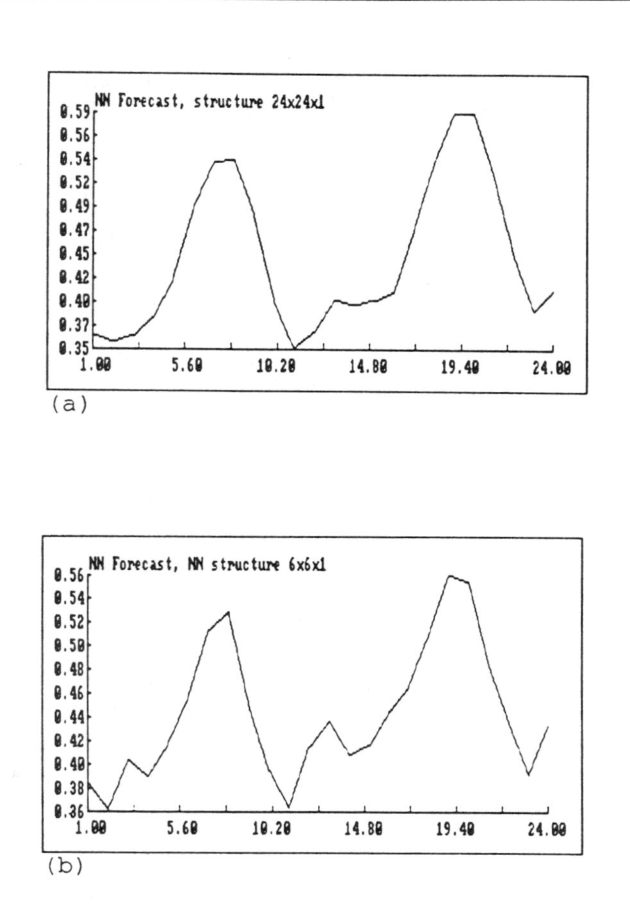

**Figure 3.** NN Forecasts with Different Input Patterns

provides somewhat smooth curve, ignoring the 'details'. There could be many factors attributing to the result. We would expect that changing the network structure and/ or the training parameter could improve the forecast of those 'details'. Changing the input pattern also helps in this aspect as can be seen from Figure 3.

When the input number increases, the forecasting performance of neural network improves, as shown in Table 2. Figure 3 depicts the forecasting differences with six and twenty four inputs. More inputs will provide more information, and hence will provide more accurate forecasts. It is interesting to note that with six inputs, the network learned the time series pattern better than with twenty four inputs, but it did not learn the increasing trend very well.

The amount of data, or equivalently, the number of training patterns also affects the forecast performance (Table 3). Although for the long memory series, more training patterns results in more accurate forecasts, the neural network can perform reasonably well with short series of input data. The Box-Jenkins model does not work well or does not work at all for short input series. This can be regarded as one of the advantages of the neural network over Box- Jenkins model.

For domestic car sale data, the Box-Jenkins model did less well than the neural network, although both result in relatively large errors due to the irregular nature of the series (Table 4). The two methods produced comparable results for foreign car sale forecast. Comparing the forecasting results for the three time series with different memory patterns, we noticed that, as the complexity of the time series increase, the Box-Jenkins model become less competitive against the neural network model.

## Neural Network Structure and Training Parameter Analysis

As we mentioned in section 2, neural network structure affects its forecasting ability. For instance, with different input patterns, which correspond to different neural network structures, the trained neural network present different forecast patterns. We also mentioned that some of the neural networks used in our forecasting may not have been trained optimally. The following explores more on how neural network structure and training parameters affect their performance.

## The Effect of Hidden Layer

We compare two neural network structures: (1) with hidden layer, and (2) without hidden layer. The training parameters are the same as described in section 2. Table 5 summarizes the forecasting results.

**Table 5.** The effect of NN structure on forecast

| NN Structure | Forecast error |
| --- | --- |
| $12 \times 12 \times 1$ | 0.0113 |
| $12 \times 1$ | 0.0131 |
| $24 \times 24 \times 1$ | 0.0105 |
| $24 \times 1$ | 0.0215 |

The results show that adding a hidden layer improves the forecasting performance of neural networks. While plotting the forecast results, we found that the neural networks without a hidden layer actually learned the pattern better. The forecast data present a pattern very close to those resulted from the Box-Jenkins model. This is not too surprising since without a hidden layer, the neural network is close functionally to a linear model. Larger errors of neural networks without the hidden layer result from improper estimation of the time series trend. With a hidden layer, the neural networks learned a smoother mapping (Figure 4a).

## The Effect of Training Parameters

The effect of training parameters on the neural network learning were studied. The same randomly generated initial weight set was used in all the experiments. Table 6 and table 7 present the results, where LR is the learning rate, MO is the momentum value, TSS is the total sum of square error, and EPO is the number of training epochs.

For the airline passenger data, which is the least complex, the network converges quite rapidly and reaches error level specified by the global error criterion. At higher learning rates the convergence is much faster. For the other two series, the convergence towards a global minimum appears to be taking place for very small values of LR while the momentum is high. As the complexity of the pattern decreases the occurrence of local minima are less frequent, and a larger LR is accommodated.

## Discussions

We began our study by asking when and why the neural networks offer superior performance to conventional methods. We have answered, at least partially, the first part of the question in the last two sections. Now let us try to answer the second part of the question by examining how the Box-Jenkins model and the neural network model perform input-output mapping.

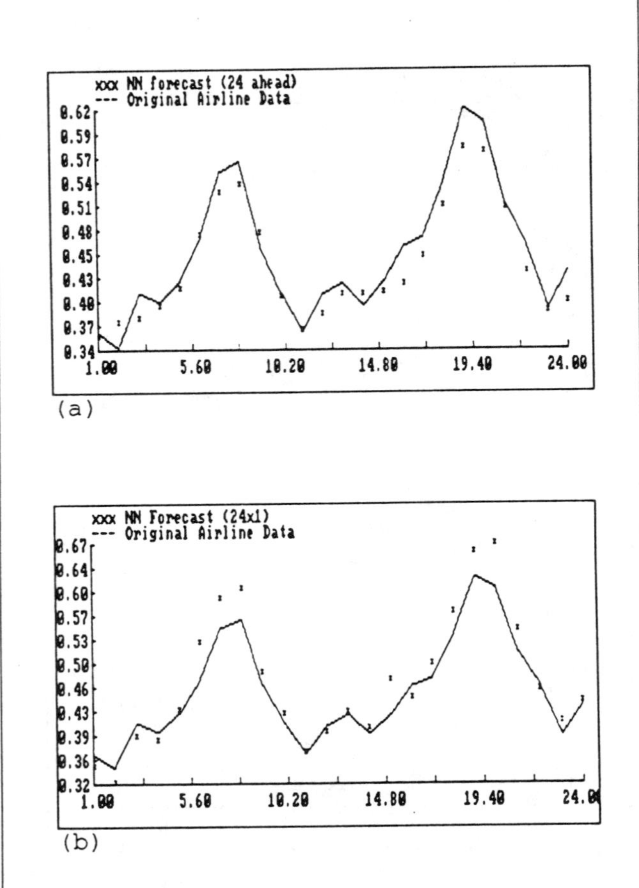



**Figure 4.** Effect of Hidden Layer on Forecast.

**Table 6.** Effect of Momentum for Fixed Learning Rate

LR $\quad = \quad$ .1

Domestic Car Sales:

| MO | = | .9 | .5 | .1 |
| --- | --- | --- | --- | --- |
| TSS | = | .2333 | .2386 | .2547 |
| EPO | = | 1000 | 1000 | 1000 |

Foreign Car Sales:

| MO | = | .9 | .5 | .1 |
| --- | --- | --- | --- | --- |
| TSS | = | .0225 | .0302 | .0362 |
| EPO | = | 1000 | 1000 | 1000 |

## Input-Output Mapping with Box-Jenkins Model

As we have stated in section 2, the model we identified for the airline data is:

$$(1 - B^{12})(1 - B)y_t = (1 - \theta_1 B)(1 - \theta_{1,12} B)a_t \qquad (4)$$

The same model has been identified by other re-

**Table 7.** Effect of Learning Rate for Fixed Momentum

```
MO    =   .9
Domestic Car Sales:
LR    =   .05      .1        .2.         5
TSS   =   .2350    .2333     5.7897      5.7897
EPO   =   1000     1000      1000        1000

Foreign Car Sales:
LR    =   .05      .1.       2           .5
TSS   =   .0242    .0225     1.6921      1.6921
EPO   =   1000     1000      1000        1000

Airline Passenger Data:
LR    =   .1       .2.       5
TSS   =   .01      .01       .01
EPO   =   324      163       68
```

searchers for the airline passenger data (Newton, 1988). Rewriting the model, we have the following:

$$(1 - B^1 - B^{12} + B^{13})y_t = (1 - \theta_1 B - \theta_{1,12}B^{12} + \theta_1\theta_{1,12}B^{13})a_t \quad (5)$$

or

$$y_t = y_{t-12} + (y_{t-1} - y_{t-13}) +$$
$$(a_t - \theta_1 a_{t-1} - \theta_{1,12}a_{t-12} + \theta_1\theta_{1,12}a_{t-13}) \quad (6)$$

Equation (6) says that the forecast for the time period t is the sum of (1) the value of the time series in the same month of the previous year; (2) a trend component determined by the difference of previous month's value and last year's previous month's value; and (3) the effects of random shocks (or residuals) of period t, t − 1, t − 12 and t − 13 on the forecast.

From above analysis, it is then easy to see why the Box-Jenkins model can provide an accurate forecast for long memory time series, even for small bumps between the large seasonal peaks (Figure 2a), as long as there is a fixed pattern of the time series. But for short memory series, there is no definite pattern. Using a model similar to (6) is apparently not sufficient.

## Input-output Mapping with Neural Network

Most neural networks use sigmoidal activation functions which make it possible for the neural network to perform a complicated input-output mapping through the back propagation procedure. In essence, a neural network model is equivalent to a set of algebraic equations arranged in a hierarchical order to form a input-output mapping. Changing the structure of a neural network is nothing more than changing the hierarchical order of the algebraic equations. Training a neural network is just another way to say estimating the parameters in the complex input-output transformation function (Fishwick, 1989), formed by activation functions.

It is difficult to study the input-output transformation function of a neural network with hidden layer(s). Without a hidden layer, the neural network output is a function of a linear combination of the input variables. Then, we would like to know how this function is related to the Box-Jenkins model. Since the Box-Jenkins model for the airline data says that the time series value at time t is determined by a the value at time t − 1, t − 12, and t − 13, and some random shocks, we would expect that these data items also play an important role in the neural network model. This is indeed true as shown in Table 8. To compare with the Box-Jenkins model, we used 13 inputs (corresponding data at time t − 1 through t − 13) to forecast the value at time t. The training methods are the same as those described in section 2.

The weights of the neural network correspond to the coefficients of the input variables (since there is no hidden layer), and the bias in the output unit corresponds to a constant term. Although the neural network model is not a linear model because of the sigmoidal activation function of the output unit, it nevertheless identified the most important inputs (inputs with lager value of coefficients), as the Box-Jenkins model did. Note that those inputs are identified only after sufficient iterations of training epochs.

One important issue in understanding the neural network's ability to learn complicated mapping was brought up by Lapedes and Farber (1987). That is, the mode decomposition perspective. They made it clear that a neural network learns the relationship of the input-output pairs by using combinations of sigmoid functions to approximate the underlying time series mapping. Consider a series $x(t + 1) = 4^*x\,(t)\,(1 - x(t))$, for instance, Lapedes and Farber trained a simple $1 \times 5 \times 1$ (1 input unit, 5 hidden units, 1 output unit) neural network, and t hey showed that using the weights and

**Table 8.** Weights and bias associated with the neural network

| Training | weights | | | | | | | | | | | | | bias |
|---|---|---|---|---|---|---|---|---|---|---|---|---|---|---|
| 100 epo. | 1.7 | −.2 | .2 | −.6 | .5 | .0 | .3 | −.6 | .0 | .0 | 1.5 | 2.3 | .0 | −2.33 |
| 500 | 2.9 | .0 | .1 | −.4 | .4 | −.1 | .4 | −.6 | .2 | .0 | .9 | 3.6 | −2.33 | −2.43 |
| 1000 | 34.5 | −.1 | .3 | −.4 | .7 | −.7 | .7 | −.7 | .5 | −.2 | .6 | 4.3 | −4.63 | −2.43 |

biases from the trained network, they could explicitly write out an input-output mapping as a linear combination of 5 sigmoid functions and a linear function of the input variable. This linear combination of functions can approximate the underlying mapping, *i.e.*, x(t + 1) = 4* x(t) (1 − x(t)), very accurately within the domain.

Figure 5 shows the neural network mapping of the airline passenger time series. Different network structures result in different mapping. The one with a hidden layer is flatter than the one without a hidden layer. We see that a neural network is capable of reproducing the underlying pattern of a time series, with a proper network structure and appropriate training.

From above discussions, we see that training the neural network is essentially finding a set of hierarchically ordered activation functions which could best approximate the underlying mapping of the time series. With this perspective, we raise the following questions:

1. How accurate is the approximation?
2. Can we use analytical approach to find the approximation?

It is beyond the scope of this project to provide rigorous answer to above questions. Here we offer some of our initial thoughts gained from this project.

(1). Theoretically, the neural network mapping approximation could be made arbitrarily accurate. In practice, however, the accuracy is affected by many factors, such as the neural network structure, the accuracy of the input data. The fact that there is no established theory concerning neural network structure and training procedure makes accurate mapping more difficult. This could be one explanation to the discrepancy of reports on neural network performance in forecasting. In time series forecasting, suppose the series has a long memory, that is, a deterministic pattern (e.g., airline passenger), then the series can be described by the Box-Jenkins model

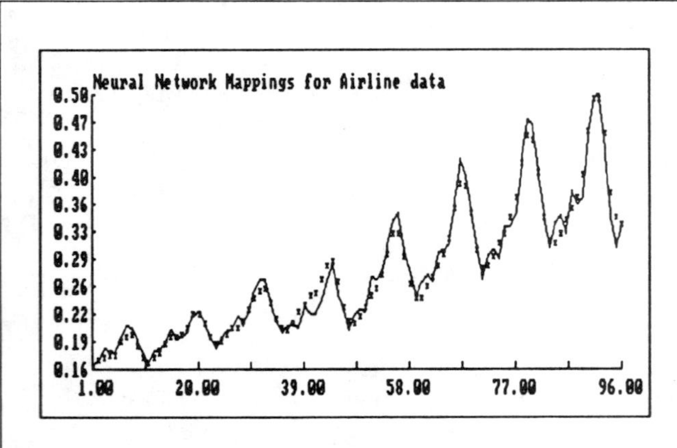


**Figure 5.** NN Mapping of the Time Series

very accurately. Using neural networks to approximate the mapping can hardly compete with Box-Jenkins model. However, Box-Jenkins model is sensitive to noise, and since it builds its forecast on previous observations, the method is only good for short term forecasting. A neural network (with a hidden layer) bases its forecasting on the approximated underlying mapping. Hence it is more robust and better in the case of long term forecasting as shown in sections 2.

(2). Training a neural network is time consuming. Since it can be regarded as an optimization problem, one would think analytical methods could be applicable, at least when the network structure is fixed. The problem is then finding a set of parameters, corresponding weights and biases in the neural network, such that the error function is minimized. Admittedly, this would be difficult since we do not have the experience of working on hierarchically ordered sigmoidal functions. But it may not be impossible. Research in improving neural network learning, such as fast learning rules, stepwise training, and so on, could lend insights to the analysis of the hierarchical mapping function. On the other hand, analytical study of the mapping approximation may, in turn, bring new ideas to improve neural network learning.

### Effect of Training on NN Learning

A proper training schedule can greatly improve both learning speed and the forecasting accuracy. Our experiments show that stepwise training does indeed help learning as reported by others in the literature. In our stepwise training case, we use, instead of different pattern, part of the total training series to train the network first, then the whole series.

Few papers have talked about changing training parameters during the training process. We found that a properly designed training schedule can improve learning speed, and increase chance of convergence. This can be thought as an analog to simulated annealing, in which the cooling schedule plays a key role in avoiding local optima and finding good solutions.

### Conclusions

Neural networks provide a promising alternative approach to time series forecasting. For time series with long memory, both Box-Jenkins model and neural network performs well, with Box-Jenkins model slightly better for short term forecasting. Neural network proved to be better in long term forecasting; however, we are still performing comparisons with alternative long term forecasting methods. For short memory time series, neural networks appear to be superior to Box-Jenkins model.

By approximating the underlying mapping of the time series, a neural network provides robust forecasting in the cases of irregular time series. The neural network model is more parsimonious in data requirement than the Box-Jenkins model.

Neural networks can be trained to approximate the underlying mapping of a time series, albeit the accuracy of the approximation depends on a number of factors such as the neural network structure, learning method, and training procedure. Without a hidden layer, the neural network model is functionally similar to the Box-Jenkins model.

The neural network structures and training procedures have great impact on its forecasting performance. Since the structures and training procedures used in our study are by no means the best, we believe there is still much room for improvement of neural network forecasting. We consider the following topics worth studying:

(1) Applying different neural network models, for instance, recurrent and cascade network, to forecasting.

(2) Building neural network causal models for time series forecasting.

(3) Comparing the neural network model with other conventional forecasting approaches.


## Acknowledgement

Dr. Chung Chen at Syracuse University provided the car sales data and some insightful discussions. The airline data is taken from *TIMESLAB* (Newton, 1988). Zaiyong Tang would like to thank the DIS Department at University of Florida for financial support. Paul Fishwick would like to thank the National Science Foundation (Award IRI8909152) for partial support during this research period.


## References

Bowerman, B.L. and O'Connell, R.T., 1987, *Time Series Forecasting*, 2nd. Ed. PWS Publishers, pp. 120.

Fishwick, P.A., 1989, "Neural Network Models in Simulation: A Comparison with Traditional Modeling Approaches," *Proceedings of Winter Simulation Conference*, Washington, DC, pp. 702-710.

Kung, S.Y. and Hwang, J.N., 1988, "An Algebraic Projection Analysis for Optimal Hidden Units Size and Learning Rates in Back-Propagation Learning," *Proceedings of IEEE International Neural Network Conference*, Vol. II.

Lapedes, A. and Farber, R., 1987, "Nonlinear Signal Processing Using Neural Network: Prediction and System Modelling," Los Alamos National Lab Technical Report, LA-UR-87 -2662.

Rumelhart, D.E. and McClelland, J.L., 1986, *Parallel Distributed Processing, Vol . 1*, MIT Press, Cambridge, Massachusetts.

McClelland, J.L. and Rumelhart, D.E., 1988, *Explorations in Parallel Distributed Processing*, MIT Press, Cambridge, Massachusetts.

Newton, H.J., 1988. *TIMESLAB: A Time Series Analysis Laboratory*, Wadsworth & Brooks/Cole Publishing Company, California.

Sharda, R. and Patil, R.B., 1990, "Neural Networks as Forecasting Experts : An Empirical Test," *Proceedings of the IJCNN Meeting*, Washington, pp. 491-494.

ZAIYONG TANG is a Ph.D. candidate in the Department of Decision and Information Sciences at the University of Florida. He received his B.E. in Mechanical Engineering from Chongqing University, China, in 1982; M.S. in MAterials Science from Chengdu University of Sci. & Tech., China, in 1984; M.S. in Transportation from Washington State University in 1987. His research interests include neural networks, machine learning, global optimization and forecasting.

CHRYSANTHUS S. DE ALMEIDA is reading for his Ph.D. in Decision and Information Sciences at the University of Florida. He obtained the B.Sc. in Electrical Engineering from the University of Sri Lanka in 1975, and the M.B.A. from the University of Florida in 1988. He has held positions of varied responsibilities, both engineering and managerial, in the national radio and television broadcasting organizations in Sri Lanka. His research interests are in knowledge-based information systems.

PAUL A. FISHWICK is an associate professor in the Department of Computer and Information Sciences at the University of Florida. He received a PhD in Computer and Information Science from the University of Pennsylvania in 1986. His research interests are in computer simulation modeling and analysis methods for complex systems. He is a member of IEEE, IEEE Society for Systems, Man and Cybernetics, IEEE Computer Society, The Society for Computer Simulation, ACM and AAAI. Dr. Fishwick was chairman of the IEEE Computer Society technical committee on simulation (TCSIM) for two years (1988-1990) and he is on the editorial boards of several journals including the *ACM Transactions on Modeling and Computer Simulation, The Transactions of The Society for Computer Simulation, International Journal of Computer Simulation,* and the *Journal of Systems Engineering*.

# Generalization by Weight-Elimination
# with Application to Forecasting


**Andreas S. Weigend**
Physics Department
Stanford University
Stanford, CA 94305

**David E. Rumelhart**
Psychology Department
Stanford University
Stanford, CA 94305

**Bernardo A. Huberman**
Dynamics of Computation
Xerox PARC
Palo Alto, CA 94304


## Abstract


Inspired by the information theoretic idea of minimum description length, we add a term to the back propagation cost function that penalizes network complexity. We give the details of the procedure, called weight-elimination, describe its dynamics, and clarify the meaning of the parameters involved. From a Bayesian perspective, the complexity term can be usefully interpreted as an assumption about prior distribution of the weights. We use this procedure to predict the sunspot time series and the notoriously noisy series of currency exchange rates.


## 1   INTRODUCTION

Learning procedures for connectionist networks are essentially statistical devices for performing inductive inference. There is a trade-off between two goals: on the one hand, we want such devices to be as general as possible so that they are able to learn a broad range of problems. This recommends large and flexible networks. On the other hand, the true measure of an inductive device is not how well it performs on the examples it has been shown, but how it performs on cases it has not yet seen, *i.e.*, its out-of-sample performance.

Too many weights of high precision make it easy for a net to fit the idiosyncrasies or "noise" of the training data and thus fail to generalize well to new cases. This *overfitting problem* is familiar in inductive inference, such as polynomial curve fitting. There are a number of potential solutions to this problem. We focus here on the so-called minimal network strategy. The underlying hypothesis is: if several nets fit the data equally well, the simplest one will on average provide the best generalization. Evaluating this hypothesis requires *(i)* some way of measuring simplicity and *(ii)* a search procedure for finding the desired net.

The complexity of an algorithm can be measured by the length of its minimal description in some language. Rissanen [Ris89] and Cheeseman [Che90] formalized the old but vague intuition of Occam's razor as the information theoretic *minimum description length (MDL) criterion:* Given some data, the most probable model is the model that minimizes

$$\underbrace{\text{description length}}_{\text{cost}} = \underbrace{\text{description length(data|model)}}_{\text{error}} + \underbrace{\text{description length(model)}}_{\text{complexity}} .$$

This sum represents the trade-off between residual error and model complexity. The goal is to find a net that has the lowest complexity while fitting the data adequately. The complexity is dominated by the number of bits needed to encode the weights. It is roughly proportional to the number of weights times the number of bits per weight. We focus here on the procedure of weight-elimination that tries to find a net with the smallest *number of weights*. We compare it with a second approach that tries to minimize the *number of bits per weight*, thereby creating a net that is not too dependent on the precise values of its weights.

## 2   WEIGHT-ELIMINATION

In 1987, Rumelhart proposed a method for finding minimal nets within the framework of back propagation learning. In this section we explain and interpret the procedure and, for the first time, give the details of its implementation. [1]

### 2.1   METHOD

The idea is indeed simple in conception: add to the usual cost function a term which counts the number of parameters, and *minimize the sum* of performance error and the number of weights by back propagation,

$$\sum_{k \in \mathcal{T}} \left(\text{target}_k - \text{output}_k\right)^2 + \lambda \sum_{i \in \mathcal{C}} \frac{w_i^2/w_0^2}{1 + w_i^2/w_0^2} \quad . \tag{1}$$

The first term measures the performance of the net. In the simplest case, it is the sum squared error over the set of training examples $\mathcal{T}$. The second term measures the size of the net. Its sum extends over all connections $\mathcal{C}$. $\lambda$ represents the relative importance of the complexity term with respect to the performance term.

The learning rule is then to change the weights according to the gradient of the *entire* cost function, continuously doing justice to the trade-off between error and complexity. This differs from methods that consider a set of fixed models, estimate the parameters for each of them, and then compare between the models by considering the number of parameters.

The complexity cost as function of $w_i/w_0$ is shown in Figure 1(b). The extreme regions of very large and very small weights are easily interpreted. For $|w_i| \gg w_0$, the cost of a weight approaches unity (times $\lambda$). This justifies the interpretation of the complexity term as a counter of significantly sized weights. For $|w_i| \ll w_0$, the cost is close to zero. "Large" and "small" are defined with respect to the scale $w_0$, a free parameter of the weight-elimination procedure that has to be chosen.

---

[1]The original formulation benefited from conversations with Paul Smolensky. Variations, and alternatives have been developed by Hinton, Hanson and Pratt, Mozer and Smolensky, le Cun, Denker and Solla, Ji, Snapp and Psaltis and others. They are discussed in Weigend [Wei91].

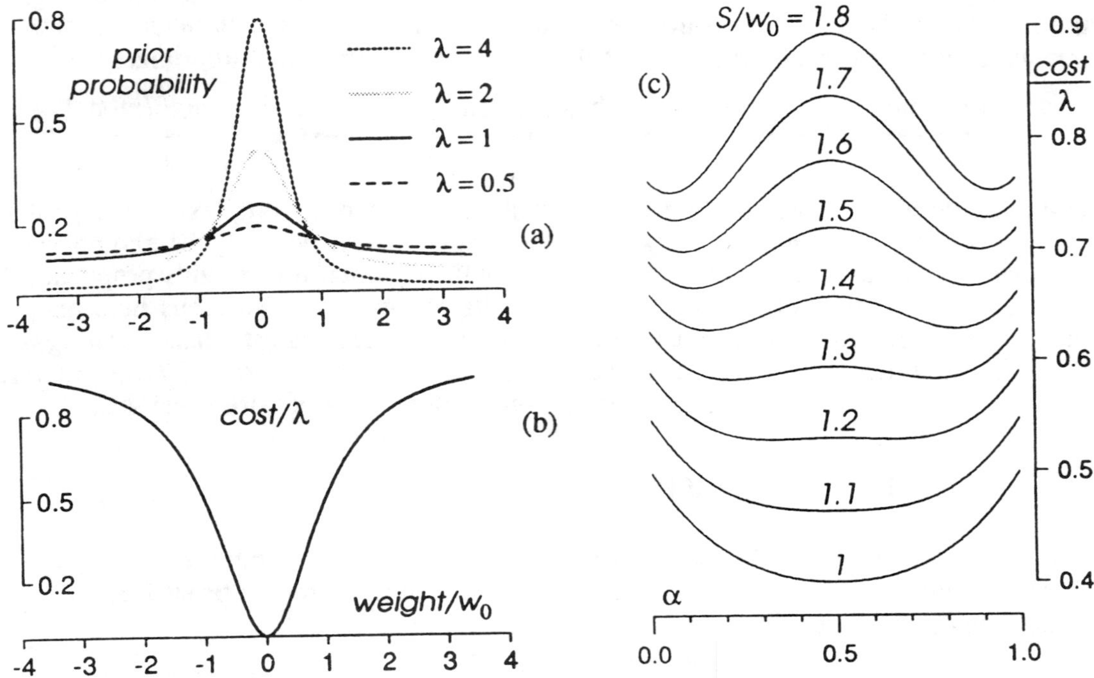

Figure 1: (a) Prior probability distribution for a weight. (b) Corresponding cost.
(c) Cost for different values of $S/w_0$ as function of $\alpha = w_1/S$, where $S = w_1 + w_2$.

To clarify the meaning of $w_0$, let us consider a unit which is connected—redundantly—by two weights ($w_1$ and $w_2$) to the same signal source. Is it cheaper to have two smaller weights or just one large weight? Interestingly, as shown in Figure 1(c), the answer depends on the ratio $S/w_0$, where $S = w_1 + w_2$ is the relevant sum for the receiving unit. For values of $S/w_0$ up to about 1.1, there is only one minimum at $\alpha := w_1/S = 0.5$, *i.e.*, both weights are present and equal. When $S/w_0$ increases, this symmetry gets broken; it is cheaper to set one weight $\approx S$ and eliminate the other one.

Weight-*decay*, proposed by Hinton and by le Cun in 1987, is contained in our method of weight-*elimination* as the special case of large $w_0$. In the statistics community, this limit (cost $\propto w_i^2$) is known as *ridge regression*. The scale parameter $w_0$ thus allows us to express a preference for fewer large weights ($w_0$ small) or many small weights ($w_0$ large). In our experience, choosing $w_0$ of order unity is good for activations of order unity.

## 2.2   INTERPRETATION AS PRIOR PROBABILITY

Further insight can be gained by viewing the *cost as the negative log likelihood of the network, given the data*. In this framework[2], the error term is the negative logarithm of the probability of the data given the net, and the complexity term is the negative logarithm of the prior probability of the weights.

The cost function corresponds approximately to the assumption that the weights come from a mixture of two distributions. Relevant weights are drawn from a uniform distribution (to

---

[2]This perspective is expanded in a forthcoming paper by Rumelhart *et al.* [RDGC92].

allow for normalization of the probability, up to a certain maximum size). Weights that are merely the result of "noise" are drawn from a Gaussian-like distribution centered on zero; they are expected to be small. We show the prior probability for our complexity term for several values of $\lambda$ in Figure 1(a). If we wish to approximate the bump around zero by a Gaussian, its variance is given by $\sigma^2 = w_0^2/\lambda$. Its width scales with $w_0$.

Perhaps surprisingly the innocent weighting factor $\lambda$ now influences the width: the variance of the "noise" is inversely proportional to $\lambda$. The larger $\lambda$ is, the closer to zero a weight must be to have a reasonable probability of being a member of the "noise" distribution. Also, the larger $\lambda$ is, the more "pressure" small weights feel to become even smaller.

The following technical section describes how $\lambda$ is dynamically adjusted in training. From the perspective taken in Section 2.1, the usual increase of $\lambda$ during training corresponds to attaching more importance to the complexity term. From the perspective developed in this section, it corresponds to sharpening the peak of the weight distribution around zero.

## 2.3 DETAILS

Although the basic form of the weight-elimination procedure is simple, it is sensitive to the choice of $\lambda$.[3] If $\lambda$ is too small, it will have no effect. If $\lambda$ is too large, all of the weights will be driven to zero. Worse, a value of $\lambda$ which is useful for a problem that is easily learned may be too large for a hard problem, and a problem which is difficult in one region (at the start, for example) may require a larger value of $\lambda$ later on. We have developed some rules that make the performance relatively insensitive to the exact values of the parameters.

We start with $\lambda = 0$ so that the network can initially use all of its resources. $\lambda$ is changed after each epoch. It is usually gently incremented, sometimes decremented, and, in emergencies, cut down. The choice among these three actions depends on the value of the error on the training set $\mathcal{E}_n$.

The subscript $n$ denotes the number of the epoch that has just finished. (Note that $\mathcal{E}_n$ is only the first term of the cost function (Equation 1). Since gradient descent minimizes the sum of both terms, $\mathcal{E}_n$ by itself can decrease or increase.) $\mathcal{E}_n$ is compared to three quantities, the first two derived from previous values of that error itself, the last one given externally:

- $\mathcal{E}_{n-1}$ Previous error.

- $\mathcal{A}_n$ Average error (exponentially weighted over the past).
  It is defined as $\mathcal{A}_n = \gamma \mathcal{A}_{n-1} + (1 - \gamma)\mathcal{E}_n$ (with $\gamma$ relatively close to 1).

- $\mathcal{D}$ Desired error, the externally provided performance criterion.
  The strategy for choosing $\mathcal{D}$ depends on the specific problem. For example, "solutions" with an error larger than $\mathcal{D}$ might not be acceptable. Or, we may have observed (by monitoring the out-of-sample performance during training) that overfitting starts when a certain in-sample error is reached. Or, we may have some other estimate of the amount of noise in the training data. For toy problems, derived from approximating analytically defined functions (where perfect performance on the training data can be expected), a good choice is $\mathcal{D} = 0$. For hard problems, such as the prediction of currency exchange rates, $\mathcal{D}$ is set just below the error that corresponds to chance performance, since overfitting would occur if the error was reduced further.

After each epoch in training, we evaluate whether $\mathcal{E}_n$ is above or below each of these quantities. This gives eight possibilities. Three actions are possible:

- $\lambda \leftarrow \lambda + \Delta\lambda$
  In six cases, we increment $\lambda$ slightly. These are the situations in which things are going well: the error is already below than the criterion ($\mathcal{E}_n < \mathcal{D}$) and/or is still falling ($\mathcal{E}_n < \mathcal{E}_{n-1}$).

---

[3]The reason that $\lambda$ appears at all is because weight-elimination only deals with a part of the complete network complexity, and this only approximately. In a theory rigidly derived from the minimum description length principle, no such parameter would appear.

Incrementing $\lambda$ means attaching more importance to the complexity term and making the Gaussian a little sharper. Note that the primary parameter is actually $\Delta\lambda$. Its size is fairly small, of order $10^{-6}$.

In the remaining two cases, the error is worse than the criterion and it has grown compared to just before ($\mathcal{E}_n \geq \mathcal{E}_{n-1}$). The action depends on its relation to its long term average $\mathcal{A}_n$.

- $\lambda \leftarrow \lambda - \Delta\lambda$ $\qquad\qquad\qquad\qquad\qquad\left[\text{if } \mathcal{E}_n \geq \mathcal{E}_{n-1} \wedge \mathcal{E}_n < \mathcal{A}_n \wedge \mathcal{E}_n \geq \mathcal{D}\right]$

  In the less severe of those two cases, the performance is still improving with respect to the long term average ($\mathcal{E}_n < \mathcal{A}$). Since the error can have grown only slightly, we reduce $\lambda$ slightly.

- $\lambda \leftarrow 0.9\,\lambda$ $\qquad\qquad\qquad\qquad\qquad\left[\text{if } \mathcal{E}_n \geq \mathcal{E}_{n-1} \wedge \mathcal{E}_n \geq \mathcal{A}_n \wedge \mathcal{E}_n \geq \mathcal{D}\right]$

  In this last case, the error has increased and exceeds its long term average. This can happen for two reasons. The error might have grown a lot in the last iteration. Or, it might not have improved by much in the whole period covered by the long term average, *i.e.*, the network might be trapped somewhere before reaching the performance criterion. The value of $\lambda$ is cut, hopefully prevent weight-elimination from devouring the whole net.

We have found that this set of heuristics for finding a minimal network while achieving a desired level of performance on the training data works rather well on a wide range of tasks. We give two examples of applications of weight-elimination. In the second example we show how $\lambda$ changes during training.


# 3  APPLICATION TO TIME SERIES PREDICTION

A central problem in science is predicting the future of temporal sequences; examples range from forecasting the weather to anticipating currency exchange rates. The desire to know the future is often the driving force behind the search for laws in science. The ability to forecast the behavior of a system hinges on two types of knowledge. The first and most powerful one is the knowledge of the laws underlying a given phenomenon. When expressed in the form of equations, the future outcome of an experiment can be predicted. The second, albeit less powerful, type of knowledge relies on the discovery of empirical regularities without resorting to knowledge of the underlying mechanism. In this case, the key problem is to determine which aspects of the data are merely idiosyncrasies and which aspects are truly indicators of the intrinsic behavior. This issue is particularly serious for real world data, which are limited in precision and sample size. We have applied nets with weight-elimination to time series of sunspots and currency exchange rates.


## 3.1  SUNSPOT SERIES [4]

When applied to predict the famous yearly sunspot averages, weight-elimination reduces the number of hidden units to three. Just having a small net, however, is not the ultimate goal: predictive power is what counts. The net has one half the out-of-sample error (on iterated single step predictions) of the benchmark model by Tong [Ton90].

What happens when we enlarge the input size from twelve, the optimal size for the benchmark model, to four times that size? As shown in [WRH90], the performance does not deteriorate (as might have been expected from a less dense distribution of data points in higher dimensional spaces). Instead, the net manages to ignore irrelevant information.

---

[4]We here only briefly summarize our results on sunspots. Details have been published in [WHR90] and [WRH90].

## 3.2 CURRENCY EXCHANGE RATES [5]

We use daily exchange rates (or *prices* with respect to the US Dollar) for five currencies (German Mark (DM), Japanese Yen, Swiss Franc, Pound Sterling and Canadian Dollar) to predict the *returns* at day $t$, defined as

$$r_t := \ln \frac{p_t}{p_{t-1}} = \ln \left( 1 + \frac{p_t - p_{t-1}}{p_{t-1}} \right) \approx \frac{p_t - p_{t-1}}{p_{t-1}} \tag{2}$$

For small changes, the return is the difference to the previous day normalized by the price $p_{t-1}$. Since different currencies and different days of the week may have different dynamics, we pick for one day (Monday) and one currency (DM). We define the task to be to learn *Monday DM dynamics:* given exchange rate information through a Monday, predict the DM - US\$ rate for the following day.

The net has 45 inputs for past daily DM returns, 5 inputs for the present Monday's returns of all available currencies, and 11 inputs for additional information (trends and volatilities), solely derived from the original exchange rates. The $k$ *day trend* at day $t$ is the mean of the returns of the $k$ last days, $\frac{1}{k} \sum_{t-k+1}^{t} r_t$ . Similarly, the $k$ *day volatility* is defined to be the standard deviation of the returns of the $k$ last days.

The inputs are fully connected to the *5 sigmoidal hidden units* with range $(-1, 1)$. The hidden units are fully connected to *two output units*. The first one is to predict the next day return, $r_{t+1}$. This is a linear unit, trained with quadratic error. The second output unit focuses on the *sign* of the change. Its target value is one when the price goes up and zero otherwise. Since we want the unit to predict the probability that the return is positive, we choose a sigmoidal unit with range $(0, 1)$ and minimize cross entropy error.

The central question is whether the net is able to extract any signal from the training set that generalizes to the test sets. The performance is given as function of training time in epochs in Figure 2. [6]

The result is that the out-of-sample prediction is *significantly better than chance*. Weight-elimination reliably extracts a signal that accounts for between 2.5 and 4.0 per cent of the variance, corresponding to a correlation coefficient of $0.21 \pm 0.03$ for both test sets. In contrast, nets without precautions against overfitting show hopeless out-of-sample performance almost before the training has started. Also, none of the control experiments (randomized series and time-reversed series) reaches any significant predictability.

The dynamics of weight-elimination, discussed in Section 2.3, is also shown in Figure 2. $\lambda$ first grows very slowly. Then, around epoch 230, the error reaches the performance

---

[5]We thank Blake LeBaron for sending us the data.

[6]The error of the unit predicting the return is expressed as the *average relative variance*

$$\mathrm{arv}_S = \frac{\sum_{k \in S} \left( \mathrm{target}_k - \mathrm{prediction}_k \right)^2}{\sum_{k \in S} \left( \mathrm{target}_k - \mathrm{mean}_S \right)^2} = \frac{1}{\sigma_S^2} \frac{1}{N_S} \sum_{k \in S} \left( r_k - \widehat{r}_k \right)^2 \quad . \tag{3}$$

The averaging (division by $N_S$, the number of observations in set $S$) makes the measure independent of the size of the set. The normalization (division by $\sigma_S^2$, the estimated variance of the data in $S$), removes the dependence on the dynamic range of the data. Since the mean of the returns is close to zero, the random walk hypothesis corresponds to $\mathrm{arv} = 1.0$.

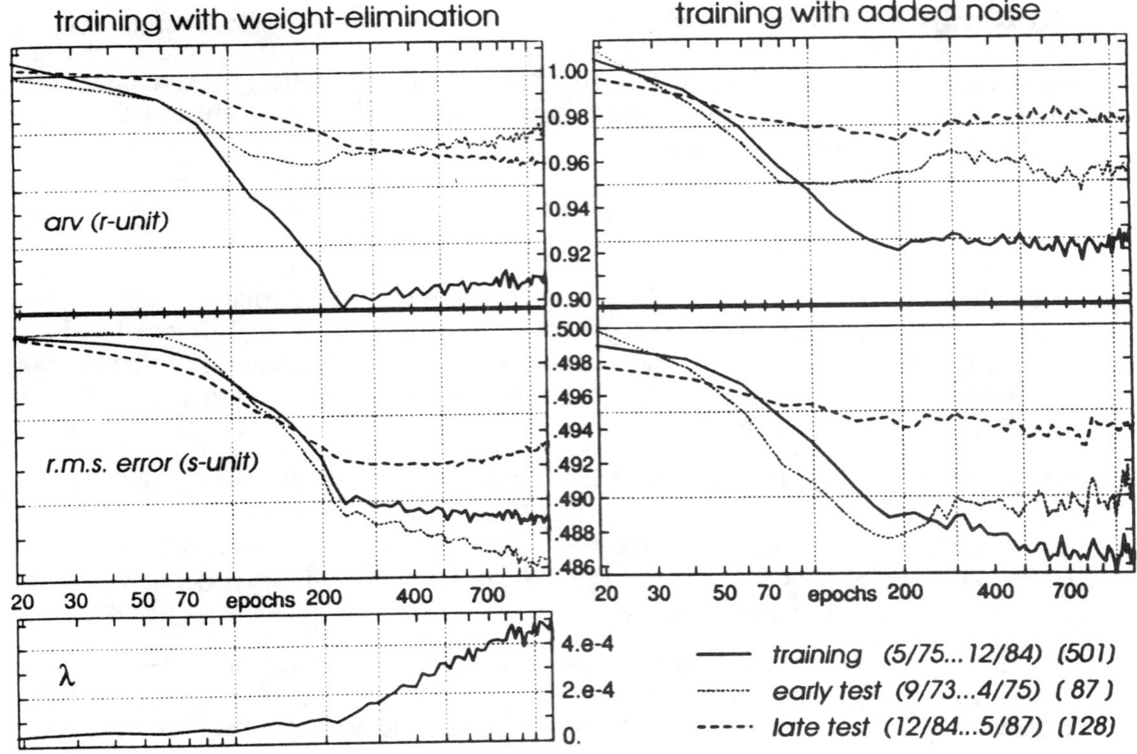



Figure 2: Learning curves of currency exchange rates for training with weight-elimination (left) and training with added noise (right). In-sample predictions are shown as solid lines, out-of sample predictions in grey and dashed. Top: average relative variance of the unit predicting the return (r-unit). Center: root-mean-square error of the unit predicting the sign (s-unit). Bottom: Weighting of the complexity term.

criterion. [7] The network starts to focus on the elimination of weights (indicated by growing $\lambda$) without further reducing its in-sample errors (solid lines), since that would probably correspond to overfitting.

We also compare training with weight-elimination with a method intended to make the parameters more robust. We add noise to the inputs, independently to each input unit, different at each presentation of each pattern.[8] This can be viewed as artificially enlarging the training set by smearing the data points around their centers. Smoother boundaries of the "basins of attraction" are the result. Viewed from the description length angle, it means saving bits by specifying the (input) weights with less precision, as opposed to eliminating some of them. The corresponding learning curves are shown on the right hand side of Figure 2. This simple method also successfully avoids overfitting.

---

[7]Guided by cross-validation, we set the criterion (for the sum of the squared errors from both outputs) to 650. With this value, the choice of the other parameters is not critical, as long as they are fairly small. We used a learning rate of $2.5 \times 10^{-4}$, no momentum, and an increment $\Delta\lambda$ of $2.5 \times 10^{-6}$. If the criterion was set to zero, the balance between error and complexity would be fragile in such a hard problem.

[8]We add Gaussian noise with a rather large standard deviation of 1.5 times the signal. The exact value is not crucial: similar performance is obtained for noise levels between 0.7 and 2.0 .

Finally, we analyze the weight-eliminated network solution. The weights from the hidden units to the outputs are in a region where the complexity term acts as a counter. In fact only one or two hidden units remain. The weights from the inputs to the dead hidden units are also eliminated. For time series prediction, weight-elimination acts as hidden-unit elimination.

The weights between inputs and remaining hidden units are fairly small. Weight-elimination is in its quadratic region and prevents them from growing too large. Consequently, the activation of the hidden units lies in $(-0.4, 0.4)$. This prompted us to try a linear net where our procedure also works surprisingly well, yielding comparable performance to sigmoids.

Since all inputs are scaled to zero mean and unit standard deviation, we can gauge the importance of different inputs directly by the size of the weights. With weight-elimination, it becomes fairly clear which quantities are important, since connections that do not manage to reduce the error are not worth their price. A detailed description will be published in [WHR91]. Weight-elimination enhances the interpretability of the solution.

To summarize, we have a working procedure that finds small nets and can help prevent overfitting. With our rules for the dynamics of $\lambda$, weight-elimination is fairly stable. values of most parameters. In the examples we analyzed, the network manages to pick out some significant part of the dynamics underlying the time series.

## References


[Che90]    Peter C. Cheeseman. **On finding the most probable model.** In J. Shrager and P. Langley (eds.) *Computational Models of Scientific Discovery and Theory Formation*, p. 73. Morgan Kaufmann, 1990.

[RDGC92]   David E. Rumelhart, Richard Durbin, Richard Golden, and Yves Chauvin. **Backpropagation: theoretical foundations.** In Y. Chauvin and D. E. Rumelhart (eds.) *Backpropagation and Connectionist Theory*. Lawrence Erlbaum, 1992.

[Ris89]    Jorma Rissanen. **Stochastic Complexity in Statistical Inquiry.** World Scientific, 1989.

[Ton90]    Howell Tong. **Non-linear Time Series: a Dynamical System Approach.** Oxford University Press, 1990.

[Wei91]    Andreas S. Weigend. **Connectionist Architectures for Time Series Prediction.** PhD thesis, Stanford University, 1991. (in preparation)

[WHR90]    Andreas S. Weigend, Bernardo A. Huberman, and David E. Rumelhart. **Predicting the future: a connectionist approach.** *International Journal of Neural Systems*, 1:193, 1990.

[WHR91]    Andreas S. Weigend, Bernardo A. Huberman, and David E. Rumelhart. **Predicting sunspots and currency rates with connectionist networks.** In M. Casdagli and S. Eubank (eds.) *Proceedings of the 1990 NATO Workshop on Nonlinear Modeling and Forecasting (Santa Fe)*. Addison-Wesley, 1991.

[WRH90]    Andreas S. Weigend, David E. Rumelhart, and Bernardo A. Huberman. **Backpropagation, weight-elimination and time series prediction.** In D. S. Touretzky, J. L. Elman, T. J. Sejnowski, and G. E. Hinton (eds.) *Proceedings of the 1990 Connectionist Models Summer School*, p 105. Morgan Kaufmann, 1990.

*Chemical Engineering Science*. Vol. 45, No. 8, pp. 2075–2081, 1990.
Printed in Great Britain.

0009–2509/90 $3.00 + 0.00
© 1990 Pergamon Press plc

# NONLINEAR SIGNAL PROCESSING AND SYSTEM IDENTIFICATION: APPLICATIONS TO TIME SERIES FROM ELECTROCHEMICAL REACTIONS

J. L. HUDSON[1], M. KUBE[1], R. A. ADOMAITIS[2], I. G. KEVREKIDIS[2], A. S. LAPEDES[3],
and R. M. FARBER[3]

[1]Department of Chemical Engineering, University of Virginia, Charlottesville, VA 22903-2442
[2]Department of Chemical Engineering, Princeton University, Princeton, NJ 08544
[3]Theoretical Division, Los Alamos National Laboratory, Los Alamos, NM 87544

## ABSTRACT

We show how nonlinear signal processing techniques can be used for extracting simple dynamic models from complex experimental time series. A neural network analysis is applied to measurements of current versus time from an experimental system where the electrodissolution of copper in a phosphoric acid solution takes place. We investigate transitions from steady to oscillatory behavior and from period-one to period-two oscillations. Such procedures can be used in the analysis of systems for which no adequate phenomenological models exist.

## KEYWORDS

Electrochemical Oscillations; Neural Networks; Signal Processing; Nonlinear Dynamics; Bifurcations.

## INTRODUCTION

Chemical reactors often operate under unsteady conditions. This unsteady behavior can result from variations in an input, such as a feed concentration, or can be caused by kinetic or thermal instabilities in the reactor system itself. Under such conditions, one obtains a transient signal, e.g., a measurement of concentration, potential, or temperature as a function of time. One way of understanding the different behaviors is by comparing the observed behaviors to the predictions of fundamental models obtained using established theories of the process. These models can then be used to characterize the process, select optimal operating conditions, and control the system. However, we are often faced with processes whose fundamental models are tentative, nonexistent, or extremely difficult to analyze because of their size and complexity. Experimentally observed dynamic behavior is often low-dimensional, suggesting that a small set of ordinary differential equations could provide an accurate model of the system, at least over the operating regime of interest. Recent developments in nonlinear time series processing, using different forms of artificial neural networks (e.g., Lapedes and Farber, 1987a, b), provide a basis for the identification of low-order, accurate dynamic models consistent with the experimental time series.

Electrochemical reactions are known to exhibit interesting dynamic behavior. For example, the electrodissolution of copper in acidic chloride solutions is known to undergo several well-defined low-dimensional transitions, such as breaking of tori, transitions to homoclinic behavior, and period-doubling of tori (e.g., Bassett and Hudson, 1988, 1989a, b). The dynamics of these systems have been investigated using several methods from nonlinear dynamics, such as Poincaré maps, dimension calculations, and attractor reconstruction through time-delays (proposed by Packard *et al.*, 1980 and by Takens, 1981). As shown in Albahadily and Schell (1988), the electrodissolution of copper in phosphoric acid also exhibits low-order, yet interesting dynamics, including Hopf bifurcations and period-doublings. In this paper, we apply neural network methods to time series obtained from the latter system. The experiments are performed under potentiostatic conditions and the current is measured as a function of time. In this early study, we limit the analysis to transitions from steady state to periodic oscillations and from single-loop to double-loop oscillations. We plan to analyze transitions to chaos in subsequent papers.

## EXPERIMENTS

The experiments were carried out with a rotating disc electrode; a copper rod, 8.26mm in diameter, was imbedded in a 2cm diameter Teflon cylinder with the copper exposed at the end. The cell was a 400ml beaker with 25ml side chambers. The counter electrode was a platinum sheet with a surface area of 25cm$^2$. The reference electrode was a saturated calomel electrode (SCE). The cell contained 300ml of 85% phosphoric acid. The temperature was maintained at 25°C by means of a water bath.

The potential was set using a Princeton Applied Research (PAR) model 362 scanning potentiostat. Steps in the potential were applied with a PAR model 175 Universal Programmer. Digital data were taken using a Keithley model 500A measurement and control system. All data were collected at 1000 Hz.

### TIME SERIES ANALYSIS

We analyze time series of the current (corresponding to the net rate of dissolution) for a range of parameter values (the operating parameter is the applied potential). The purpose of the analysis is to obtain a nonlinear input-output map which, given the operating parameter values, the present measurement, and possibly some recent history, will predict the state of the system at the next time step. The resulting map is used for short-term prediction of the time series, to generate the system's attractor(s), and for analyzing the stability and bifurcation behavior of the system. In the last few years, several alternative techniques for obtaining such maps for nonlinear dynamical systems have been proposed (e.g., Bayly *et al.*, 1987; Casdagli, 1989; Crutchfield and McNamara, 1987; Lapedes and Farber, 1987a; Farmer and Sidorowich, 1987, 1988). Past research efforts have focused mainly on time series prediction, rather than system identification.

We have used two of these techniques, both based on artificial neural networks, in characterizing our experimental time series. The first involves a feedforward neural network with several inputs (four in our case), two hidden layers (each with ten neurons), and a continuous, nonlinear, nonpolynomial, sigmoidal activation function. We first discuss, for the sake of simplicity, the method for a fixed value of the operating parameter (three inputs). The framework, shown schematically in Fig.1, consists of a set of identical simple computing elements (neurons) wired together into a network. The input to each neuron is a weighted sum of the outputs of the neurons in the previous layer. Each hidden layer neuron performs a simple nonlinear transformation of its input:

$$O_i = g\left(\sum_j T_{ij} I_j + \theta_i\right) \tag{1}$$

where $O_i$ is the neuron output, $I_j$ are the neuron inputs (outputs of the previous layers), $T_{ij}$ are the synaptic weights, and $\theta_i$ are offsets (the $T_{ij}$ and the $\theta_i$ are the adjustable parameters of the model). The activation function $g(\,.\,)$ is usually a sigmoidal function with range from 0 to 1. The motivation for choosing this form of a function comes from smoothing an "on-off" step function. The exact shape of this sigmoidal function is not critical; we have used the function $g(x)=0.5(1+\tanh(x))$ following Rummelhart and McClelland (1986). The inputs consist of the time series $x(t)$ and a suitable number of delays $[x(t-\tau_1), x(t-\tau_2), ..., (x(t-\tau_n)]$. The final network output is the predicted value of the time series at the next sampling instant, $x(t+\tau)$. The output layer neuron is a simple linear scaling, so that the predicted values can be outside the range 0 to 1. The network is trained using nonlinear least squares - this gives values of $T_{ij}$ and $\theta_i$ that minimize the sum of squares of the differences between the predicted and measured values of the output sampled over the entire time series. A conjugate gradient method was used for the minimization. The calculations were carried out on the 64,000 processor Connection Machine at Los Alamos. At every iteration of the conjugate gradient method, we simultaneously evaluate the prediction of the current net for every point of the time series. Individual processors evaluate this predicted output for individual points in the time series, thus exploiting the massively parallel architecture of the CM-2. In some cases, we also "pruned" the net: during the optimization, when certain synaptic weights came very close to zero, they were set identically equal to zero and the minimization with respect to the remaining weights was then continued. In this manner, we reduced the number of connections from ~150 to approximately 40. This connection pruning perhaps can be considered as a type of noise filtering: eliminating superfluous weights may prevent the model from fine-tuning to the experimental noise.

After the iterative optimization procedure has converged (not necessarily to a global minimum), we have an explicit nonlinear map

$$x_{n+1} = f(x_n, x_{n-1}, ..., x_{n-m}) \tag{2}$$

where m is the number of delays chosen. By "bootstrapping" the net into the future, this map can be iterated to give

$$x_{n+1} = f(\, f(x_n, x_{n-1}, ..., x_{n-m}), x_n, x_{n-1}, ..., x_{n-m+1}\,) \tag{3}$$

or, using an m+1 dimensional vector $x_n \equiv (x_n, x_{n-1}, ..., x_{n-m})^T$, we can define the map

$$x_{n+1} = F(x_n). \tag{4}$$

In this formalism, a measurement or a prediction in the time series becomes a phase point in an m+1-dimensional space with coordinates defined by the present value and the m previous values. Trajectories in phase space approach an *attractor*

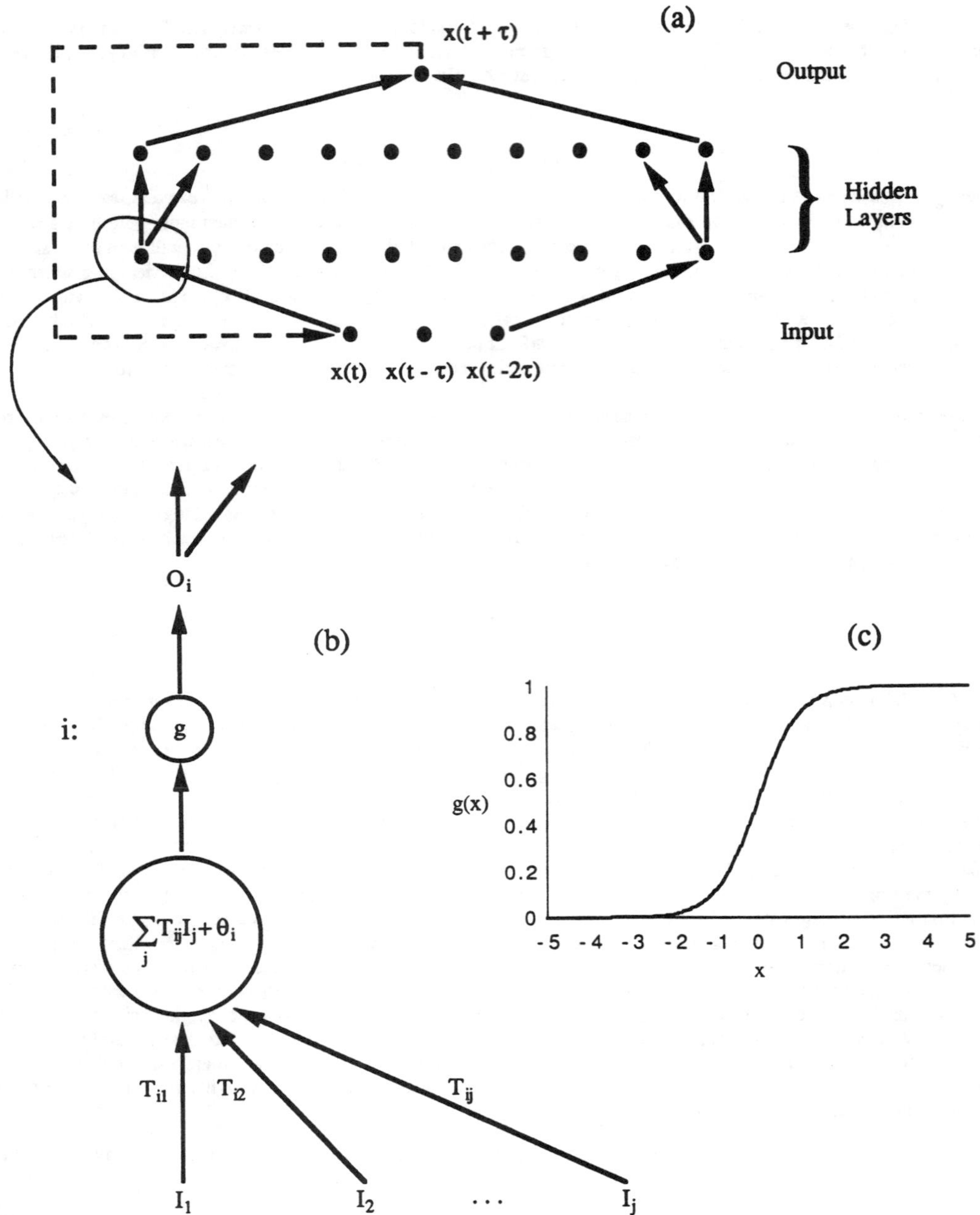



Fig. 1. (a): A neural network with two hidden layers, three input neurons (two time delays) and one output (predicted time series). (b): A blowup of the operations performed by one neuron. (c): The graph of a typical nonlinear activation function g(x).

as initial transients die out. Comparing the attractors reconstructed using time delays from the original time series and the attractors resulting from iteration of eq. (4) is a useful method for evaluating the long-term predictive capabilities of the network.

We have incorporated the dependence of the map (4) on the operating parameter by simply reserving one of the neural network inputs for the value of the fixed potential, i.e., we let

$$x_{n+1} = F(x_n, E). \tag{4'}$$

Equation (4') can now be used to analyze the stability and bifurcation behavior of the system as the operating parameter varies. A comparison of experimental and predicted bifurcation diagrams gives insight into specific dynamic instabilities of the system and is useful in designing experiments to elucidate their nature.

The second technique we use can be interpreted as a particular kind of a neural network and is shown schematically in Fig. 2. Here the network is of the simpler "perceptron" type and does not involve hidden layers. Every "point" in (phase)×(parameter) space consists of a vector $x = (x_n, x_{n-1}, x_{n-2}, E)^T$ which includes the present value of the current, $x_n$, two time delayed values, $x_{n-1}$ and $x_{n-2}$, as well as the potential, E, at which these measurements were obtained. We select k such data points, $Y_j$ ( with elements $Y_{ji}$, i=1, ..., 4, and j=1, ..., k), randomly from the measured time series. Given a "point" x, the k inputs to the network consist of the k distances, $d_j$ (j=1, ..., k), of the vector x from the vectors $Y_j$ defined as

$$d_j^2 = \sum_{i=1}^{4} (x_i - Y_{ji})^2 \qquad j = 1, \ldots, k.$$

(5)

These k distances are the inputs to the k neurons of the single layer of the network (see Fig. 2). The output (the predicted value of the current at the next time step) is given by a linear combination of the k distances. This network is a special case of fitting input-output maps using *radial basis functions* (Aizermann *et al.*, 1964; Broomhead and Lowe, 1988; Casdagli, 1989; Powell, 1985). Training begins with a large number (k=1000) of data points selected randomly from all available experimental time series at several parameter values, and we again prune this network to a smaller number of connections. Because of the simple, linear dependence of the output on the synaptic weights, training this network is a linear least squares problem, which is solved using the singular value decomposition.

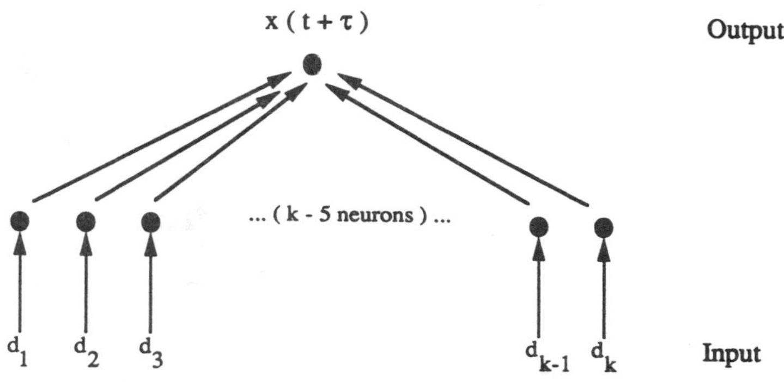


Fig. 2.  A schematic of the radial basis function network with k neurons.

### RESULTS

We first describe an example of using the two-hidden-layer network approach. This network was trained on two experimental time series, the first at a potential of 820mV yielding a single peak oscillation and the second at a potential of 766mV which gave a two-peak oscillation. The resulting pruned network was capable of predicting both the single and the two-peak oscillations at the corresponding parameter values. Figures 3a and 3b show the experimental transients at 769mV and 788mV respectively, including a relatively long startup period. Figures 3c and 3d show two-dimensional projections of the phase portraits reconstructed using two time delays (of 10 and 20 sampling periods). Figures 3e and 3f show the same projection of the phase portraits of the attractors predicted by the pruned neural network. Although not shown in the figure, short-term prediction of the time series is excellent. What is demonstrated in this figure is that the network can also semi-quantitatively capture the asymptotic, long-term system behavior (i.e., its attractors).

The behaviors shown in Figs 3a and 3b are far removed in parameter space from each other (i.e., there is no simple bifurcation between the two states). We now discuss a series of transitions which occur in a well-defined manner as the parameter is changed. Figures 4a, b, and c show experimentally-determined attractors for potential values of 748mV (steady state), 753mV (a triangle-shaped oscillation), and 759mV (a double-loop oscillation), respectively. Experimental time series at intermediate parameter values (a total of eight time series between 748mV and 763mV) indicate that the transitions observed are most probably a Hopf bifurcation to a limit cycle followed by a simple period-doubling of the limit cycle. For this set of eight time series, we obtained our best results using the pruned radial-basis network. Again, it is important to note that the parameter is part of the fitting, since the radial distances which constitute the input to the network are calculated in the four-dimensional (phase)×(parameter) space. Figures 4d and 4e compare a segment of

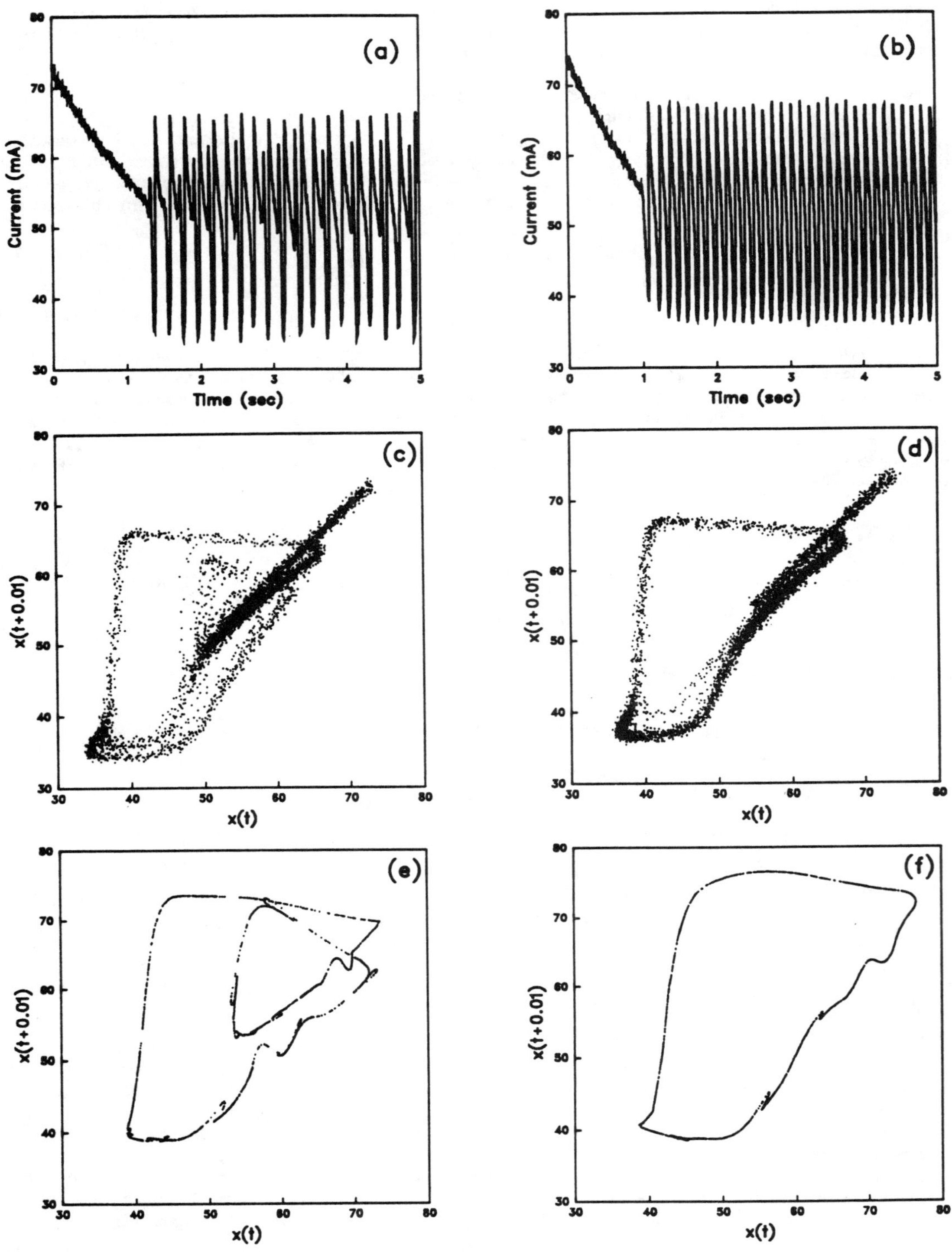

Fig. 3.  (a, b): Experimental measurements of electrodissolution current vs. time at 769mV and 788mV, respectively.  (c, d): The same transients plotted in delay space, leading to a double loop (769mV, 3c) and a single loop (788mV, 3d) attractor. The long straight segment corresponds to the startup part of the transient.  (e, f): Attractors predicted by a two-hidden-layer network.

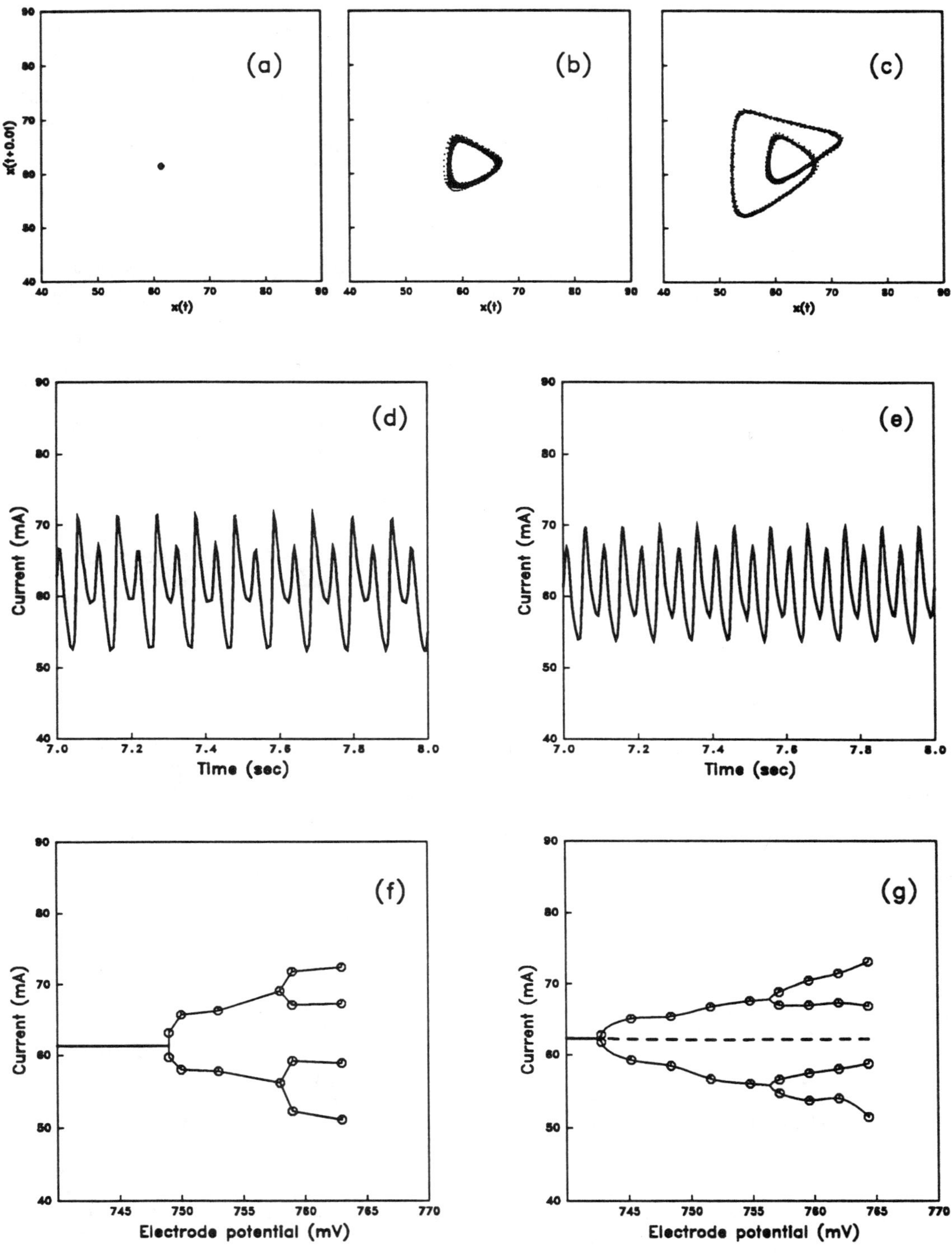

Fig. 4. (a, b, c): Phase portraits reconstructed in delay space using experimental measurements at 748mV, 753mV, and 759mV, respectively. (d, e): Segments of experimental (d) and predicted time series (e) at 759mV. (f, g): Bifurcation diagrams generated by experimental data (f) and the radial basis function network (g).

experimental and predicted time series in the period-doubled regime (V=759mV). We see again that short term prediction of the time series itself is very good, but prediction accuracy deteriorates as the map is iterated farther into the future (notice the shift in peaks towards the end of the time series segments shown). Nevertheless, the nature of the two-peak oscillation (double-loop attractor) is retained here, as it was in Fig. 3e. Finally, in Figs 4f and 4g, we include the experimental and predicted bifurcation diagrams, respectively. For the oscillatory branches, we plot the maximum and minimum of the oscillations. Since the fitted map is available in closed form, we can find both stable and unstable solutions, quantify their stability, and accurately detect bifurcation points using numerical analysis techniques (we have included the predicted unstable steady state in Fig. 4g).

## CONCLUDING REMARKS

The results presented here constitute our initial attempt to apply neural network analysis to chemical reaction data. These initial examples involved relatively simple dynamic phenomena. The methods, however, should be applicable to more complex dynamic behavior, and the extension to incorporate the dependence on more than one parameter is straightforward. It appears that this approach is indeed capable of producing accurate *nonlinear* dynamic models of processes exhibiting low-order dynamics (this does not necessarily mean simple dynamics!). Predictive models can be used to simulate and/or control a process. We should mention that the training in our examples was performed off-line, i.e., the time series were first obtained, and the training was performed subsequently. On-line training, however, is also possible, and the development of special purpose hardware for neural network configurations can find use in real-time chemical process identification and control (see for example Ydstie, 1989; Bhat and Mc Avoy, 1989).

## ACKNOWLEDGEMENTS

This work was partially supported by the National Science Foundation (JLH and IGK), the Center for Innovative Technology, Commonwealth of Virginia (JLH), a Packard Foundation Fellowship (IGK) and the Air Force Office of Scientific Research (ASL and RMF). The hospitality of the Center for Nonlinear Studies at Los Alamos is gratefully acknowledged.

## REFERENCES

Aizerman, M. A., E. M. Braverman, and L. I. Rozonoer (1964). Theoretical Foundations of the Potential Function Method in Pattern Recognition Learning. Translated from *Avtomatika i Telemekhanika*, 25, 917-936.

Albahadily, F. N. and M. Schell (1988). An experimental investigation of periodic and chaotic electrochemical oscillations in the anodic dissolution of copper in phosphoric acid. *J. Chem. Phys.*, 88, 4312-4318.

Bassett, M. R. and J. L. Hudson (1988). S'ilnikov Chaos During Copper Electrodissolution. *J.Phys.Chem.*, 92, 6963-6966.

Bassett, M. R. and J. L. Hudson (1989a). Quasiperiodicity and Chaos During an Electrochemical Reaction. *J. Phys. Chem.*, 93, 2731-2737.

Bassett, M. R. and J. L. Hudson (1989b). Experimental Evidence for Period-Doubling of Tori during an Electrochemical Reaction. *Physica D,* 35, 289-298.

Bayly, B. J., I. Goldhirsch, and S. A. Orszag (1987). Independent Degrees of Freedom of Dynamical Systems. *J. Sci. Comp.*, 2, 111-121.

Bhat, N. and T. J. Mc Avoy (1989). Use of neural nets for dynamic modeling and control of chemical process systems. *Proc. 1989 American Control Conf.*, Pittsburgh, PA, June, 1989, 1342-1347.

Broomhead, D. S. and D. Lowe (1988). Radial Basis Functions, Multi-Variable Functional Interpolation and Adaptive Networks. Royal Signals and Radar Establishment memorandum # 4148, London.

Casdagli, M. (1989). Nonlinear Prediction of Chaotic Time Series. *Physica D,* 35, 335-356.

Crutchfield, J. P., and B. S. McNamara (1987). Equations of motion from a data series. *Complex Systems*, 1, 417-452.

Farmer, J. D. and J. J. Sidorowich (1987). Predicting Chaotic Time Series. *Phys. Rev. Letters*, 59, 845-848.

Farmer, J. D. and J. J. Sidorowich (1988). Exploiting Chaos to Predict the Future and Reduce Noise. In: *Evolution, Learning and Cognition* (Y. C. Lee, ed.), World Scientific, Singapore, 277-330.

Lapedes, A. S. and R. M. Farber (1987a). Nonlinear Signal Processing Using Neural Networks: Prediction and System Modeling. Los Alamos Report LA-UR 87-2662.

Lapedes, A. S. and R. M. Farber (1987b). How Neural Nets Work. In: *Neural Information Proessing Systems* (D. Z. Anderson, ed.), AIP Press, 442-456.

Packard, N. H., J. P. Crutchfield, J. D. Farmer, and R. S. Shaw (1980). Geometry from a Time Series. *Phys. Rev. Lett.*, 45, 712-716.

Powell, M. J. D. (1985). Radial Basis Functions for Multivariable Interpolation: A Review. Technical report, University of Cambridge.

Rummelhart, D. and J. McClelland (1986). In: *Parallel Distributed Processing*, Vol. 1, MIT Press, Cambridge MA.

Takens, F. (1981). Detecting Strange Attractors in Turbulence. In: *Dynamical Systems and Turbulence* (D. A. Rand and L. -S. Young, eds.), *Lect. Notes in Math*, 898, Springer, Heidelberg, 366-381.

Ydstie, B. E. (1989) Forecasting and control using adaptive connectionist networks. *Comp. Chem. Eng.*, in press.

# Electric Load Forecasting Using An Artificial Neural Network


D.C. Park, M.A. El-Sharkawi, R.J. Marks II,
L.E. Atlas and M.J. Damborg

Department of Electrical Engineering, FT-10
University of Washington
Seattle, WA 98195



## Abstract

This paper presents an artificial neural network(ANN) approach to electric load forecasting. The ANN is used to learn the relationship among past, current and future temperatures and loads. In order to provide the forecasted load, the ANN interpolates among the load and temperature data in a training data set. The average absolute errors of the one-hour and 24-hour ahead forecasts in our test on actual utility data are shown to be 1.40% and 2.06%, respectively. This compares with an average error of 4.22% for 24-hour ahead forecasts with a currently used forecasting technique applied to the same data.

**Keywords** - Load Forecasting, Artificial Neural Network


## 1 Introduction

Various techniques for power system load forecasting have been proposed in the last few decades. Load forecasting with lead-times, from a few minutes to several days, helps the system operator to efficiently schedule spinning reserve allocation. In addition, load forecasting can provide information which is able to be used for possible energy interchange with other utilities. In addition to these economical reasons, load forecasting is also useful for system security. If applied to the system security assessment problem, it can provide valuable information to detect many vulnerable situations in advance.

Traditional computationally economic approaches, such as regression and interpolation, may not give sufficiently accurate results. Conversely, complex algorithmic methods with heavy computational burden can converge slowly and may diverge in certain cases.

A number of algorithms have been suggested for the load forecasting problem. Previous approaches can be generally classified into two categories in accordance with techniques they employ. One approach treats the load pattern as a time series signal and predicts the future load by using various time series analysis techniques [1-7]. The second approach recognizes that the load pattern is heavily dependent on weather variables, and finds a functional relationship between the weather variables and the system load. The future load is then predicted by inserting the predicted weather information into the predetermined functional relationship [8-11].

General problems with the time series approach include the inaccuracy of prediction and numerical instability. One of the reasons this method often gives inaccurate results is that it does not utilize weather information. There is a strong correlation between the behavior of power consumption and weather variables such as temperature, humidity, wind speed, and cloud cover. This is especially true in residential areas. The time series approach mostly utilizes computationally cumbersome matrix-oriented adaptive algorithms which, in certain cases, may be unstable.

Most regression approaches try to find functional relationships between weather variables and current load demands. The conventional regression approaches use linear or piecewise-linear representations for the forecasting functions. By a linear combination of these representations, the regression approach finds the functional relationships between selected weather variables and load demand. Conventional techniques assume, without justification, a linear relationship. The functional relationship between load and weather variables, however, is not stationary, but depends on spatio-temporal elements. Conventional regression approach does not have the versatility to address this temporal variation. It, rather, will produce an averaged result. Therefore, an adaptable technique is needed.

In this paper, we present an algorithm which combines both time series and regressional approaches. Our algorithm utilizes a layered perceptron *artificial neural network* (ANN). As is the case with time series approach, the ANN traces previous load patterns and predicts(*i.e.* extrapolates) a load pattern using recent load data. Our algorithm uses weather information for modeling. The ANN is able to perform non-linear modeling and adaptation. It does not require assumption of any functional relationship between load and weather variables in advance. We can adapt the ANN by exposing it to new data. The ANN is also currently being investigated as a tool in other power system problems such as security assessment, harmonic load identification, alarm processing, fault diagnosis, and topological observability [12-18].


90 SM 377-2 PWRS    A paper recommended and approved by the IEEE Power System Engineering Committee of the IEEE Power Engineering Society for presentation at the IEEE/PES 1990 Summer Meeting, Minneapolis, Minnesota, July 15-19, 1990. Manuscript submitted August 31, 1989; made available for printing April 24, 1990.

In the next section, we briefly review various load forecasting algorithms. These include both the time series and regression approach. The generalized Delta rule used to train the ANN is shown in Section 3. In Section 4, we define the load forecasting problems, show the topologies of the ANN used in our simulations, and analyze the performance in terms of errors (the differences between actual and forecasted loads). A discussion of our results and conclusions are presented in Section 5.

## 2  Previous Approaches

### 2.1  Time Series

The idea of the time series approach is based on the understanding that a load pattern is nothing more than a time series signal with known seasonal, weekly, and daily periodicities. These periodicities give a rough prediction of the load at the given season, day of the week, and time of the day. The difference between the prediction and the actual load can be considered as a stochastic process. By the analysis of this random signal, we may get more accurate prediction. The techniques used for the analysis of this random signal include the Kalman filtering [1], the Box-Jenkins method [3,4], the auto-regressive moving average (ARMA) model [2], and spectral expansion technique [5].

The Kalman filter approach requires estimation of a covariance matrix. The possible high nonstationarity of the load pattern, however, typically may not allow an accurate estimate to be made [6,7].

The Box-Jenkins method requires the autocorrelation function for identifying proper ARMA models. This can be accomplished by using pattern recognition techniques. A major obstacle here is its slow performance [2].

The ARMA model is used to describe the stochastic behavior of hourly load pattern on a power system. The ARMA model assumes the load at the hour can be estimated by a linear combination of the previous few hours. Generally, the larger the data set, the better is the result in terms of accuracy. A longer computational time for the parameter identification, however, is required.

The spectral expansion technique utilizes the Fourier Series. Since load pattern can be approximately considered as a periodic signal, load pattern can be decomposed into a number of sinusoids with different frequencies. Each sinusoid with a specific frequency represents an orthogonal base [19]. A linear combination of these orthogonal basis with proper coefficients can represent a perfectly periodic load pattern if the orthogonal basis span the whole signal space. However, load patterns are not perfectly periodic. This technique usually employs only a small fraction of possible orthogonal basis set, and therefore is limited to slowly varying signals. Abrupt changes of weather cause fast variations of load pattern which result in high frequency components in frequency domain. Therefore, the spectral expansion technique can not provide any accurate forecasting for the case of fast weather change unless sufficiently large number of base elements are used.

Generally, techniques in time series approaches work well unless there is an abrupt change in the environmental or sociological variables which are believed to affect load pattern. If there is any change in those variables, the time series technique is no longer useful. On the other hand, these techniques use a large number of complex relationships, require a long computational time [20] and result in a possible numerical instabilities.

### 2.2  Regression

The general procedure for the regression approach is: 1) select the proper and/or available weather variables, 2) assume basic functional elements, and 3) find proper coefficients for the linear combination of the assumed basic functional elements.

Since temperature is the most important information of all weather variables, it is used most commonly in the regression approach (possibly nonlinear). However, if we use additional variables such as humidity, wind velocity, and cloud cover, better results should be obtained.

Most regression approaches have simply linear or piecewise linear functions as the basic functional elements [8-11, 21-23]. A widely used functional relationship between load, $L$, and temperature, $T$, is

$$L = \sum_{i=1}^{N} a_i T\{U(T - T_{i1}) - U(T - T_{i2})\} + C \qquad (1)$$

where

$$U(T) = \left\{ \begin{array}{ll} 1, & \text{if } T \geq 0 \\ 0, & \text{otherwise} \end{array} \right. \qquad (2)$$

and $a_i$, $T_{i1}$, $T_{i2}$, and $C$ are constant, and $T_{i1} > T_{i2}$ for all $i$.

The variables ($L$, $a_i$, $T$, $T_{i1}$, $T_{i2}$, and $C$) are temporally varying. The time-dependency, however, is not explicitly noted for reasons of notational compactness.

After the basic functional forms of each subclass of temperature range are decided, the proper coefficients of the functional forms are found in order to make a representative linear combination of the basic functions.

Approaches other than regression have been proposed for finding functional coefficients:

1. Jabbour *et al.*[11] used a pattern recognition technique to find the nearest neighbor for best 8 hourly matches for a given weather pattern. The corresponding linear regression coefficients were used.

2. An application of the Generalized Linear Square Algorithm(GLSA) was proposed by Irisarri *et al.*[23]. The GLSA, however, is often faced with numerical instabilities when applied to a large data base.

3. Rahman *et al.*[10] have applied an expert system approach. The expert system takes the advantages of the expert knowledge of the operator. It makes many subdivisions of temperature range and forms different functional relationships according to the hour of interest. It shows fairly accurate forecasting. As pointed out in the discussion of [10] by Tsoi, it is not easy to extract a knowledge base from an expert and can be rather difficult for the expert to articulate their experience and knowledge.

4. Lu *et al.*[24] utilize the *modified Gram-Schmidt orthogonalization process* (MGSOP) to find an orthogonal basis set which spans the output signal space formed by load information. The MGSOP requires a predetermined cardinality of the orthogonal basis set

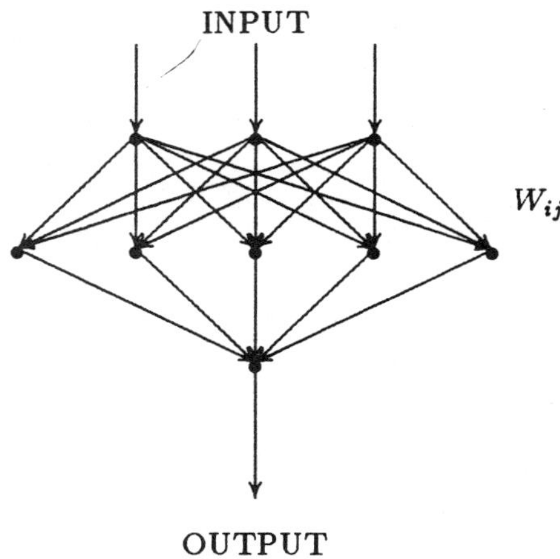

INPUT

$W_{ij}$

OUTPUT

Figure 1: Structure of a Three-Layered Perceptron Type ANN

and the threshold value of error used in adaptation procedure. If the cardinality of the basis set is too small or the threshold is not small enough, the accuracy of the approach suffers severely. On the other hand, if the threshold is too small, numerical instability can result. The MGSOP also has an ambiguity problem in the sequence of input vectors. Different exposition of input vectors result in different sets of orthogonal basis and different forecasting outputs.

## 3  A Layered ANN

### 3.1  Architecture

An ANN can be defined as a highly connected array of elementary processors called *neurons*. A widely used model called the multi-layered perceptron(MLP) ANN is shown in Figure 1. The MLP type ANN consists of one input layer, one or more hidden layers and one output layer. Each layer employs several neurons and each neuron in a layer is connected to the neurons in the adjacent layer with different weights. Signals flow into the input layer, pass through the hidden layers, and arrive at the output layer. With the exception of the input layer, each neuron receives signals from the neurons of the previous layer linearly weighted by the interconnect values between neurons. The neuron then produces its output signal by passing the summed signal through a sigmoid function [12-18].

A total of $Q$ sets of training data are assumed to be available. Inputs of $\{\vec{i}_1, \vec{i}_2, \ldots, \vec{i}_Q\}$ are imposed on the top layer. The ANN is trained to respond to the corresponding target vectors, $\{\vec{t}_i, \vec{t}_2, \ldots, \vec{t}_Q\}$, on the bottom layer. The training continues until a certain stop-criterion is satisfied. Typically, training is halted when the average error between the desired and actual outputs of the neural network over the $Q$ training data sets is less than a predetermined threshold. The training time required is dictated by various elements including the complexity of the problem, the number of data, the structure of network, and the training parameters used.

## 3.2  ANN Training

In this paper, the *generalized Delta rule* (GDR) [25,26] is used to train a layered perceptron-type ANN. An output vector is produced by presenting an input pattern to the network. According to the difference between the produced and target outputs, the network's weights $\{W_{ij}\}$ are adjusted to reduce the output error. The error at the output layer propagates backward to the hidden layer, until it reaches the input layer. Because of backward propagation of error, the GDR is also called *error back propagation algorithm*.

The output from neuron $i$, $O_i$, is connected to the input of neuron $j$ through the interconnection weight $W_{ij}$. Unless neuron $k$ is one of the input neurons, the state of the neuron $k$ is:

$$O_k = f(\Sigma_i W_{ik} O_i) \tag{3}$$

where $f(x) = 1/(1 + e^{-x})$, and the sum is over all neurons in the adjacent layer. Let the target state of the output neuron be $t$. Thus, the error at the output neuron can be defined as

$$E = \frac{1}{2}(t_k - O_k)^2 \tag{4}$$

where neuron $k$ is the output neuron.

The gradient descent algorithm adapts the weights according to the gradient error, *i.e.*,

$$\Delta W_{ij} \propto -\frac{\partial E}{\partial W_{ij}} = -\frac{\partial E}{\partial O_j}\frac{\partial O_j}{\partial W_{ij}} \tag{5}$$

Specifically, we define the error signal as

$$\delta_j = -\frac{\partial E}{\partial O_j} \tag{6}$$

With some manipulation, we can get the following GDR:

$$\Delta W_{ij} = \epsilon \delta_j O_i \tag{7}$$

where $\epsilon$ is an adaptation gain. $\delta_j$ is computed based on whether or not neuron $j$ is in the output layer. If neuron $j$ is one of the output neurons,

$$\delta_j = (t - O_j)O_j(1 - O_j) \tag{8}$$

If neuron $j$ is not in the output layer,

$$\delta_j = O_j(1 - O_j)\Sigma_k \delta_k W_{jk} \tag{9}$$

In order to improve the convergence characteristics, we can introduce a momentum term with momentum gain $\alpha$ to Equation 7.

$$\Delta W_{ij}(n + 1) = \epsilon \delta_j O_i + \alpha \Delta W_{ij}(n) \tag{10}$$

where $n$ represents the iteration index.

Once the neural network is trained, it produces very fast output for a given input data. It only requires a few multiplications, additions, and calculations of sigmoid function [14].

Table 1: Test Data Sets

| sets | Test data from |
|------|----------------|
| Set 1 | 01/23/'89 - 01/30/'89 |
| Set 2 | 11/09/'88 - 11/17/'88 |
| Set 3 | 11/18/'88 - 11/29/'88 |
| Set 4 | 12/08/'88 - 12/15/'88 |
| Set 5 | 12/27/'88 - 01/04/'89 |

## 4  Test Cases and Results

Hourly temperature and load data for Seattle/Tacoma area in the interval of Nov. 1, 1988 - Jan. 30, 1989 were collected by the Puget Sound Power and Light Company. We used this data to train the ANN and test its performance. Our focus is on a normal weekday (*i.e.* no holiday or weekends).

Table 1 shows five sets used to test the neural network. Each set contains 6 normal days. These test data were not used in the training process of the neural network. This approach of classifier evaluation is known as a *jack-knife* method.

The ANN was trained to recognize the following cases:

- Case 1: Peak load of the day

- Case 2: Total load of the day

- Case 3: Hourly load

where

$$\text{Peak load at day } d = \max \{L(1,d), \cdots, L(24,d)\} \quad (11)$$

$$\text{Total load at day } d = \sum_{h=1}^{24} L(h,d) \quad (12)$$

$L(h,d)$ is the load at hour $h$ on day $d$.

The neural network structures used in this paper, including the size of the hidden layer, were chosen from among several structures. The chosen structure is the one that gave the best network performance in terms of accuracy. In most cases, we found that adding one or two hidden neurons did not significantly effect the neural network accuracy.

To evaluate the resulting ANN's performance, the following percentage error measure is used throughout this paper:

$$\text{error} = \frac{|\text{ actual load - forecasted load }|}{\text{actual load}} \times 100 \quad (13)$$

### 4.1  Case 1

The topology of the ANN for the peak load forecasting is as follows;

| Input neurons: | T1(k), T2(k), and T3(k) |
|---|---|
| Hidden neurons: | 5 hidden neurons |
| Output neuron : | L(k) |

where
k = day of predicted load,
L(k) = *peak load* at day k,
T1(k) = average temperature at day k,
T2(k) = peak temperature at day k,
T3(k) = lowest temperature at day k.

Table 2: Error(%) of Peak Load Forecasting

| days | set1 | set2 | set3 | set4 | set5 |
|------|------|------|------|------|------|
| day1 | 4.19 | 1.89 | 0.72 | 1.69 | 1.83 |
| day2 | 0.24 | 1.85 | 3.03 | 0.31 | 3.25 |
| day3 | 0.58 | 2.44 | 0.95 | 2.72 | 2.68 |
| day4 | 2.39 | 3.85 | 3.29 | 2.84 | 1.10 |
| day5 | 0.35 | 4.26 | 0.65 | 6.64 | 0.56 |
| day6 | 2.81 | 0.13 | 0.63 | 1.40 | 2.04 |
| Avg. | 1.73 | 2.40 | 1.55 | 2.60 | 1.91 |

Table 3: Error(%) of Total Load Forecasting

| days | set1 | set2 | set3 | set4 | set5 |
|------|------|------|------|------|------|
| day1 | 0.34 | 0.26 | 2.66 | 1.03 | 0.42 |
| day2 | 1.02 | 1.99 | 1.82 | 0.70 | 0.92 |
| day3 | 3.47 | 1.03 | 3.25 | 0.66 | 1.42 |
| day4 | 1.63 | 1.73 | 5.64 | 1.89 | 2.11 |
| day5 | 1.04 | 0.88 | 4.14 | 0.03 | 0.27 |
| day6 | 1.77 | 1.10 | 2.96 | 1.20 | 1.05 |
| Avg. | 1.78 | 1.07 | 3.39 | 1.15 | 1.03 |

Table 2 shows the error(%) of each day in the test sets. The average error for all 5 sets is 2.04 %.

### 4.2  Case 2

The topology of the ANN for the total load forecasting is as follows;

| Input neurons: | T1(k), T2(k), and T3(k) |
|---|---|
| Hidden neurons: | 5 hidden neurons |
| Output neuron : | L(k) |

where
k = day of predicted load,
L(k) = *total load* at day k,
T1(k) = average temperature at day k,
T2(k) = peak temperature at day k,
T3(k) = lowest temperature at day k.

Table 3 shows the error(%) of each day in test sets. The average error for all 5 sets is 1.68 %.

### 4.3  Case 3

The topology of the ANN for the hourly load forecasting with one hour of lead time is as follows;

| Input neurons: | k, L(k-2), L(k-1), |
|---|---|
| | T(k-2), T(k-1), and $\tilde{T}(k)$ |
| Hidden neurons: | 10 hidden neurons |
| Output neuron : | L(k) |

k = hour of predicted load
L(x) = load at hour x,
T(x) = temperature at hour x,
$\tilde{T}(x)$ = predicted temp. for hour x

In training stage, T(x) was used instead of $\tilde{T}(x)$. The lead times of predicted temperatures, $\tilde{T}(x)$, vary from 16 to 40 hours.

Table 4 shows the error(%) of each day in the test sets. The average error for all 5 sets is found to be 1.40 %. Note that each day's result is averaged over a 24 hour period.

Table 4: Error(%) of Hourly Load Forecasting
with One Hour Lead Time

| days | set1 | set2 | set3 | set4 | set5 |
|------|------|------|------|------|------|
| day1 | (*) | 1.20 | 1.41 | 1.17 | (*) |
| day2 | 1.67 | 1.48 | (*) | 1.58 | 2.18 |
| day3 | 1.08 | (*) | 1.04 | (*) | 1.68 |
| day4 | 1.40 | 1.34 | 1.42 | 1.20 | 1.73 |
| day5 | 1.30 | 1.41 | (*) | 1.20 | (*) |
| day6 | (*) | 1.51 | 1.29 | 1.68 | 0.98 |
| avg. | 1.35 | 1.39 | 1.29 | 1.36 | 1.64 |

(*: Predicted temperatures, $\tilde{T}$, are not available.)

In order to find the effect of the lead time on the ANN
load forecasting, we used set 2 whose performance in Table 4 was the closest to the average. The lead time was
varied from 1 to 24 hours with a 3 hour interval. The
topology of ANN was as follows:

    input neurons :    $k$, $L(24,k)$, $T(24,k)$,
                             $L(m,k)$, $T(m,k)$, and $\tilde{T}(k)$
    hidden neurons :  1 hidden neuron
    ouput neuron :    $L(k)$

where
    $k$ = hour of predicted load
    $m$ = lead time,
    $L(x,k)$ = load x hours before hour k
    $T(x,k)$ = temperature x hours before hour k
    $\tilde{T}(k)$ =   predicted temperature for hour k

In the training stage, $T(x)$ was used instead of $\tilde{T}(x)$. The
lead times of predicted temperatures, $\tilde{T}(x)$, vary from 16
to 40 hours.

Figure 2 shows examples of the hourly actual and forecasted loads with one-hour and 24-hour lead times. Figure 3 shows the average errors (%) of the forecasted loads
with different lead hours for test set 2.

From Figure 3, the error gradually increases as the lead
hour grows. This is true up to 18 hours of lead time. One
of the reasons for this error pattern is the periodicity of
temperature and load pattern. Even though they are not
quite the same as those of the previous day, the temperature and system load are very similar to those of the
previous day.

We compare our results with the prediction of Puget
Sound Power and Light Co. (PSPL) in Figure 4. Since
the PSPL forecasts loads with lead times of 16- to 40-
hour, there are 3 overlaps(18-, 21-, and 24-hour) with our
results. As shown in Figure 4, the average errors for the
18-, 21- and 24-hour lead times are 2.79, 2.65, and 2.06 %,
respectively. This compares quite favorably with errors of
2.72, 6.44, and 4.22 % (18-, 21-, and 24-hour lead times)
obtained by current load forecasting technique using the
same data from PSPL [27]. The current load forecasting
method, in addition, uses cloud cover, opaque cover, and
relative humidity information.

## 5   Conclusions

We have presented an electric load forecasting methodology using an artificial neural network(ANN). This technique was inspired by the work of Lapedes and Farber
[28]. The performance of this technique is similar to the
ANN with locally tuned receptive field [29]. We find it no-

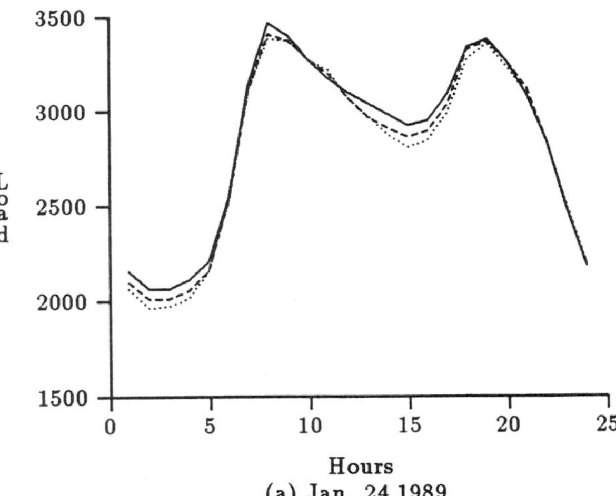

(a) Jan. 24,1989

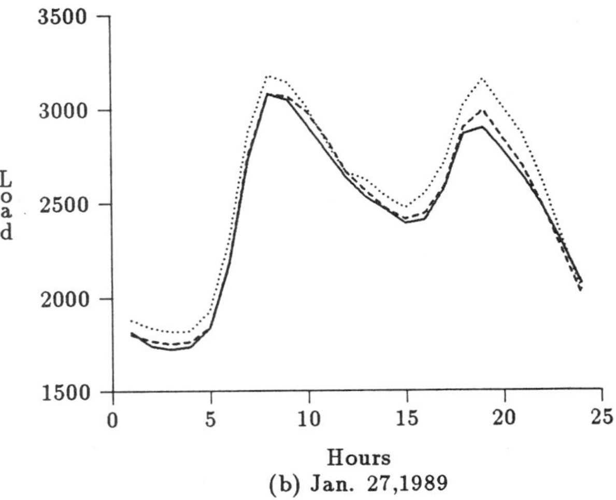

(b) Jan. 27,1989

Figure 2: Hourly Load Forecasting and Actual Load
(in MW) (solid: actual load, dash: 1-hour lead
forecast, dot: 24-hour lead forecast)

table that Moody and Darken's technique is remarkably
similar to the estimation of Gaussian mixture models.

The results shows that the ANN is suitable to interpolate among the load and temperature pattern data of
training sets to provide the future load pattern. In order
to forecast the future load from the trained ANN, we need
to use the recent load and temperature data in addition
to the predicted future temperature. Compared to the
other regression methods, the ANN allows more flexible
relationships between temperature and load pattern. A
more intensive comparison can be found in [30].

Since the neural network simply interpolates among the
training data, it will give high error with the test data
that is not close enough to any one of the training data.

In general, the neural network requires training data
well spread in the feature space in order to provide highly
accurate results. The training times required in our experiments vary, depending on the cases studied, from 3
to 7 hours of CPU time using the SUN SPARK Station
1. However, a trained ANN requires only 3 to 10 millisec-

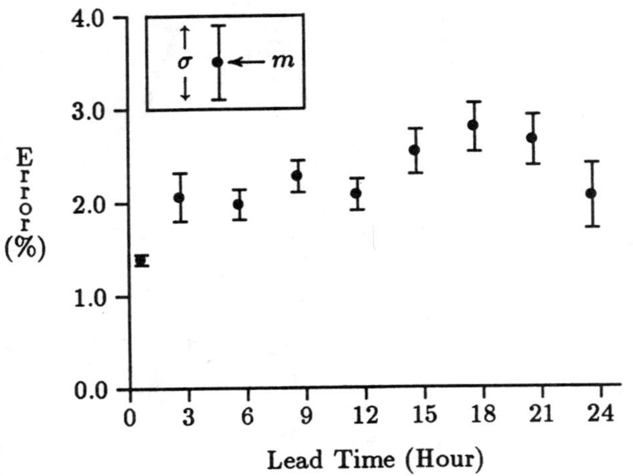

Figure 3: Mean($m$) and Standard Deviation($\sigma$) of Errors Vs. Lead Time

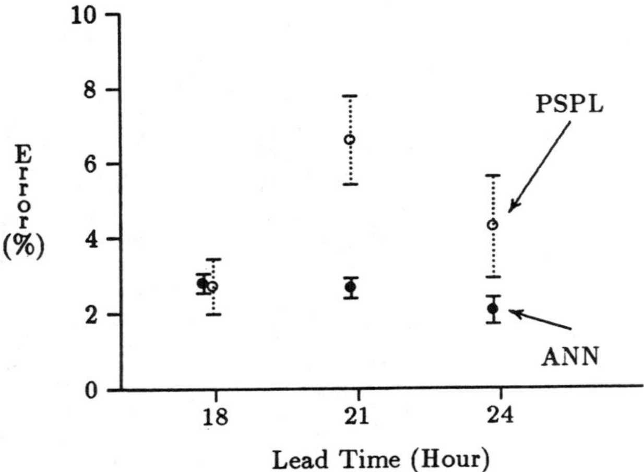


Figure 4: Mean and Standard Deviation of Errors: ANN Vs. Conventional Technique Used in PSPL

onds for testing.

The neural network typically shows higher error in the days when people have specific start-up activities such as Monday (for example, on day 1 of set 1 in Table 2), or variant activities such as during the holiday seasons (for example, on days 4 & 5 of set 3 in Table 3). In order to have more accurate results, we may need to have more sophisticated topology for the neural network which can discriminate start-up days from other days.

We utilize only temperature information among weather variables since it is the only information available to us. Use of additional weather variables such as cloud coverage and wind speed should yield even better results.

## 6    Acknowledgments

This work was supported by the Puget Sound Power and Light Co., the National Science Foundation, and the Washington Technology Center at the University of Washington. The authors thank Mr. Milan L. Bruce of the Puget Sound Power and Light Co. for his contribution.

## References

[1] J. Toyoda, M. Chen, and Y. Inoue, "An Application of State Estimation to short-Term Load Forecasting, Part1: Forecasting Modeling," "—— Part2: Implementation," IEEE Tr. on Power App. and Sys., vol. PAS-89, pp.1678-1688, Oct., 1970

[2] S. Vemuri, W. Huang, and D. Nelson, "On-line Algorithms For Forecasting Hourly Loads of an Electric Utility," IEEE Tr. on Power App. and Sys., vol., PAS-100, pp.3775-3784, Aug., 1981

[3] G.E. Box and G.M. Jenkins, *Time Series Analysis - Forecasting and Control*, Holden-day, San Francisco, 1976

[4] S. Vemuri, D. Hill, R. Balasubramanian, "Load Forecasting Using Stochastic Models," Paper No. TPI-B, Proc. of 8th PICA conference, Minneapolis, Minn., pp.31-37, 1973

[5] W. Christiaanse, "Short-Term Load Forecasting Using General Exponential Smoothing," IEEE Tr. on Power App. and Sys., vol. PAS-90, pp. 900 - 910, Apr., 1971

[6] A. Sage and G. Husa, "Algorithms for Sequential Adaptive Estimation of Prior Statistics," Proc. of IEEE Symp. on Adaptive Processes, State College, Pa., Nov., 1969

[7] R. Mehra, " On the Identification of Variance and Adaptive Kalman Filtering, " Proc. of JACC (Boulder, Colo.), pp.494-505, 1969

[8] P. Gupta and K. Yamada, "Adaptive Short-Term Forecasting of Hourly Loads Using Weather Information," IEEE Tr. on Power App. and Sys., vol. PAS-91, pp.2085-2094, 1972

[9] C. Asbury, "Weather Load Model for Electric Demand Energy Forecasting," IEEE Tr. on Power App. and Sys., vol. PAS-94, no.4, pp.1111-1116, 1975

[10] S. Rahman and R. Bhatnagar, " An Expert System Based Algorithm for Short Load Forecast," IEEE Tr. on Power Systems, vol.3, no.2, pp.392-399, May, 1988

[11] K. Jabbour, J. Riveros, D. Landbergen, and W. Meyer, "ALFA: Automated Load Forecasting Assistant," IEEE Tr. on Power Systems, vol.3, no.3, pp.908-914, Aug., 1988

[12] D. Sobajic and Y. Pao, "Artificial Neural-Net Based Dynamic Security Assessment for Electric Power Systems," IEEE Tr. on Power Systems, vol.4, no.1, pp.220-228, Feb, 1989

[13] M. Aggoune, M. El-Sharkawi, D. Park, M. Damborg, and R. Marks II, "Preliminary Results on Using Artificial Neural Networks for Security Assessment," Proc. of PICA, pp.252-258, May, 1989

[14] M. El-Sharkawi, R. Marks II, M. Aggoune, D. Park, M. Damborg, and L. Atlas, " Dynamic Security Assessment of Power Systems Using Back Error Propagation Artificial Neural Networks," Proc. of 2nd Sym. on Expert Systems Applications to Power Systems, pp.366-370, July, 1989

[15] H. Mori, H. Uematsu, S. Tsuzuki, T. Sakurai, Y. Kojima, K. Suzuki, "Identification of Harmonic Loads in Power Systems Using An Artificial Neural Network," Proc. of 2nd Sym. on Expert Systems Applications to Power Systems, pp.371-377, July, 1989

[16] E.H. Chan, "Application of Neural-Network Computing in Intelligent Alarm Processing," Proc. of PICA, pp.246-251, May, 1989

[17] H. Tanaka, S. Matsuda, H. Ogi, Y. Izui, H. Taoka, and T. Sakaguchi, "Design and Evaluation of Neural Network for Fault Diagnosis," Proc. of 2nd Sym. on Expert Systems Application to Power Systems, pp.378-384, July, 1989

[18] H. Mori and S. Tsuzuki, "Power System Topological Observability Analysis Using a Neural Network Model," Proc. of 2nd Sym. on Expert Systems Application to Power Systems, pp.385-391, July, 1989

[19] N. Naylor and G. Sell, *Linear Operator Theory*, New York, Holt, Rinehart and Winston, 1971

[20] M. Honig and D. Messerschmitt, *Adaptive Filters, Structures, Algorithms, and Applications*, Klumer Academic Publishers, Hingham, Massachusetts, 1984

[21] J. Davey, J. Saacks, G. Cunningham, and K. Priest, "Practical Application of Weather Sensitive Load Forecasting to System Planning," IEEE Tr. on Power App. and Sys., vol.PAS-91, pp.971-977, 1972

[22] R. Thompson, "Weather Sensitive Electric Demand and Energy Analysis on a Large Geographically Diverse Power System - Application to Short Term Hourly Electric Demand Forecasting," IEEE Tr. on Power App. and Sys., vol. PAS-95, no.1, pp.385-393, Jan., 1976

[23] G. Irisarri, S. Widergren, and P. Yehsakul, "On-Line Load Forecasting for Energy Control Center Application," IEEE Tr. on Power App. and Sys., vol. PAS-101, no.1, pp.71-78, Jan., 1982

[24] Q. Lu, W. Grady, M. Crawford, and G. Anderson, "An Adaptive Nonlinear Predictor with Orthogonal Escalator Structure for Short-Term Load Forecasting," IEEE Tr. on Power Systems, vol.4, No.1, pp.158-164, Feb., 1989

[25] Y.-H. Pao, *Adaptive Pattern Recognition and Neural Network*, Addison-Wesley Pub. Co. Inc., Reading, MA., 1989

[26] D. Rumelhart, G. Hinton, and R. Williams, "Learning Internal Representations by Error Propagation," in *Parallel Distributed Processing Explorations in the Microstructures of Cognition, vol.1: Foundations*, pp.318-362, MIT Press, 1986

[27] S. Mitten-Lewis, *Short-Term Weather Load Forecasting Project Final Report*, Puget Sound Power and Light Co., Bellevue, Washington, 1989

[28] A. Lapedes and R. Farber, *Nonlinear Signal Processing Using Neural Networks: Prediction and System Modeling*, Technical Report, Los Alamos National Laboratory, Los Alamos, New Mexico, 1987

[29] J. Moody and C. Darken, "Learning with Localized Receptive Fields ," Proc. of the 1988 Connectionist Models Summer School, Morgan Kaufmann, 1988

[30] L. Atlas, J. Connor, D. Park, M. El-Sharkawi, R. Marks II, A. Lippman, and Y. Muthusamy, "A Performance Comparison of Trained Multi-Layer Perceptrons and Trained Classification Trees," Proc. of the 1989 IEEE International Conference on Systems, Man, and Cybernetics, pp.915-920, Nov. 1989



**Dong C. Park** received his B.S. Degree in Electronic Engineering in 1980 from Sogang University and the M.S. degree in Electrical Engineering in 1982 from the Korea Advanced Institute of Science and Technology, Seoul, Korea. From 1982 through 1985, he had been with the Goldstar Central Research Laboratory. Since September 1985, he has been working toward the Ph.D. degree in the Department of Electrical Engineering at the University of Washington. His research interests include artificial neural network application to nonlinear system modeling, signal processing and optical computing.

**M. A. El-Sharkawi** (SM'76-M'80-SrM'83) was born in Cairo, Egypt, in 1948. He received his B.Sc. in Electrical Engineering in 1971 from Cairo High Institute of Technology, Egypt. His M.A.SC and Ph.D. in Electrical Engineering were received from University of British Columbia in 1977 and 1980 respectively. In 1980 he joined University of Washington as a faculty member where he is presently an associate professor. He is the Chairman of IEEE Task Force on "Application of Artificial Neural Networks for Power Systems". His major areas of research include neural network applications to power systems, electric devices, high performance tracking control, power system dynamics and control. Most of his research in these areas are funded by the US government, and by public and private industrial organizations.

**Robert J. Marks II** received his Ph.D. in 1977 from Texas Tech University in Lubbock. He joined the faculty of the Department of Electrical Engineering at the University of Washington, Seattle, in December of 1977 where he currently holds the title of Professor. Prof. Marks was awarded the Outstanding Branch Councillor award in 1982 by IEEE and, in 1984, was presented with an IEEE Centennial Medal. He is President of the IEEE Council on Neural Networks and former Chair of the IEEE Neural Network Committee. He was also the co-founder and first Chair of the IEEE Circuit & Systems Society Technical Committee on Neural Systems & Applications. He is a Fellow of the Optical Society of America and a Senior Member of IEEE. He has over eighty archival journal and proceedings publications in the areas of signal analysis, detection theory, signal recovery, optical computing and artificial neural processing. Dr. Marks is a co-founder of the Christian Faculty Fellowship at the University of Washington. He is a member of Eta Kappa Nu and Sigma Xi.

**Les E. Atlas** (Member, IEEE) received his B.S.E.E. degree from the University of Wisconsin and his M.S. and Ph.D. degrees from Stanford University. He joined the University of Washington College of Engineering in 1984 and is currently an Associate Professor of Electrical Engineering. He is currently doing research in speech processing and recognition, neural network classifiers, and biologically-inspired signal processing algorithms and architectures. His research in these areas is funded by the National Science Foundation, the Office of Naval Research, and the Washington Technology Center. Dr. Atlas was a 1985 recipient of a National Science Foundation's Presidential Young Investigator Award.

**M. J. Damborg** received his B.S. Degree in Electrical Engineering in 1962 from Iowa State University, and the M.S. and Ph.D. degrees from the University of Michigan in 1963 and 1969, respectively. Since 1969, Dr. Damborg has been at the University of Washington where he is now Professor of Electrical Engineering. His research interests concern analysis and control of dynamic systems with emphasis on power systems.

Discussion

**O. A. Mohammed** (Florida International University Miami, FL): The authors are to be thanked on their excellent work applying this new ANN technique to load forecasting. I would like the authors to clarify or explain the followings points:

1. The authors presented a new method for load forecast which shows a promise for providing accurate forecasts. This discussor feels that the ANN method would be adequate for providing the base forecast which might be combined with an expert system approach to fine tune the load forecast for additional factors.
2. If one experiments with additional factors which may affect the load forecast such as humidity, load inertia, wind velocity, etc., how much additional training time would be required compared with the data size.
3. The authors presented results for hourly load forecast for weekdays but not weekends because of the variation in load pattern. Will this be handled by a separate neural network? and if so, how would it be combined with previous day forecasts. For example, to forecase Monday's load.
4. Have the authors experimented with different ANN architectures other than the ones explained in the paper. It seems to this discussor that the proposed architectures will not work all the time or it may yield larger errors because of the continual change in weather and load information. May be a methodology which updates the weights of the ANN based on the new short term weather and load information.

Manuscript received August 13, 1990.

**M. A. El-Sharkawi and M. J. Damborg**: The authors would like to thank the discusser for their interest and encouraging comments. The research work reported in this paper is preliminary. Several key issues, such as those raised by the discusser, need to be carefully addressed before a viable electric load forecasting system is deployed. The purpose of the paper, however, is to investigate the potentials of the Neural Network (NN) in load forecasting. Future work should certainly address questions related to weather conditions, distinct load profiles, cold snaps, etc.

To respond to the specific issues raised by the reviewer, we would like to offer the following comments:

1. The role of expert systems in NN environment, and vise versa, is a topic that is being proposed for several applications. In load forecasting applications, as an example, the selection of relevant training sets from load and weather data base is currently accomplished manually and off-line. Also, the convergency of the NN is currently observed and controlled at only discrete training steps. These functions, for example, may be effectively accomplished by a supervisory layer employing a rule-based system.

2. Other weather variables such as wind speed and humidity may result in more accurate load forecasting. The problem, however, is that the forecasting errors of these variables are usually high which may lead to a biased training or erroneous network.

3. Except for Tuesday to Thursday, the load profile of the each other day of the week is distinct. For example, the profile of Monday morning include the "pickup loads". Due to these differences in load profiles, we have used one NN for the days with similar load profiles and one NN for each day with distinct load profile.

When we forecasted the electric loads of Saturday, Sunday or Monday, we used weather and load data obtained up to Friday morning (9:00 am) to conform with Puget Power practice.

4. We have tried several architectures for load forecasting. The key issue in selecting a particular NN configuration is to achieve low training error without "memorization". This can be accomplished by first selecting an over sized network then "prune" the network to eliminate any memorization problem that might exist without jeopardizing the training accuracy.

Manuscript received September 23, 1990.

*Neural Networks.* Vol. 5, pp. 961–970, 1992
Printed in the USA. All rights reserved.





*ORIGINAL CONTRIBUTION*

# Forecasting the Behavior of Multivariate Time Series Using Neural Networks

KANAD CHAKRABORTY, KISHAN MEHROTRA, CHILUKURI K. MOHAN,
AND SANJAY RANKA

Syracuse University

(*Received* 13 *December* 1990; *revised and accepted* 6 *April* 1992)

**Abstract**—*This paper presents a neural network approach to multivariate time-series analysis. Real world observations of flour prices in three cities have been used as a benchmark in our experiments. Feedforward connectionist networks have been designed to model flour prices over the period from August 1972 to November 1980 for the cities of Buffalo, Minneapolis, and Kansas City. Remarkable success has been achieved in training the networks to learn the price curve for each of these cities and in making accurate price predictions. Our results show that the neural network approach is a leading contender with the statistical modeling approaches.*

**Keywords**—Neural networks, Back propagation, Multivariate time-series, Statistical models, Training, One-lag prediction, Multi-lag prediction, Combined modeling, Forecasting.

## 1. INTRODUCTION

Predicting the future is the prime motivation behind the search for laws that explain certain phenomena. As observed by Weigend, Huberman, & Rumelhart (1990), it hinges on two types of knowledge: knowledge of underlying laws, a very powerful and accurate means of prediction, and the discovery of strong empirical regularities in observations of a given system. However, there are problems with both approaches—discovery of laws underlying the behavior of a system is often a difficult task, and empirical regularities or periodicities are not always evident and can often be masked by noise.

Multivariate time-series analysis is an important statistical tool to study the behavior of time dependent data and forecast future values depending on the history of variations in the data. A time-series is a sequence of values measured over time, in discrete or continuous time units. By studying many related variables together, rather than by studying just one, a better understanding is often obtained. A multivariate time-series consists of sequences of values of several contemporaneous variables changing with time. An important case is when the variables being measured are significantly corre-

lated, e.g., when similar attributes are being measured at different geographic locations. In forecasting new values for each variable, better prediction capabilities are available if variations in the other variables are also taken into account. Robust forecasting must rely on all available correlations and empirical interdependencies among different temporal sequences.

Many available techniques for time-series analysis assume linear relationships among variables (see Box and Jenkins, 1970). But in the real world, temporal variations in data do not exhibit simple regularities and are difficult to analyze and predict accurately. Linear recurrence relations and their combinations for describing the behavior of such data are often found to be inadequate. It seems necessary, therefore, that nonlinear models be used for the analysis of real-world temporal data. Tong (1983) describes some of the drawbacks of linear modeling for time series analyses. These include, e.g., their inability to explain sudden bursts of very large amplitudes at irregular time intervals. Discussion following the Tiao and Tsay (1989) paper also addresses some of the problems with linear models for multivariate time series. In order to accommodate for such inabilities, nonlinear statistical models, such as the threshold model and the bilinear model, have been suggested and discussed in Tong (1990), whereas Granger and Newbold (1986) suggest the use of nonlinear transformation of the original data before performing the "usual" linear modeling. Farmer and Sidorowich (1987) report a significantly better predic-

---

Requests for reprints should be sent to Kishan Mehrotra, 4-116 Center for Science and Technology, School of Computer and Information Science, Syracuse University, Syracuse, NY 13244.

tion for chaotic time series by using a local approximation approach involving use of nearest $k$ neighbors with respect to the magnitudes of the values rather than with respect to time points to which the values belong. Despite considerable progress over the last decade, formulation of reasonable nonlinear models is an extremely difficult task because of simplifications made in the modeling stage, e.g., omitting parameters which are unknown or which do not seem to affect the observed data directly. Also, the relationships between known parameters and observed values can only be hypothesized with no simple laws governing their mutual behavior. See, for example, Saikkonen and Luukkonen (1991). Hence, we resort to a "neural network" approach for nonlinear modeling of multivariate time-series; in earlier work, we have successfully used this approach in analyzing univariate time-series (see Li, Mehrotra, Mohan, & Ranka, 1990).

Neural networks belong to the class of *data-driven* approaches, as opposed to model-driven approaches. The analysis depends on available data, with little rationalization about possible interactions. Relationships between variables, models, laws, and predictions are constructed post-facto after building a machine whose behavior simulates the data being studied. The process of constructing such a machine based on available data is addressed by certain general-purpose algorithms such as "back propagation" (see Rumelhart, Hinton, & Williams, 1986).

In this paper, we use neural networks to predict future values of possibly noisy multivariate time-series based on past histories. The particular data analyzed are monthly flour prices for Buffalo, Minneapolis, and Kansas City over a period of 100 months. For impartial evaluation of the prediction performance of the approach, data for different periods are used in the "training" (modeling) and "testing" (prediction) phases. The performance exceeded expectations and the root mean squared errors (in long-term, or multi-lag prediction) obtained using this approach are better than those obtained from the statistical model of Tiao and Tsay (1989) by at least one order of magnitude. We expect such results to be obtained in other applications of interdependent time-series as well.

Section 2 presents the architecture of the neural networks used for our analysis, the experiments performed and the training paradigm used. In Section 2.3, a model of statistical prediction is described and its performance compared in Section 3 with the network performance. Discussion and concluding remarks then follow.

As stated before, several other statistical approaches have been suggested for modeling and analysis of time-series data. We use the model proposed by Tiao and Tsay as a benchmark to judge the neural network performance. Our results indicate that the back propagation network approach provides a competitive alternative to the existing procedures for learning as well as forecasting of interdependent data.

## 2. METHODOLOGY

### 2.1. Neural Networks

Artificial neural networks are computing systems containing many simple nonlinear computing units or nodes interconnected by links. In a "feedforward" network, the units can be partitioned into layers, with links from each unit in the $k^{th}$ layer being directed (only) to each unit in the $(k + 1)^{st}$ layer. Inputs from the environment enter the first layer, and outputs from the network are manifested at the last layer. A $d - n - 1$ network, shown in Figure 1, refers to a network with $d$ inputs, $n$ units in the intermediate "hidden" layer, and one unit in the output layer (see Weigend et al., 1990). A weight or "connection strength" is associated with each link, and a network "learns" or is trained by modifying these weights, thereby modifying the network function which maps inputs to outputs.

We use such $d - n - 1$ networks to learn and then predict the behavior of multivariate time-series. The hidden and output nodes realize nonlinear functions of the form $(1 + \exp(-\sum_{i=1}^{m} w_i x_i + \theta))^{-1}$, where $w_i$'s denote real-valued weights of edges incident on a node, $\theta$ denotes the adjustable "threshold" for that node, and $m$ denotes the number of inputs to the node from the previous layer. The training algorithm is detailed in Section 2.2.

### 2.2. Procedure for Training the Networks

We use the error back propagation algorithm of Rumelhart et al. (1986) to train the networks, using mean squared error (MSE) over the training samples as the objective function. From the given $p$-variate time-series $S = \{\langle v_1(t), \ldots, v_p(t) \rangle : 1 \leq t \leq N\}$, we obtain two sets: a training set $S_{\text{train}} = \{\langle v_1(t), \ldots, v_p(t) \rangle : 1 \leq t \leq T\}$, and a test set $S_{\text{test}} = \{\langle v_1(t), \ldots, v_p(t) \rangle : T < t \leq N\}$. A set $P_{\text{train}}$ of $(d + 1)$-tuples (the first $d$

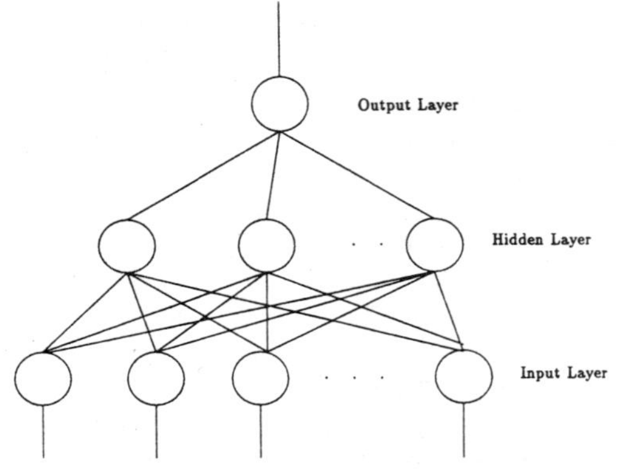

**FIGURE 1. A feedforward neural net with one hidden layer.**

components representing inputs and the last component representing the desired outputs) and a set $P_{\text{test}}$ of $d$-tuples (each component representing an input) are then created from $S_{\text{train}}$ and $S_{\text{test}}$, respectively. The MSE(training) is calculated as $\sum_{k=1}^{M} (u^k - \hat{u}_k)^2/M$, where $u_k$ and $\hat{u}_k$, $1 \leq k \leq M$ are the desired and the actual network outputs, respectively, for each of the $M$ training patterns. The MSE(test) is similarly defined for the test patterns.

In each step in the training phase, a $d$-tuple (recent history) of normalized input data is presented to the network. The network is asked to predict the next value in the time sequence. The error between the value predicted (by the network) and the value actually observed (known data) is then measured and propagated backwards along the feedforward connections. The weights of links between units and node thresholds are modified to various extents, using a technique which apportions "blame" for the error to various nodes and links as prescribed by the back propagation algorithm. If the MSE exceeds some small predetermined value, a new "epoch" (cycle of presentations of all training inputs) is started after termination of the current epoch. After training the network, its performance on test samples is measured in terms of MSE(test), the mean squared error on the test samples alone.

The parameters of the back propagation algorithm are the "learning rate" and "momentum," which roughly describe the relative importance given to the current and past error-values in modifying connection strengths. For better performance in our experiments, we found that it was best to use a small learning rate in training the network. In all training cases, we chose a learning rate of 0.3 and an associated momentum term of 0.6. The number of epochs varied between 25,000 to 50,000 in all cases.

## 2.3. Experiments

In our experiments, we analyzed a trivariate time-series $X_T = \{(x_t, y_t, z_t) : t = 1, 2, \ldots, T\}$, where $T$ ranges up to 100. The data used are logarithms of the indices of monthly flour prices for Buffalo ($x_t$), Minneapolis ($y_t$), and Kansas City ($z_t$), over the period from August 1972 to November 1980, obtained from Tiao and Tsay (1989). In all cases, we train the network over a certain part of our data, and once training is completed, test the network over the remaining data, i.e., make the network predict the so-called "future" values.

Both "one-lag" and "multi-lag" output predictions for the test samples are done with the given models. In one-lag prediction, we forecast flour prices of each year based only on actual past values. In multi-lag prediction, on the other hand, we append the predicted values to our input database and use these values also to predict future values. For instance, if the network is used

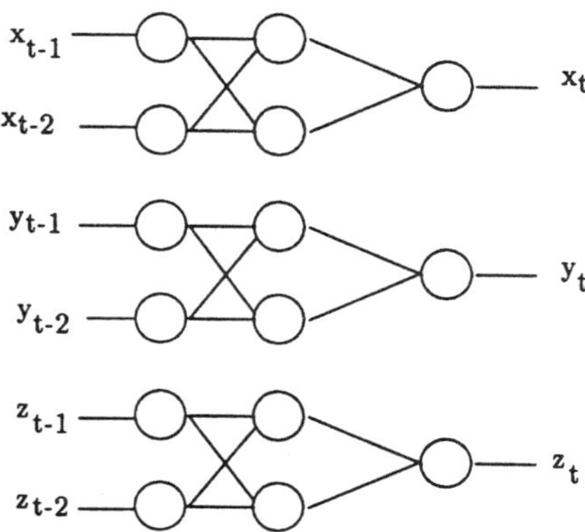

**FIGURE 2. Separate architectures schema.**

to predict a value $n_6$ from observed input data $i_1, \ldots i_5$, then the next network prediction $n_7$ is made using inputs $i_2, \ldots i_5, n_6$, and the subsequent network prediction $n_8$ is made using inputs $i_3, i_4, i_5, n_6, n_7$. With one-lag prediction, on the other hand, the prediction at the eighth instant is made using only the actual input data values $i_3, i_4, i_5, i_6, i_7$. The following three sets of experiments were performed in this study.

1. **Separate Modeling:** Each univariate time-series $x_T = \{x_t : t = 1, 2, \ldots, T\}$, $y_T = \{y_t : t = 1, 2, \ldots, T\}$, and $z_T = \{z_t : t = 1, 2, \ldots, T\}$, was analyzed separately, without utilizing their interdependencies. For example, only the values of $x_1, \ldots, x_k$ were used to predict $x_{k+1}$. A separate neural network was used for each of the three series, as illustrated in Figure 2, and trained with 90 input data values ranging from August 1972 to January 1980. The training phase was followed by output prediction for the next 10 time points (for February 1980 to November 1980) using the weights and thresholds generated during training. These predictions were compared with the test data set

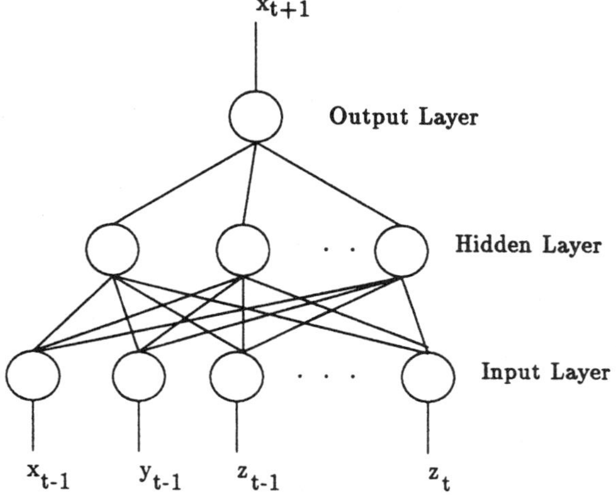

**FIGURE 3. Combined architectures schema.**

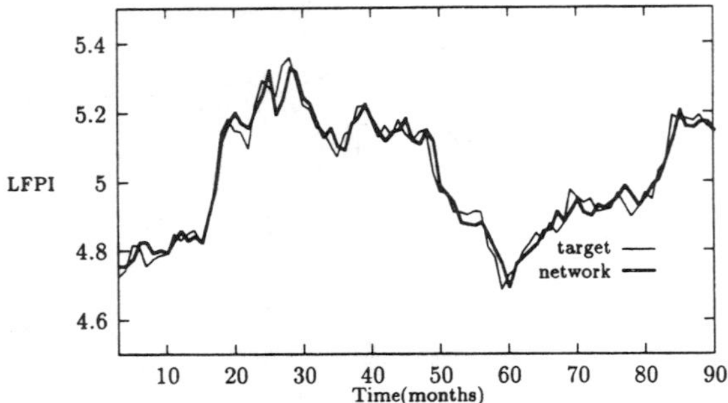

**FIGURE 4. 6-6-1 network modeling: Buffalo (training).**

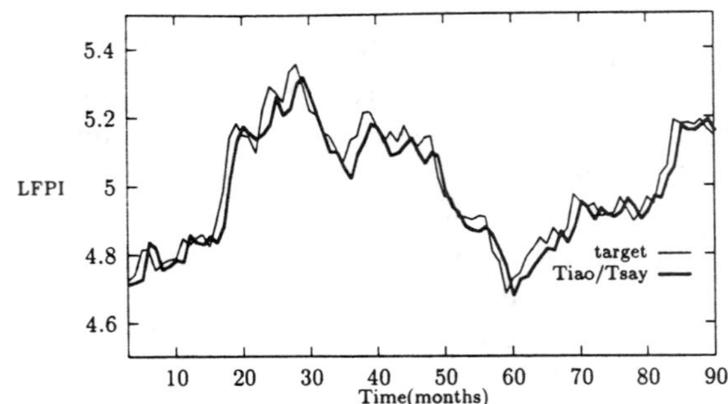

**FIGURE 6. Tiao & Tsay's model: Buffalo (90 months).**

to judge the performance of the network in terms of MSE(test). Experiments were performed with 2-2-1, 4-4-1, 6-6-1, and 8-8-1 networks. These experiments were done in order to compare with the combined modeling approach, described below.

2. **Combined Modeling:** We obtained a considerably improved performance using (for each series) information from all three series, instead of treating each series individually. Two kinds of experiments were performed using this approach. The first kind is illustrated in Figure 3 in which $x_{t+1}$ is shown as being learned/predicted using six preceding values (recorded at time points $t$ and $t - 1$ only) from all the three series, i.e., $(x_t, y_t, z_t, x_{t-1}, y_{t-1}, z_{t-1})$. Similar experiments were performed to predict $y_{t+1}$ and $z_{t+1}$ also. This method determines the value of a variable at any time $t$ using strictly past data for all the variables in each training input; it does *not* utilize contemporaneous data for the other variables. We experimented with 6-6-1 networks of this kind and the results are shown in Table 2. We experimented with a variety of 6-$h$-1 networks and obtained the best results with 6-6-1 networks. The reason for choosing 6 input nodes is mentioned in Section 3.

However, for the data studied, there was an implicit ordering among the three series: $x_t$ values were available before $y_t$ values, and $y_t$ values were available before $z_t$ values, and (naturally) all these were available before $x_{t+1}$ values. This observation led to our second kind of combined modeling approach. In this approach, each training input pattern consists of "past" data items by

the above criterion. For instance, in the $d - n - 1$ feedforward network used to predict $y_t$, if $d = 8$, the chosen input values would be $x_t$, $z_{t-1}$, $y_{t-1}$, $x_{t-1}$, $z_{t-2}$, $x_{t-2}$, $y_{t-2}$, $z_{t-3}$. In both cases, the training set consisted of the first 90 items of trivariate data and the test set consisted of the remaining 10. The results shown in Figures 4 through 30 compare performances of both a 6-6-1 network (the first approach) and an 8-8-1 network (the second approach) with that of Tiao and Tsay's model. As before, we have explained our choice of an 8-$h$-1 network in Section 3. The best performances were obtained with $h = 8$ for such networks that were experimented with. In all the graphs shown, the $y$-axis is labeled "LFPI," an abbreviation for "<u>L</u>ogarithms of monthly <u>F</u>lour <u>P</u>rice <u>I</u>ndices."

3. **Statistical Model:** Tiao and Tsay (1989) developed a statistical model of prediction which involves computation of the overall order of the temporal process with the help of normalized criterion and root tables, followed by estimation of unknown parameters. For this example, it was found that a trivariate ARMA(1,1) model or AR(2) model would be appropriate for the data. Subsequently, Tiao and Tsay (1989) modeled the data as described below.

First, each trivariate input vector $\mathbf{z}_t$ has to be transformed by premultiplication with a $3 \times 3$ matrix $\mathbf{T}$, called the transformation matrix. The transformed data conforms to a trivariate equation of the form

$$(\mathbf{I} - \Phi_1 B)\mathbf{y}_t = \mathbf{c} + (\mathbf{I} - \Phi_1 B)\mathbf{a}_t$$

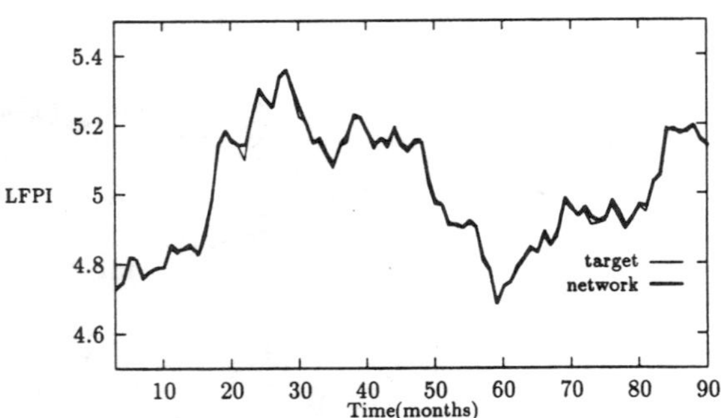

**FIGURE 5. 8-8-1 network modeling: Buffalo (training).**

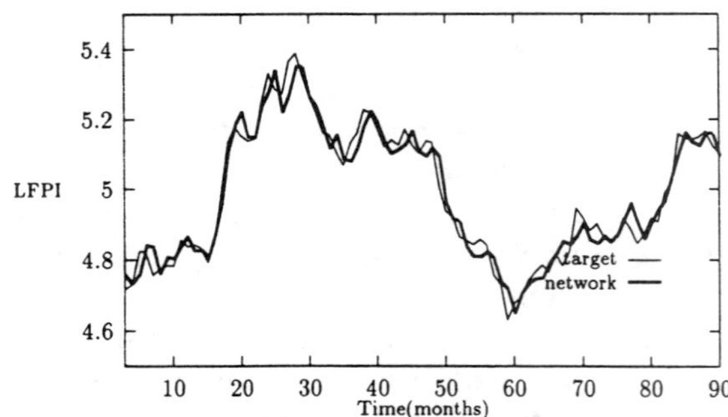

**FIGURE 7. 6-6-1 network modeling: Minneapolis (training).**

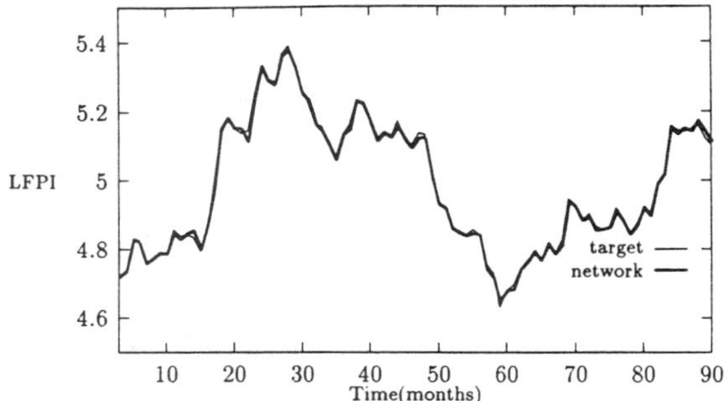

**FIGURE 8. 8-8-1 network modeling: Minneapolis (training).**

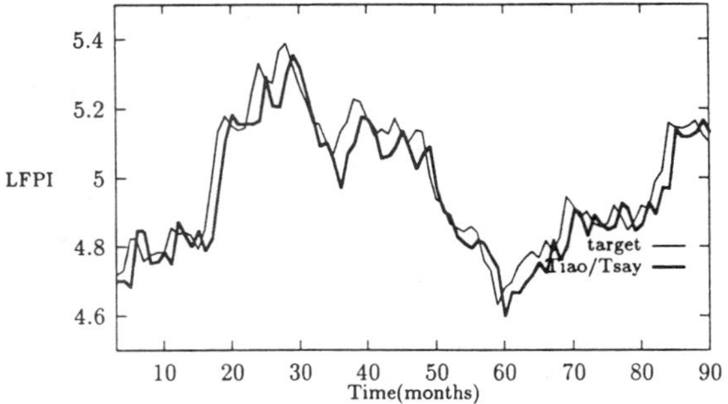

**FIGURE 9. Tiao & Tsay's model: Minneapolis (90 months).**

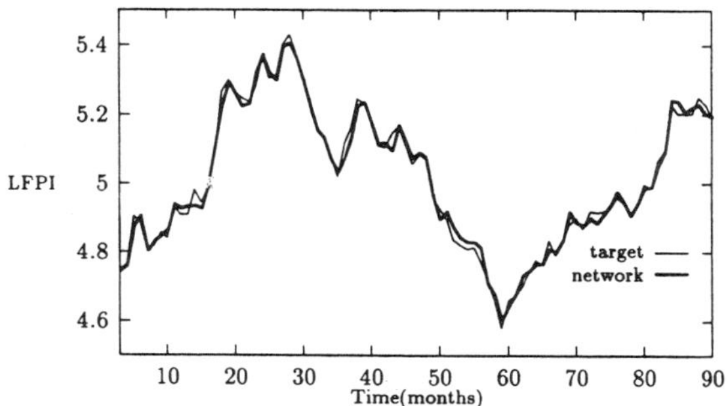

**FIGURE 11. 8-8-1 network modeling: Kansas City (training).**

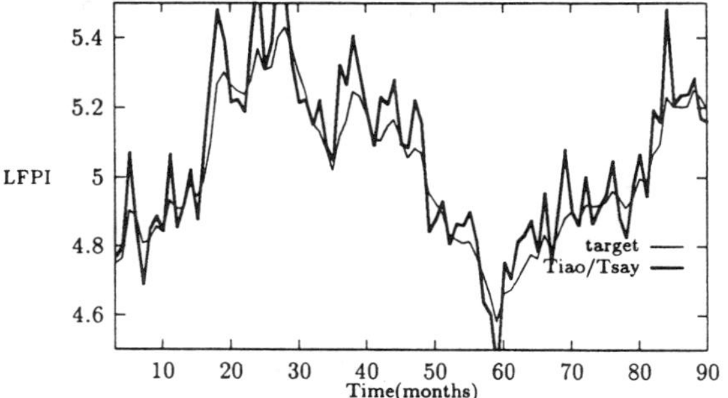

**FIGURE 12. Tiao & Tsay's model: Kansas City (90 months).**

where the transformed series $\mathbf{y}_t = \mathbf{T}\mathbf{z}_t$ is a $3 \times 1$ (trivariate) column vector, $B$ represents the backshift operator (i.e., $B\mathbf{y}_t = \mathbf{y}_{t-1}$), and the $3 \times 1$ column vectors $\mathbf{a}_t$ comprise the error components of the model. The matrix coefficients $(\mathbf{I} - \Phi_1 B)$ and $(\mathbf{I} - \Theta_1 B)$ represent the autoregressive and moving average components, respectively. The estimated values of the $3 \times 3$ matrices $\Phi_1$, $\Theta_1$, and the $3 \times 1$ vector $\mathbf{c}$ are given in Tiao and Tsay (1989).

In the above trivariate model, the mean squared errors are obtained from $\mathbf{a}_t$'s, after premultiplying each such vector by the inverse of the transformation matrix $\mathbf{T}$. The manner of computing the $\mathbf{a}_t$ vectors is as follows. We initialize $\mathbf{a}_1$ to zero; and for $t = 1, 2 \ldots 89$, compute $\mathbf{y}_{t+1}$ by the recipe of the model by using known values of $\mathbf{y}_t$, $\mathbf{a}_t$. The error vector $\mathbf{a}_t$ is obtained at each step by taking the difference between the computed and the actual values of $\mathbf{y}_t$, for $t = 2, 3 \ldots 90$. One-lag prediction is merely a continuation of the above process for $t = 91, 92 \ldots$, and multi-lag prediction is performed in a similar fashion but using estimated values of $\mathbf{y}_t$ for $t = 91, 92, \ldots, 99$ instead of actual values $\mathbf{y}_{91}, \ldots, \mathbf{y}_{99}$.

## 3. COMPARATIVE ANALYSIS OF EXPERIMENTAL RESULTS

The mean squared errors obtained for three different models of separate modeling networks are presented in Table 1. The values correspond to the mean squared errors observed for (a) the first 90 univariate data items, which correspond to the training data, (b) one-lag, and (c) multi-lag predictions over the remaining 10 univariate data items for each of the three time-series. It is interesting to observe that the training performance

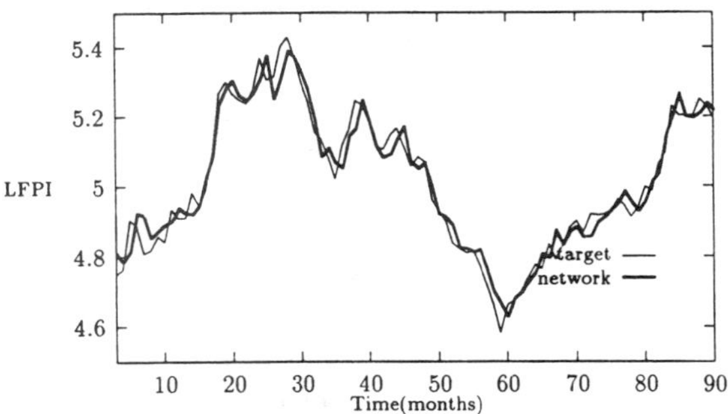

**FIGURE 10. 6-6-1 network modeling: Kansas City (training).**

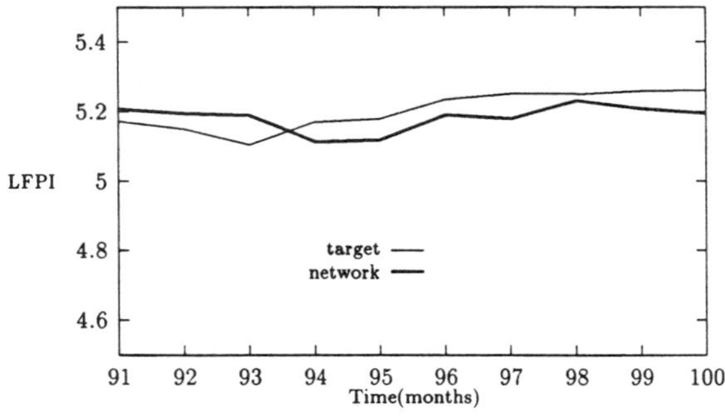

**FIGURE 13. 6-6-1 network prediction, one-lag (Buffalo).**

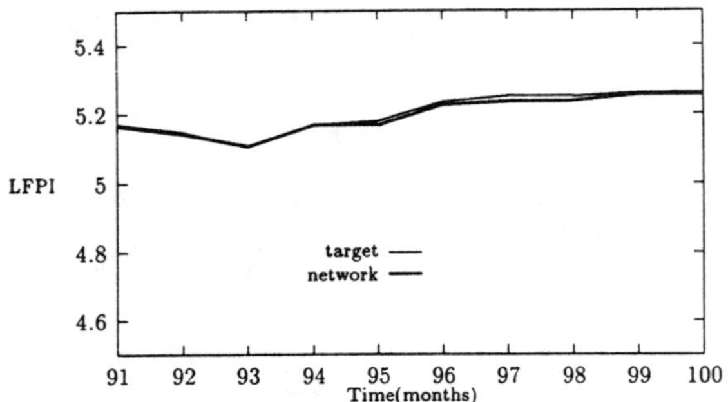

FIGURE 14. 8-8-1 network prediction, one-lag (Buffalo).

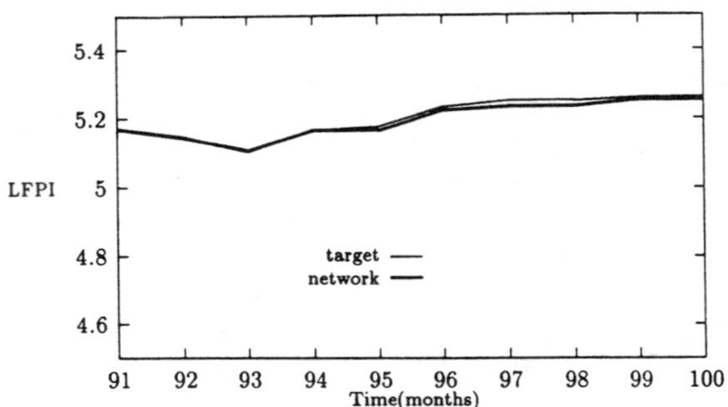

FIGURE 17. 8-8-1 network prediction, multi-lag (Buffalo).

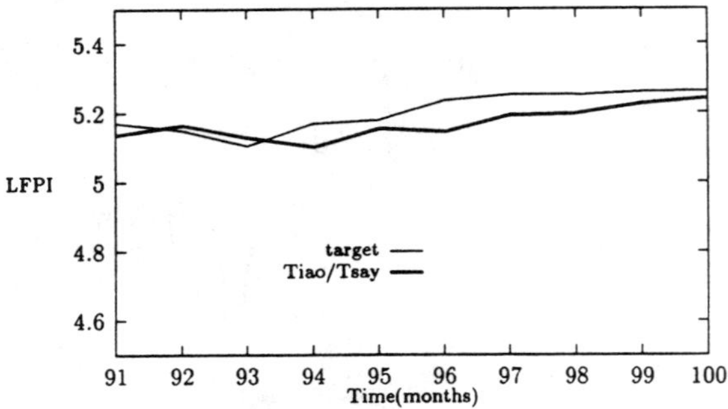

FIGURE 15. Tiao & Tsay's model, one-lag (Buffalo).

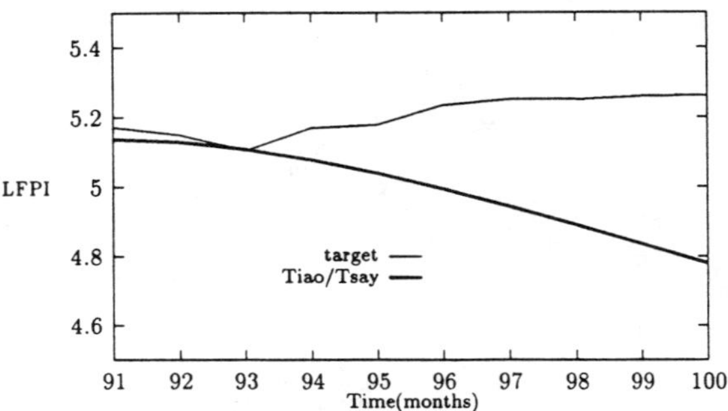

FIGURE 18. Tiao & Tsay's model, multi-lag (Buffalo).

improves whereas one-lag and multi-lag performances deteriorate (in terms of MSE(training) and MSE(test), respectively), as the size of the networks is increased. This suggests that the 4-4-1 and 6-6-1 networks are oversized for the given univariate data and a 2-2-1 network is more suitable for prediction. Thus, every data item in each time-series considered individually is found to be strongly dependent on the past two values only, a fact which agrees with Tiao and Tsay's AR(2) model. This observation also led us to experiment with 6-$h$-1 and 8-$h$-1 networks for the two combined modeling approaches, respectively. Since combined modeling uses trivariate data in our example, the choice of 6 for the number of inputs in the first case is obvious. For the second combined modeling approach, we uniformly chose an 8-$h$-1 network for modeling each city because 8 is the least number of network inputs which

ensures that there are two data items belonging to strictly past time points for each city.

Considerably improved performance, as measured in terms of mean squared errors in training and testing, resulted by following the combined modeling approach for the given data. We believe that separate modeling gives poorer results than combined modeling for two reasons. First, since the three series have a high pairwise positive correlation, each series carries information valuable not only for prediction of its own future values but also for those of the other two series. Second, the combined modeling training set contains three times as many observations as are available for each single modeling training set.

The mean squared errors and coefficients of variation for three different sets of experiments are listed in Table 2. The values correspond, respectively, to the

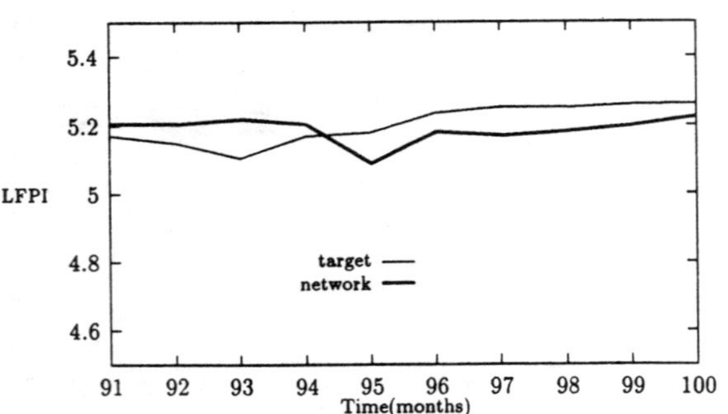

FIGURE 16. 6-6-1 network prediction, multi-lag (Buffalo).

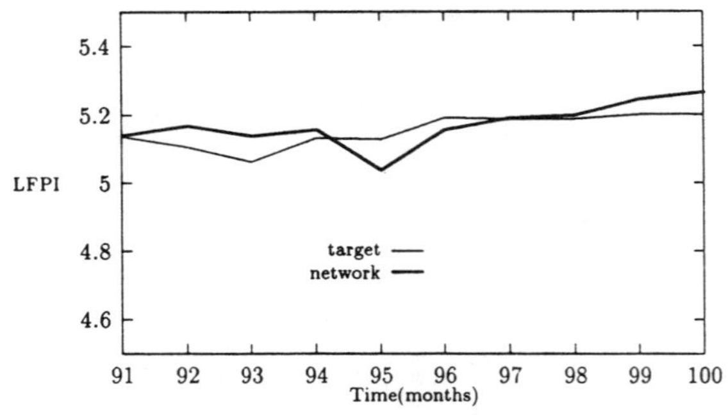

FIGURE 19. 6-6-1 network prediction, one-lag (Minneapolis).

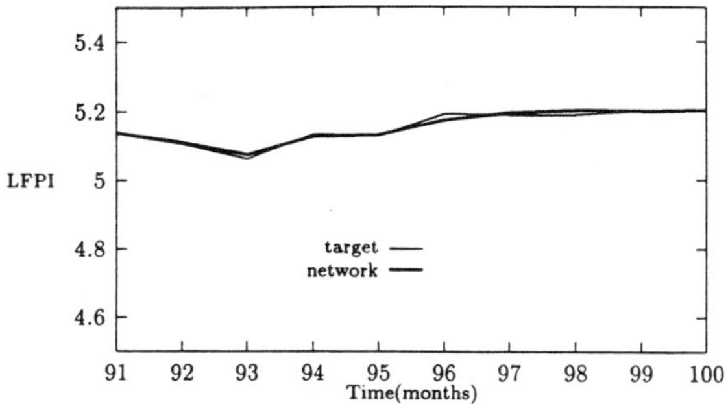

**FIGURE 20. 8-8-1 network prediction, one-lag (Minneapolis).**

mean squared errors and coefficients of variation observed for (a) the first 90 trivariate data items, which correspond to the training data for the combined modeling networks, (b) one-lag, and (c) multi-lag predictions of the combined modeling network and statistical models. Tiao and Tsay's model is seen to produce greater mean squared errors in training and prediction than the combined modeling networks in all but one case (one-lag prediction for Buffalo, for which Tiao and Tsay's model outperforms the 6-6-1 model.) A word of caution is in order at this point. The model of Tiao and Tsay was derived using all 100 trivariate observations. For comparison with our network errors, we obtained two sets of MSE values from their model. In this sense, the neural network is in a slightly disadvantageous position because the network modeling is based on the first 90 trivariate observations only. Yet this method is a simple and desirable way to perform comparisons between the two approaches.

We also notice that the 8-8-1 combined modeling network, which assumes ordering among the three series, performs considerably better than the 6-6-1 network, which utilizes strictly past data in both modeling and prediction. This proves that for the example studied, contemporaneous values of the two other variables have a great role to play in determining the behavior of a variable at any time instant. This fact indicates that there is a strong pairwise correlation between the data for the three cities.

The performance of the neural networks did not vary much for different choices of input sizes in the training

and prediction phases of our experiments and the results shown in Table 2 are fairly representative. Since back propagation is a gradient-descent optimization technique, training a network may result in its sinking into a local minimum of the MSE that may be far removed from the global one (see Tesauro & Janssens, 1988). Hence, to ensure that the MSE(training) was not trapped in such a local minimum, several training runs were conducted for each network. The MSE values achieved in these runs were found to be extremely small quantities that differed only slightly from one another.

A small value of MSE(training) does not necessarily imply a small value of MSE(test) as well. However, our experimental results generally indicate that if the neural network performs well on the training samples, it also has good generalization capabilities, i.e., MSE(test) is also quite small. This is to be expected if the training and test samples are drawn from the same distribution and the network is not overtrained. In most of our experiments, the MSE(training) and MSE(test) values for the network were highly correlated.

## 4. DISCUSSION

Most statistical models for learning and predicting time-series are based only on linear recurrences. Though computationally inexpensive, such functions do not often accurately represent temporal variations. Nonlinear functions, on the other hand, are more useful for tracing temporal sequences. This is probably the main reason for the significantly better performance of the neural

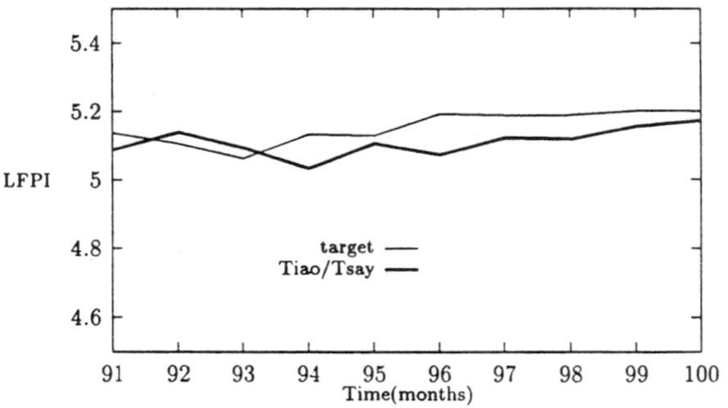

**FIGURE 21. Tiao & Tsay's model, one-lag (Minneapolis).**

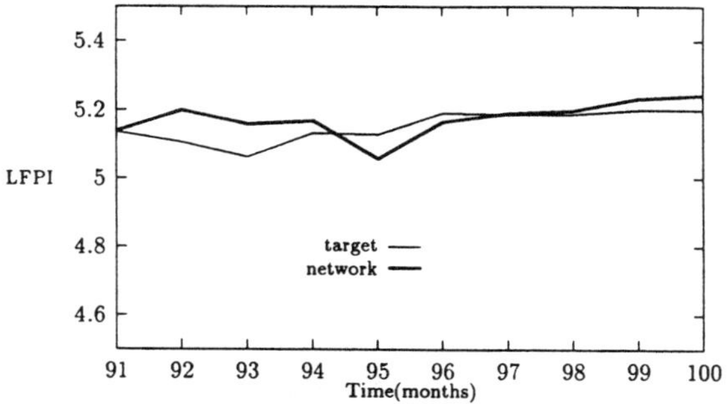

**FIGURE 22. 6-6-1 network prediction, multi-lag (Minneapolis).**

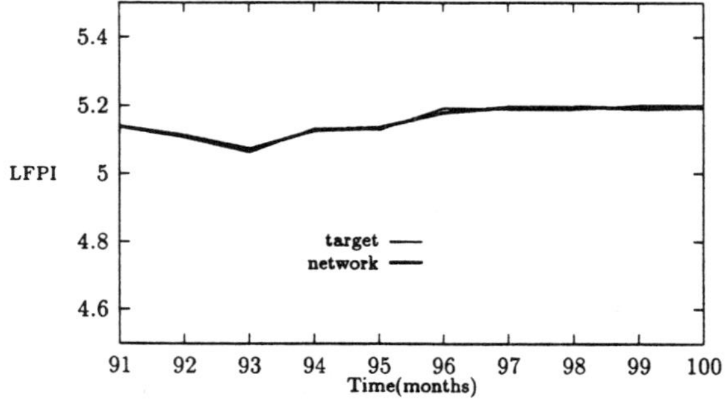

**FIGURE 23. 8-8-1 network prediction, multi-lag (Minneapolis).**

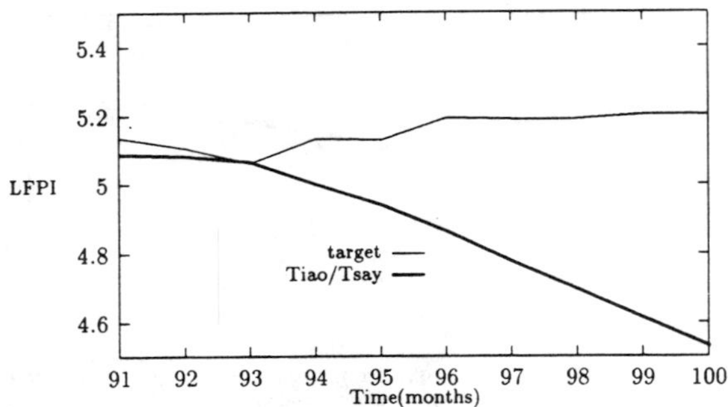

FIGURE 24. Tiao & Tsay's model, multi-lag (Minneapolis).

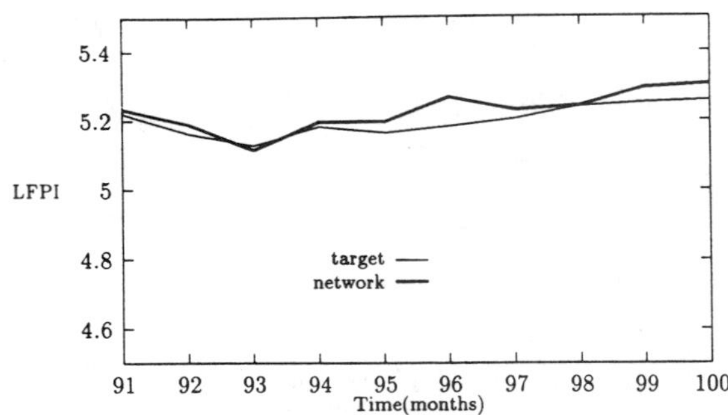

FIGURE 26. 8-8-1 network prediction, one-lag (Kansas City).

network approach (with nonlinearities at each node) as compared to statistical modeling.

In any nontrivial time-series, new values depend not only on the immediately prior value but also on many preceding values. Using too few inputs can result in inadequate modeling, whereas too many inputs can excessively complicate the model. In the context of neural networks, too many inputs would imply slower training and slower convergence, and may in fact worsen the generalization capabilities (applicability to test cases) of the network. Weigend et al. (1990) have a rule of thumb for determining the number of weights in the network as a function of the number of training samples. But this rule was found to be too restrictive for the data set of 100 patterns we worked with, and hence, had to be disregarded.

Different types of connectionist models have been proposed for learning temporal variations of data. It has generally been held in the past that recurrent networks are more suitable for learning temporal data. There were two reasons why recurrent networks were not used for modeling the trivariate data on flour-prices—we observed experimentally that unfolding them into simple feedforward networks would cause worse training and output predictions than single hidden layer feedforward nets; the network would become inherently slower because of a much greater amount of computation involved. An unfolded version of a recurrent network is an approximation of it and implementing an exact recurrent network is a computation-

ally expensive task. The main reason for this is that the units in hidden layers must be made to iterate among themselves until their outputs converge, and there is no way of knowing a priori how many iterations it would take before all the hidden units have stable outputs. Simple feedforward nets are less computationally intensive and in many applications give good performance in less time.

A potential objection to the claim of improved performance using the neural network approach, in comparison to the statistical approach, is that neural networks are more complex and have many more parameters (weights and thresholds): Would a more complex statistical model perform equally well? The answer is essentially methodological. Often, the real-world phenomena being modeled are so complex that it is impossible to theorize and generate statistical models. A large investment of experts' domain-specific research studies must precede the formulation of an adequate model for each separate phenomenon. When a large number of parameters are involved, it is difficult to predict data even when the laws which govern their behavior are known, e.g., in the gravitational interactions between a large number of bodies. With neural networks, on the contrary, an essentially similar architecture can be quickly modified and trained for a variety of different phenomena. The procedure is data-driven rather than model-driven and gives good results in many cases despite the unavailability of a good theory/model underlying observed phenomena.

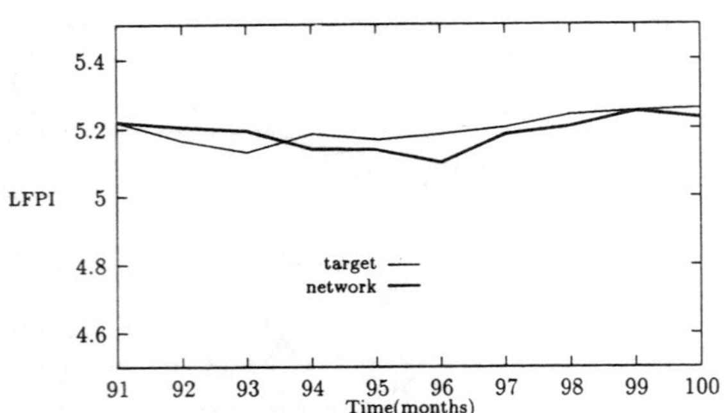

FIGURE 25. 6-6-1 network prediction, one-lag (Kansas City).

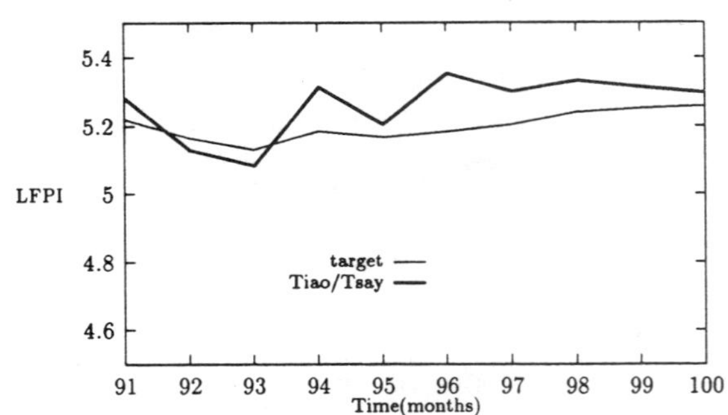

FIGURE 27. Tiao & Tsay's model, one-lag (Kansas City).

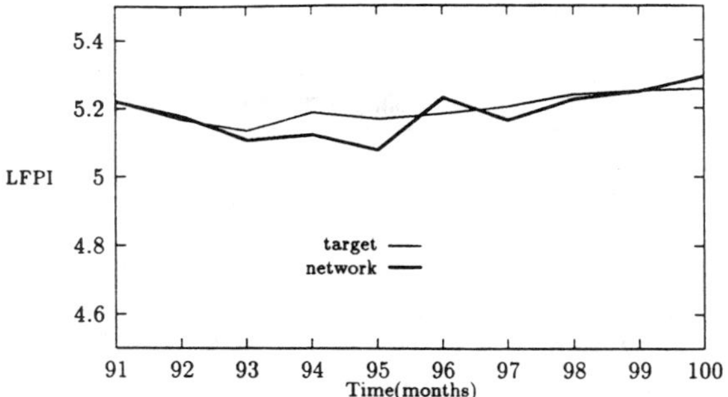

**FIGURE 28. 6-6-1 network prediction, multi-lag (Kansas City).**

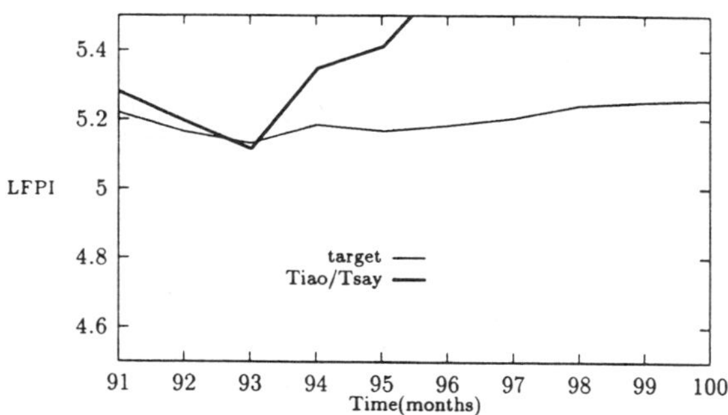

**FIGURE 30. Tiao & Tsay's model, multi-lag (Kansas City).**

We now evaluate the neural network approach with respect to the following criteria for a good model suggested in the literature, see Harvey (1989):

1. *Parsimony:* The neural network does contain a large number of parameters and is, hence, not parsimonious. However, the method of training does not impose any external biases and networks started with different random weights successfully converged to approximate the time-series very well.

2. *Data coherence:* The neural network model provides a very good fit with the data, as shown by the low MSE values for the training samples.

3. *Consistency with prior knowledge:* No explicit theory was constructed using the neural networks, hence, this criterion is largely irrelevant. In the best neural network model, the assumption that flour prices become known in a fixed order $(x_1, y_1, z_1, x_2, \ldots)$ is consistent with the information that the data are available slightly earlier for some cities than for others. So the network modeling can easily accommodate contemporaneous data which become known in a fixed predetermined order.

4. *Data admissibility:* The values in a time-series predicted by the neural networks are always close to the immediately preceding values and do not violate any obvious definitional or reasonable constraints.

5. *Structural stability:* The neural networks seem to satisfy this criterion because they give a good fit for test data, which are outside the set of training samples. Multiple training runs started with changed random initial weights for the same network architecture produced remarkably consistent MSE values after training. In all our experiments, the MSE values after training were very close to zero.

6. *Encompassing:* The results obtained using the neural networks are better than those obtained using an alternative statistical model, indicating that the network exhibits the potential of a competitive alternative tool for analysis and especially, prediction, of multivariate time-series. However, no theory is directly suggested by the neural networks developed so far. The design of forecasting models utilizing the parameters of the trained neural networks is currently under way.

### 4.1. Conclusions

We have presented a neural network approach to multivariate time-series analysis. In our experiments, real world observations of flour prices in three cities have been used to train and test the predictive power of feedforward neural networks. Remarkable success has been achieved in training the networks to learn the price curve for each of these cities, and thereby to make accurate price predictions. Our results show that the neural network approach leads to better predictions

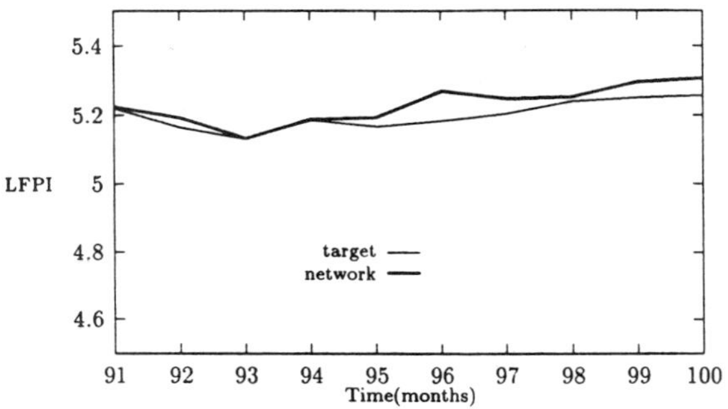

**FIGURE 29. 8-8-1 network prediction, multi-lag (Kansas City).**

**TABLE 1**
**Mean-Squared Errors for Separate Modeling & Prediction $\times 10^3$**

| Network | | Buffalo MSE | Minneapolis MSE | Kansas City MSE |
|---|---|---|---|---|
| 2-2-1 | Training | 3.398 | 3.174 | 3.526 |
| | One-lag | 4.441 | 4.169 | 4.318 |
| | Multi-lag | 4.483 | 5.003 | 5.909 |
| 4-4-1 | Training | 3.352 | 3.076 | 3.383 |
| | One-lag | 9.787 | 8.047 | 3.370 |
| | Multi-lag | 10.317 | 9.069 | 6.483 |
| 6-6-1 | Training | 2.774 | 2.835 | 1.633 |
| | One-lag | 12.102 | 9.655 | 8.872 |
| | Multi-lag | 17.646 | 14.909 | 13.776 |

**TABLE 2**
**Mean-Squared Errors and Coeffs. of Variation for Combined vs. Tiao/Tsay's Modeling/Prediction $\times 10^3$**

| Model | | Buffalo | | Minneapolis | | Kansas City | |
|---|---|---|---|---|---|---|---|
| | | MSE | CV | MSE | CV | MSE | CV |
| 6-6-1 | Training | 1.446 | 7.573 | 1.554 | 7.889 | 1.799 | 8.437 |
| Network | One-lag | 3.101 | 11.091 | 3.169 | 11.265 | 2.067 | 9.044 |
| | Multi-lag | 3.770 | 12.229 | 3.244 | 11.389 | 2.975 | 10.850 |
| 8-8-1 | Training | 0.103 | 2.021 | 0.090 | 1.898 | 0.383 | 3.892 |
| Network | One-lag | 0.087 | 1.857 | 0.072 | 1.697 | 1.353 | 7.316 |
| | Multi-lag | 0.107 | 2.059 | 0.070 | 1.674 | 1.521 | 7.757 |
| Tiao/Tsay | Training | 2.549 | 10.054 | 5.097 | 14.285 | 8.645 | 18.493 |
| | One-lag | 2.373 | 9.701 | 4.168 | 12.917 | 7.497 | 17.222 |
| | Multi-lag | 72.346 | 53.564 | 137.534 | 74.204 | 233.413 | 96.096 |

than a well-known autoregressive moving average model given by Tiao and Tsay (1989).

We obtained a very close fit during the training phase and the networks we developed consistently outperformed statistical models during the prediction phase.

We are currently exploring the combination of statistical and neural approaches for time-series analyses. We expect that model-based statistical preprocessing can further improve the performance or help in obtaining faster convergence of neural networks in the task of time-series predictions.

## REFERENCES


Box, G. E. P., & Jenkins, G. M. (1970). *Time series analysis: Forecasting and control.* San Francisco, CA: Holden-Day.

Farmer, J. D., & Sidorowich, J. J. (1987). Predicting chaotic time series. *Physical Review Letters,* **59,** 845–848.

Granger, C. W. J., & Newbold, P. (1986). *Forecasting economic time series* (2nd ed.). Orlando, FL: Academic Press.

Harvey, A. C. (1989). *Forecasting, time series models and the Kalman Filter.* U.K.: Cambridge University Press.

Li, M., Mehrotra, K., Mohan, C. K., & Ranka, S. (1990). Sunspot numbers forecasting using neural networks. *Proceedings of the IEEE Symposium on Intelligent Control,* **1,** 524–529.

Rumelhart, D. E., Hinton, G. E., & Williams, R. J. (1986). Learning internal representations by error propagation. In D. E. Rumelhart, & J. L. McClelland (Eds.), *Parallel distributed processing* (pp. 318–362). Cambridge, MA: MIT Press.

Saikkonen, P., & Luukkonen, R. (1991). Power properties of a time series linearity test against some simple bilinear alternatives. *Statistica Sinica,* **1,** 453–464.

Tesauro, G., & Janssens, B. (1988). Scaling relationships in back-propagation learning. *Complex Systems,* **2,** 39–44.

Tiao, G. C., & Tsay, R. S. (1989). Model specification in multivariate time series. *Journal of the Royal Statistical Society,* **B 51,** 157–213.

Tong, H. (1983). *Threshold models in non-linear time series analysis.* Lecture Notes in Statistics, **21,** New York: Springer-Verlag.

Tong, H. (1990). *Non-linear time series: A dynamical system approach.* Oxford: Oxford University Press.

Weigend, A. S., Huberman, B. A., & Rumelhart, D. E. (1990). Predicting the future: A connectionist approach. *International Journal of Neural Systems,* **1,** 193–209.

# Chaotic Time Series

# PHYSICAL REVIEW

# LETTERS

VOLUME 59      24 AUGUST 1987      NUMBER 8

## Predicting Chaotic Time Series

J. Doyne Farmer and John J. Sidorowich[a]

*Theoretical Division and Center for Nonlinear Studies, Los Alamos National Laboratory,
Los Alamos, New Mexico 87545*
(Received 22 April 1987)

We present a forecasting technique for chaotic data. After embedding a time series in a state space using delay coordinates, we "learn" the induced nonlinear mapping using a local approximation. This allows us to make short-term predictions of the future behavior of a time series, using information based only on past values. We present an error estimate for this technique, and demonstrate its effectiveness by applying it to several examples, including data from the Mackey-Glass delay differential equation, Rayleigh-Bénard convection, and Taylor-Couette flow.

PACS numbers: 05.45.+b, 02.60.+y, 03.40.Gc

One of the central problems of science is forecasting: Given the past, how can we predict the future? The classic approach is to build an explanatory model from first principles and measure initial data. Unfortunately, this is not always possible. In fields such as economics, we still lack the "first principles" necessary to make good models. In other cases, such as fluid flow, the models are good, but initial data are difficult to obtain. We can derive partial differential equations that allow us to predict the evolution of a fluid (at least in principle), but specification of an initial state requires the measurement of functions over a three-dimensional domain. Acquisition of such large amounts of data is usually impossible. Typical experiments employ only a few probes, each of which produces a single time series. Partial differential equations simply cannot operate on such data. In either case, when we lack proper initial data or when we lack a good model, we must resort to alternative approaches.

Such an alternative is exemplified by the work of Yule,[1] who in 1927 attempted to predict the sunspot cycle by building an *ad hoc* linear model directly from the data. The modern theory of forecasting[2] as it has evolved since then views a time series $x(t_i)$ as a realization of a random process. This is appropriate when effective randomness arises from complicated motion involving many independent, irreducible degrees of freedom.

An alternative cause of randomness is chaos,[3] which can occur even in very simple deterministic systems. While chaos places a fundamental limit on long-term prediction,[3] it suggests possibilities for *short-term* prediction: Random-looking data may contain simple deterministic relationships, involving only a few irreducible degrees of freedom. In chaotic fluid flows, for instance, experimental[4] and theoretical results[5] indicate that in some cases the state space collapses onto an attractor of only a few dimensions.

In this paper we present a method to make predictions about chaotic time series. These ideas were originally inspired by efforts to beat the game of roulette, in collaboration with Packard.[6]

If the data are a single time series, the first step is to embed it in a state space. Following the approach introduced by Packard *et al.*,[7] and put on a firm mathematical basis by Takens,[7] we create a state vector $\mathbf{x}(t)$ by assigning coordinates $x_1(t) = x(t)$, $x_2(t) = x(t-\tau)$, ..., $x_d(t) = x(t-(d-1)\tau)$, where $\tau$ is a delay time. If the attractor is of dimension $D$, a minimal requirement is that $d \geq D$.

The next step is to assume a functional relationship between the current state $\mathbf{x}(t)$ and the future state $\mathbf{x}(t+T)$,

$$\mathbf{x}(t+T) = f_T(\mathbf{x}(t)). \tag{1}$$

We want to find a predictor $F_T$ which approximates $f_T$.

If the data are chaotic, then $f_T$ is necessarily nonlinear. There are several possible approaches: One can assume a standard functional form, such as an $m$th-order polynomial in $d$ dimensions, and fit the coefficients to the data set using least squares.[8] Forecasts for longer times $2T, 3T, \ldots$, can then be made by composing $F_T$ with itself. This approach has the disadvantage that errors in approximation grow exponentially with composition. An alternative is to fit a new function $F_T$ for each time $T$. This has the advantage that global approximation techniques only work well for smooth functions—and higher iterates of chaotic mappings are *not* smooth. Yet another approach is to recast Eq. (1) as a differential equation and write $\mathbf{x}(t+T)$ as its integral. All of these approaches suffer from the problem that the number of free parameters for a general polynomial is $(m+d)!/(m!d!) \approx d^m$, which is intractable for large $d$.

Our preliminary results suggest that a more effective approach is the *local approximation*, using only nearby states to make predictions. To predict $x(t+T)$ we first impose a metric on the state space, denoted by $\| \ \|$, and find the $k$ nearest neighbors of $\mathbf{x}(t)$, i.e., the $k$ states $\mathbf{x}(t')$ with $t' < t$ that minimize $\|\mathbf{x}(t) - \mathbf{x}(t')\|$. We then construct a local predictor, regarding each neighbor $\mathbf{x}(t')$ as a point in the domain and $x(t'+T)$ as the corresponding point in the range. The simplest approach to construct a local predictor is approximation by nearest neighbor, or *zeroth-order approximation*, i.e., $k=1$ and $x_{\text{pred}}(t,T) = x(t'+T)$. A superior approach is the first-order, or linear, approximation, with our taking $k$ greater than $d$, and fitting a linear polynomial to the pairs $(\mathbf{x}(t'), x(t'+T))$. For convenience we usually treat the range as a scalar, mapping $d$-dimensional states into one-dimensional values, although for some purposes it is desirable to let the range be $d$ dimensional. The fit can be made in any of several ways; for the work reported here we did least squares by singular-value decomposition. When $k = d+1$ this is equivalent to linear interpolation, but to ensure stability of the solution it is fre-

quently advantageous to take $k > d+1$. We have also experimented with approximation using higher-order polynomials, but in higher dimensions our results are not significantly better than those obtained with first order.

If done in the most straightforward manner, finding a neighboring value in a data base of $N$ points requires the order of $N$ computational steps. This can be reduced to $\log N$ by the partitioning of the data in a decision tree.[9] Furthermore, once the neighbors are found predictors for many times $T$ can be computed in parallel. With these speedups the computations reported here can be done on small computers.

To facilitate the comparison of results, in this paper we simply build the data base from the first part of the time series, and hold it fixed as we make predictions on the remainder. Alternatively, it is possible for one to optimize the performance with respect to either memory or data limitations by dynamically updating the data base.

To evaluate the accuracy of our predictions, we compute the root-mean-square error, $\sigma_\Delta(T) = \langle [x_{\text{pred}}(t,T) - x(t+T)]^2 \rangle^{1/2}$. For convenience we normalize this by the rms deviation of the data $\sigma_x = \langle (x - \langle x \rangle)^2 \rangle^{1/2}$, forming the *normalized error* $E = \sigma_\Delta(T)/\sigma_x$. If $E=0$, the predictions are perfect; $E=1$ indicates that the performance is no better than a constant predictor $x_{\text{pred}}(t,T) = \langle x \rangle$. To estimate $E$ we make as many predictions as we need for reasonable convergence, typically on the order of 1000.

We have applied our method to several artificial and experimental systems, including the logistic map,[3] the Hénon map,[3] the Mackey-Glass delay-differential equation,[10] Taylor-Couette flow,[11] and Rayleigh-Bénard convection in an $^3$He-$^4$He mixture.[12] Our results are summarized in Table I.

An illustration of the performance of the local linear approximation is given in Fig. 1, with use of convection data obtained by Haucke and Ecke.[12] The dimension of this time series is $D \approx 3.1$ (see Ref. 12). To compare with a "standard forecasting technique," we also show

TABLE I. A summary of forecasts using local linear approximation for several different data sets. $D$ is an estimate of the attractor dimension, $d$ is the embedding dimension, $N$ is the number of data points used, $T_{\text{max}}$ is the rough prediction time (Ref. 13) at which the normalized error approached 1, and $t_{\text{char}}$ is the "characteristic time" for the time series estimated as the inverse of the mean frequency in the power spectrum. In comparison, a standard forecasting technique (global linear autoregression) gave $T_{\text{max}}$ values that were typically about one characteristic time.

| | Differential delay[a] $t_d =$ | | | | Rayleigh-Bénard[b] $R/R_c =$ | | | Couette[c] $R/R_c =$ | | |
| | 17 | 23 | 30 | 100 | 10.55 | 12.19 | 12.24 | 10.2 | 12.9 | 13.7 |
|---|---|---|---|---|---|---|---|---|---|---|
| $D$ | 2.1 | 2.7 | 3.5 | 10 | 2.0 | 2.6 | 3.1 | 2.0 | 2.7 | 3.1 |
| $d$ | 4 | 4 | 6 | 18 | 5 | 6 | 6 | 10 | 6 | 6 |
| $N$ | $10^4$ | $2 \times 10^4$ | $2 \times 10^4$ | $10^5$ | $10^4$ | $10^4$ | $3 \times 10^4$ | $10^4$ | $3 \times 10^4$ | $3 \times 10^4$ |
| $T_{\text{max}}$ | 600 | 300 | 300 | 150 | $\infty$ | 1000 s | 100 s | $\infty$ | 3 s | 1 s |
| $t_{\text{char}}$ | 50 | 55 | 60 | 65 | 3 s | 2 s | 1.5 s | 0.5 s | 0.4 s | 0.1 s |

[a]Reference 10.
[b]Reference 12.
[c]Reference 11.

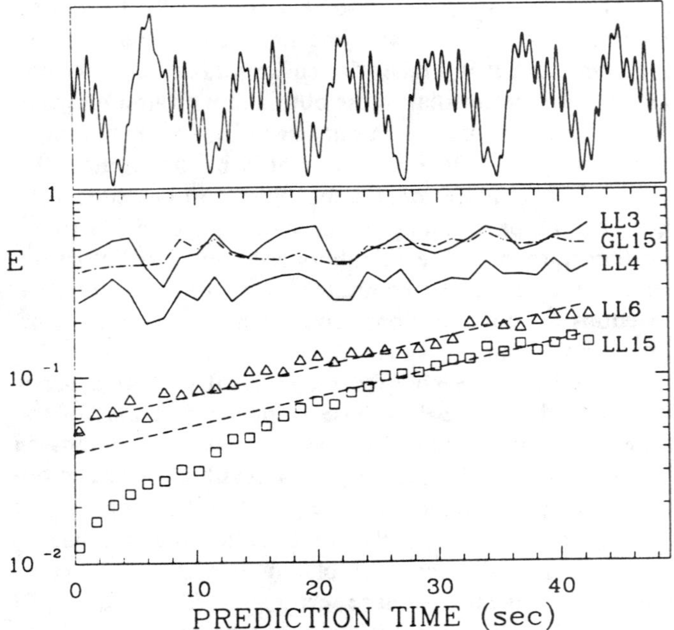

FIG. 1. Top: A time series obtained from Rayleigh-Bénard convection in an $^3$He-$^4$He mixture (Ref. 12), with Rayleigh number $R/R_c = 12.24$, and dimension $D \approx 3.1$. Bottom: The normalized error $E(T) = \sigma_\Delta(T)/\sigma_x$. The top and bottom time scales are the same. We show results for the local linear (LL) and global linear (GL) methods; numbers following the initials indicate the embedding dimension. The dashed lines are from Eq. (2), with $k$ equal to the computed metric entropy from Ref. 12, and $C$ determined by a least-squares fit.

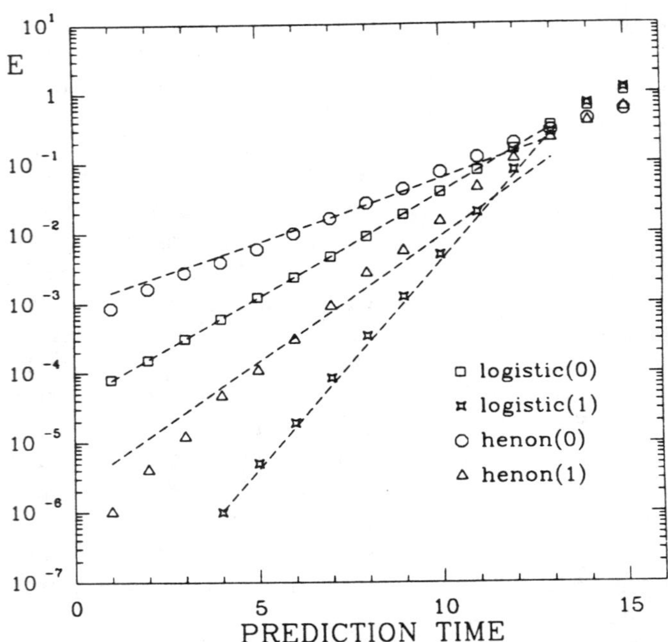

FIG. 2. The normalized error as a function of the prediction time $T$, for the logistic and Hénon maps (Ref. 3). Results are shown using zeroth-order (0) and first-order (1) local approximation. The dashed lines are from Eq. (2), with a least-squares fit for $C$ and the positive Lyapunov exponents, $k = \log 2$ for the logistic map, and $k \approx 0.42$ for the Hénon map (Ref. 14).

results obtained using a global linear approximation (linear autoregression[2]). When $d < D$, the quality of prediction for the local approximation is roughly the same as that obtained with the global linear approach, but for $d$ sufficiently large the predictions are significantly better.

How well does this local approximation work? This depends on the parameters of the problem, including the number of data points $N$, the attractor dimension $D$, the metric entropy $h$, the signal-to-noise ratio $S$, and the prediction time $T$. There are two distinct regimes: If the typical spacing between data points, $\epsilon \approx N^{-1/D} < S^{-1}$, then the forecast is limited by noise. Following Shaw,[3] the average information in a prediction is $\langle I(T) \rangle \approx \ln S - hT$. For a narrowly peaked distribution with $E \ll 1$, to first order $\langle I(T) \rangle$ is proportional to $-\ln E$.

The second regime occurs when $\epsilon > S^{-1}$ and the accuracy of forecasts is limited by the number of data points. In this case, providing $d$ is sufficiently greater than $D$, in the limit that $E \ll 1$ we propose the following error estimate:

$$E \approx C e^{(m+1)kT} N^{-(m+1)/D}, \qquad (2)$$

where $m$ is the order of approximation and $C$ is a constant. $k$ equals the largest Lyapunov exponent when $m = 0$, and equals the metric entropy otherwise. The ar-

guments leading to this formula are too involved to report here, but they are based on the following facts: The error of interpolation in one dimension is proportional to $f^{(m+1)} \epsilon^{m+1}$; to leading order the $m$th derivative grows under iteration as the $m$th power of the first derivative, and the average derivatives along the unstable manifold grow according to the positive Lyapunov exponents. Detailed arguments leading to this result will be presented elsewhere.[14]

The scalings predicted by Eq. (2) are illustrated in Figs. 2 and 3. The exponential increase of $E(T)$ is demonstrated in Fig. 2, for numerical experiments on the logistic and Hénon maps.[3] For the logistic map the slopes are very close to those predicted. For the Hénon map, a least-squares fit gives slopes about 10% greater than those expected with the positive Lyapunov exponent, indicating a possible correction[14] to Eq. (2). For the convection data on Fig. 1, agreement with computed values of the metric entropy[12] is very good as indicated in the figure.

Note that setting $E(T_{max}) = 1$ in Eq. (2) yields $T_{max} = (\ln N)/kD$, independent of the order $m$. Thus zeroth-order interpolation is less effective than first order, except when $E$ is the order of 1. Equation (2) suggests that higher-order polynomial interpolation might be more effective, but this is difficult in more than two dimensions.

The power-law variation of $E$ with $N$ is illustrated in

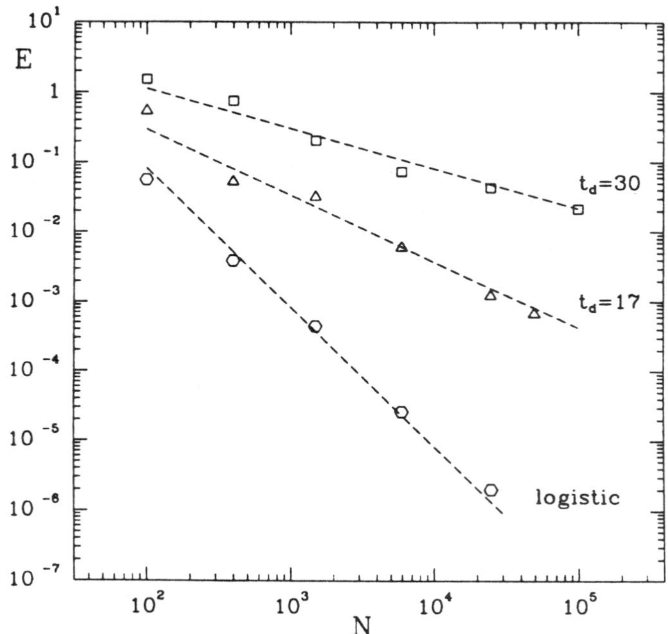

FIG. 3. The normalized error with use of local linear approximation as a function of the number of data points $N$, at fixed prediction time $T$. For the logistic map (Ref. 3) $r=4$ and $T=3$; for the Mackey-Glass delay-differential equation (Ref. 10) $T=40$, with two values of the delay parameter $t_d$. The dashed lines are from Eq. (2), with $D=1$ for the logistic map and $D=D_L$, the Lyapunov dimension, from Ref. 10 for Mackey-Glass equation.

Fig. 3, where we show the behavior for the logistic map and the Mackey-Glass equation. The agreement of the slopes with the expected values of $(m+1)/D$ based on computations of the Lyapunov dimension[10] is quite good. This scaling law breaks down for large $N$, on account of an approach to the noise floor (when $\epsilon < S^{-1}$).

In addition to the obvious practical applications of forecasting, the construction of approximate models can be a useful diagnostic tool to investigate chaos. Equation (2) demonstrates how forecasting can be used to estimate dimension and entropy; Lyapunov exponents are also easily obtained. Forecasting provides a way to determine whether the resulting numerical values of dimension and entropy are reliable. Ultimately, the ability to forecast successfully with deterministic methods may be the strongest test of whether or not low-dimensionality chaos is present.

At this point, this work is still in a preliminary stage and many possibilities remain to be investigated. In a future paper we plan to compare the local approximation in more detail to some other approaches, in particular recursive–ordinary-differential-equation models such as neural nets.

In this paper we have shown that a forecasting approach based on deterministic chaos can be quite effective in predicting low- to moderate-dimensionality time series. Furthermore, this can be done with reasonable amounts of data and computer time. The most im-

portant point is not the specific technique, but rather the demonstration that approaches based on deterministic chaos can be effective; we expect that new and better techniques will emerge rapidly as more attention is focused on this problem. Such methods should be effective for problems in fluid dynamics, control theory, artificial intelligence, and possibly even economics.

We would like to thank Scott Konishi for assistance on numerical procedures, Glenn Carter for assistance in reading nonstandard computer tape formats, and Ian Percival, Josh Deutsch, and particularly Norman Packard for valuable conversations. We would also like to thank Steve Omohundro for making us aware of the literature on decision trees. In a different context, he has recently independently proposed a local linear approximation as an efficient means of performing artificial-intelligence tasks.[15]

---


[(a)]Permanent address: Department of Physics, University of California at Santa Cruz, Santa Cruz, CA 95064.

[1]G. U. Yule, Philos. Trans. Roy. Soc. London A **226**, 267 (1927).

[2]For example, S. M. Pandit and S.-M. Yu, *Time Series and System Analysis with Applications* (Wiley, New York, 1983).

[3]For reviews see, for example, R. S. Shaw, Z. Naturforsch. **36a**, 80 (1981); J. P. Crutchfield, J. D. Farmer, N. H. Packard, and R. S. Shaw, Sci. Am. **254** (No. 12), 46 (1986); J. Ford, Phys. Today **36** (No. 4), 40 (1983).

[4]For example, G. Mayer-Kress, *Dimensions and Entropies in Chaotic Systems* (Springer-Verlag, Berlin, 1986).

[5]N. Aubry, P. Holmes, J. L. Lumley, and E. Stone, Cornell University Report No. FDA-86-15, 1986 (to be published).

[6]T. A. Bass, *The Eudaemonic Pie* (Houghton-Mifflin, New York, 1985).

[7]N. H. Packard, J. P. Crutchfield, J. D. Farmer, and R. S. Shaw, Phys. Rev. Lett. **45**, 712 (1980); F. Takens, in *Dynamical Systems and Turbulence,* edited by D. A. Rand and L.-S. Young (Springer-Verlag, Berlin, 1981).

[8]D. Gabor, W. P. Wilby, and R. Woodcock, Proc. IEEE **108B**, 422 (1960).

[9]J. L. Bentley and J. H. Friedman, A. C. M. Comput. Surv. **11**, 297 (1979).

[10]M. C. Mackey and L. Glass, Science **197**, 287 (1977); J. D. Farmer, Physica (Amsterdam) **4D**, 366 (1982).

[11]A. Brandtstater, J. Swift, H. L. Swinney, A. Wolf, J. D. Farmer, E. Jen, and J. P. Crutchfield, Phys. Rev. Lett. **51**, 1442 (1983); A. Brandtstater and H. L. Swinney, Phys. Rev. A **35**, 2207 (1987).

[12]H. Haucke and R. Ecke, Physica (Amsterdam) **25D**, 307 (1987).

[13]$T_{max}$ is a crude estimate of our ability to forecast. In some cases $E(T)$ reaches a plateau at a level less than 1. In these cases we estimate $T_{max}$ by extrapolating the initial rate of increase. (In some cases such as GL15 in Fig. 1, it is necessary to expand the $T$ axis to see the initial increase.)

[14]Detailed arguments suggest that there may be a correction to the $T$ scaling in Eq. (2), but we have not yet resolved this.

[15]S. Omohundro, "Efficient algorithms with neural network behavior" (to be published).

Physics Letters A 158 (1991) 57–62
North-Holland



# Hierarchical training of neural networks and prediction of chaotic time series ☆

J. Deppisch, H.-U. Bauer and T. Geisel
*Institut für Theoretische Physik und SFB Nichtlineare Dynamik, Universität Frankfurt, W-6000 Frankfurt/Main 11, Germany*

Received 9 October 1990; revised manuscript received 10 June 1991; accepted for publication 13 June 1991
Communicated by A.P. Fordy

We present a new procedure for hierarchical training of multilayer perceptrons to outputs of high precision. It achieves a dramatic increase in accuracy, e.g. by three orders of magnitude, and can reduce training time considerably. The method is applied to the prediction of chaotic systems where we obtain the optimum error evolution for iterated predictions as well as a substantial reduction of the absolute prediction error.

## 1. Introduction

Neural networks are nowadays applied to an increasing number of cognitive tasks, such as reading [1], motion detection [2,3], and speech recognition [4] to mention a few. A promising network type are multilayer perceptrons or feed-forward nets [5] consisting of three of more layers of nonlinear processing units. Their recent success can be attributed mainly to the introduction of an appropriate training method, the error-backpropagation algorithm [5]. The training phase, however, can become extremely time consuming, especially when the networks become large or when very accurate outputs are required. Thus many realistic applications can only be tackled if more powerful training techniques become available.

In the present article we propose a training algorithm which dramatically reduces training time and the learning error (by three orders of magnitude compared to standard backpropagation in the example considered). It is based on successive training of a hierarchical architecture and makes use of the backpropagation and conjugate gradient algorithms. It is well suited for applications requiring outputs of high precision.

As an example we treat the prediction of chaotic

times series. It is well known that chaotic behavior impedes long-term prediction of a system, as initial errors grow exponentially. It is possible, however, to improve traditional forecasting methods designed for noisy systems by exploiting the deterministic character of chaotic systems. The maximum forecasting time can be extended by reducing the error of an elementary prediction step, where very high precision output is required. Below we define a new measure determining the best possible error evolution for iterated predictions. We apply the hierarchical training algorithm to the forecasting of the logistic map and the Rössler system [6] and obtain the optimum error evolution in both cases. The absolute prediction error is reduced considerably compared to nonhierarchical training.

Prediction of chaotic systems is based on the possibility of reconstructing strange attractors from an observed times-series $x(t)$ [7,8]. It was shown that an embedding of the attractor can be obtained [9] by constructing a vector $x_t = (x(t), x(t-\tau), ..., x(t-(m-1)\tau))$ from time-delayed coordinates, where $m$ is the embedding dimension and $\tau$ the delay time. The dynamics on the attractor is a map $x_t \rightarrow x_{t+\tau}$. Farmer and Sidorowich [10] have suggested a prediction method based on local linear approximations of the map. Sugihara and May [11] derived a more simple local nonparametric simplex method thereof. In a different approach, Pawelzik and Schuster have

☆ Work supported by Deutsche Forschungsgemeinschaft.

used unstable periodic orbits for iterated predictions [12]. Multilayer preceptrons for prediction were used by Lapedes and Farber [13] and applied to sunspot data by Weigend et al. [14].

In this application the neural network must be trained to approximate a scalar map $x(t+\tau) = f(x_t)$ for a vectorial input $x_t$. The same problem arises in other applications, and extensions to vectorial outputs are straightforward. In general, we assume that a task is defined by a pattern set $\mathscr{P}$, where each pattern is a pair $(x_p, f(x_p))$ of an input $x_p$ and a desired output $f(x_p)$. In contrast to classification tasks, however, where the output only needs to fall into certain intervals, iterated prediction of chaotic systems requires outputs of extremely high precision.

## 2. Hierarchical training of multilayer perceptrons

A customary approach [5,13,15] when using neural network techniques is to set up a three-layer perceptron with an input layer supplying the $K$ components of the input vector $x$, a hidden layer with a variable number $L$ of hidden units $l$, and a linear output unit, capable of rescaling the output to any range. We classify these networks by specifying the number of units in each layer in a triple $(K, L, 1)$. Individual units perform a weighted sum of the outputs of the preceding layer and in addition the hidden units carry out a transformation by a sigmoidal transfer function $g$. The outputs of the second and third layer are given by

$$o_l = g\left(\sum_k \omega_{lk} x_k + \Theta_l\right), \quad o = \sum_l \omega_l o_l + \Theta, \tag{1}$$

where $\omega_l$, $\Theta$, $\omega_{lk}$, and $\Theta_l$ are parameters of the system. In a training phase these parameters are adjusted so as to produce the desired output using the backpropagation algorithm or modifications thereof [5]. We assume a general task defined by a pattern set $\mathscr{P}$ as mentioned above. An error measure can be defined as the quadratic average over the pattern set $\mathscr{P}_1 \subset \mathscr{P}$ by

$$F = \left\langle \left(\frac{\tilde{f}(x_p) - f(x_p)}{\sigma}\right)^2 \right\rangle_{\mathscr{A}}^{1/2}, \tag{2}$$

where $\tilde{f}$ is the approximation of $f$ given by the output $o$ of the network and $\sigma$ is the standard deviation of $f$. If $\mathscr{P}_1$ is the pattern set used for training, $F$ is called the learning error. For the evaluation of the prediction error we use a disjunct pattern set $\mathscr{P}_2 \subset \mathscr{P}$, with $\mathscr{P}_1 \cap \mathscr{P}_2 = \{\}$. The following observations can typically be made with standard learning algorithms.

– Training is hard. The training phase takes a huge amount of computing time, e.g. a day of computing on a workstation for network sizes of about 100 connections and pattern set sizes of the order of $10^4$.

– Different random initializations of the weights require a different number of learning steps to reduce the error measure and they give different final errors.

– Large networks are more powerful in principle.

– If a problem can also be solved with a smaller network, however, the smaller network not only needs less computing time for a single learning step, but also less learning steps to reach the required error measure. Moreover the ability to generalize is improved compared to the larger networks, which have too many degrees of freedom.

This means that the common learning algorithms such as variations of the backpropagation and the conjugate gradient algorithm are not able to exploit the advantages of larger networks.

Starting from an idea of Moody [16], we have developed a new learning algorithm for multilayer perceptrons which circumvents this problem and allows convenient training of large networks. Fig. 1 shows the principle of the scheme. An input signal is fed into several networks, which actually are separate parts of one large network. These parts are subsequently trained with a target signal in such a way that

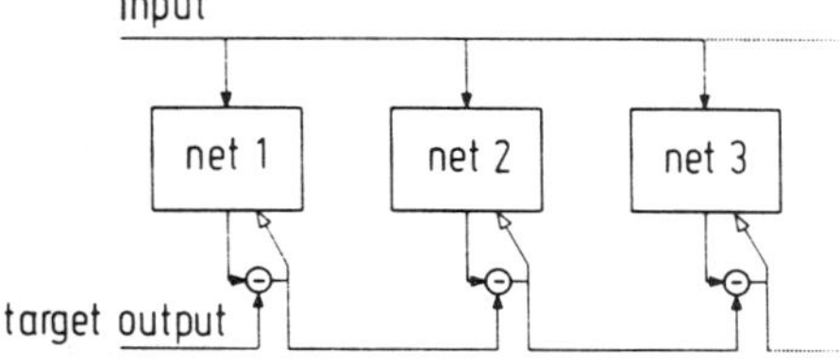


Fig. 1. The hierarchical training scheme: the input signal is fed into all subnetworks. The error, i.e. the difference between the current output of network 1 and target output is first propagated back through network 1 (open arrows) to modify its weights. After the training of net 1, this difference is used as target output for the subsequent network, and so on.

the sum of all the outputs approaches the target signal. The first step is to train network 1 until saturation of the learning error. Next, we leave network 1 unchanged and train network 2 to correct the difference between the target and the output of network 1. We successively add more parts of the network, ideally reducing the error made by the total network by one order of magnitude per part. Finally, we connect the trained parts to form a single parallel network. As the generalization from a scalar output to a vector output is straightforward, we explain the procedure for networks with just one output unit. Fig. 2 shows a simple example how to connect two networks. The input units are nonprocessing units supplying only the input values and can therefore be identified. The hidden units remain unchanged, while the two output units are now combined into one. This unit adds up all previous outputs to give an approximation of the target output.

For comparison we have also trained the entire network as a whole as usually and determined the learning speed and the learning error. As a typical example, we mention the results of training different multilayer perceptrons to forecast the logistic map with one hidden layer (2 to 15 hidden sigmoidal units) using a pattern set $\mathscr{P}_1$ of 200 samples for training. The logistic map may be used as a test system and benchmark to compare different forecasting methods [11,13,17,18]. We used the conjugate gradient algorithm [19] (where the gradients were obtained by backpropagation) to minimize the error of both the complete network on one hand, and the successive network parts on the other hand. With the non-hierarchical method the normalized root-mean-square learning error $F$ (eq. (2)) saturated at a value of $4 \cdot 10^{-4}$. The hierarchical method arrived at a $10^3$ times higher accuracy in less computing time (for statistics see fig 4). In both cases, the prediction error (based on a pattern set $\mathscr{P}_2$ with 1000 samples)

was only a few percent above the learning error. In particular, the overfitting problem mentioned in ref. [14] did not occur. Fig. 3 shows the statistical increase in accuracy of a second hierarchy level over the first level. Training of the first hierarchy was stopped after the indicated training errors $F^{(1)}$ were reached. The figure demonstrates the advantage of training the first hierarchy level until saturation before starting with a second level. Additionally, the results of the non-hierarchical training are plotted. In any case, a dramatic increase in accuracy is obtained by the hierarchical method.

Fig. 4 shows the dependence of the error measure on the computing power consumed, which we measure in terms of the number of learning steps multiplied by the number $W$ of connections in the network. Typical training curves are plotted for a minimal $(1,2,1)$-network and a larger $(1,8,1)$-network (both trained non-hierarchically) together with the hierarchical training curves of appending $(1,6,1)$-networks to the above $(1,2,1)$-network at different stages of learning. One observes that the same accuracy can be achieved with much less cpu-power by our hierarchical method. Alternatively, the accuracy can be improved by orders of magnitude while

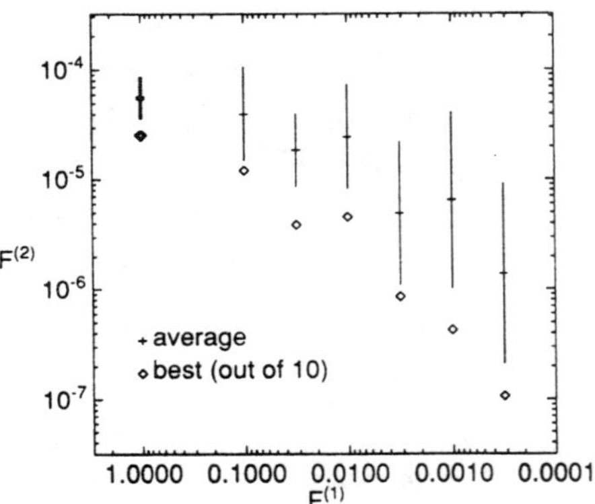

Fig. 3. Increase in accuracy due to hierarchical training: several $(1,2,1)$-networks were trained for different training times. Training was stopped when the indicated learning errors $F^{(1)}$ were achieved. For each network, a second $(1,6,1)$-network was trained hierarchically until saturation. Both were combined to a $(1,8,1)$-network and the learning error $F^{(2)}$ was plotted against $F^{(1)}$ after averaging over 10 trials, each with different initializations of the networks. For comparison, we also show the saturated learning error $F$ of non-hierarchically trained $(1,8,1)$-networks (thick lines). Averages are plotted with error bars given by their standard deviations and with a diamond marking the best trial.

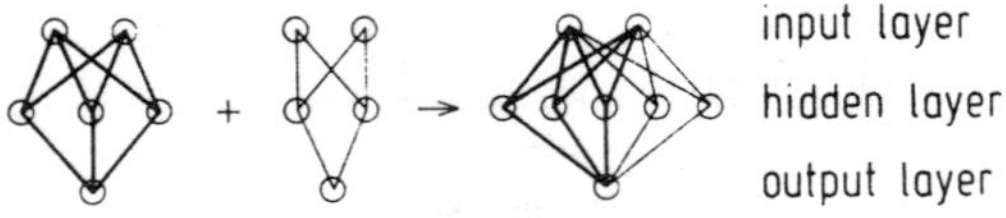


Fig. 2. Separately trained networks are combined to a single network: input units are identified, hidden units remain unchanged, while the output units are replaced by a unit which performs the sum of the previous output units.

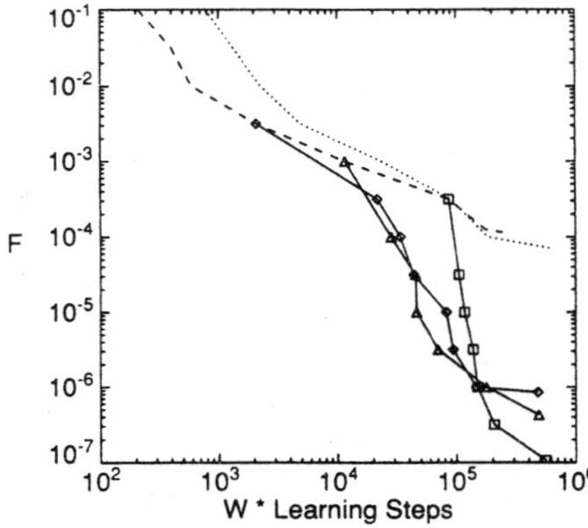

Fig. 4. Error reduction as a function of training time. The consumed computing power is measured in terms of the number of learning steps multiplied by the number of connections in the network. Typical training curves are plotted for a minimal $(1,2,1)$-network (dashed line) and a larger $(1,8,1)$-network (dot-dashed line). The solid lines show hierarchical training curves of appending $(1,6,1)$-networks to the above $(1,2,1)$-network at different stages of learning.

spending the same amount of cpu-power.


## 3. Predicting chaotic time series

Our hierarchical algorithm is a suitable tool for training high precision networks in a reasonable amount of time. We have applied it to the prediction of two chaotic systems, the logistic map and the Rössler system [6]. The networks were trained to globally fit the map $x(t+\tau)=f(x_t)$ for all elements $(x_t, f(x_t))$ of the pattern set $\mathscr{P}_1 \subset \mathscr{P}$. The scalar value $x(t+\tau)$ is thus predicted from time delayed coordinates $x(t)$, $x(t-\tau)$, ..., $x(t-(m-1)\tau)$ where $m$ is the embedding dimension and $\tau$ is a time delay. The right choice of $m$ and $\tau$ for an optimum phase-space reconstruction out of the time delayed coordinates is discussed in ref. [20]. To predict further values in the future we iterate the procedure feeding the predicted value back to the input. Thus we iteratively get values for $x(t+2\tau)$, $x(t+3\tau)$, .... The straightforward extension of the learning error (eq. (2)) after $n$ iterations is

$$F_n = \left\langle \left(\frac{\tilde{f}^n(x_t)-f^n(x_t)}{\sigma}\right)^2 \right\rangle_{\mathscr{P}_2}^{1/2}, \tag{3}$$

the root-mean-square prediction error (based on $\mathscr{P}_2$),

which is normally used in the literature [15,12,13]. For chaotic systems, neighboring trajectories in phase-space diverge exponentially on a time scale governed by the largest Liapunov exponent. We will show, however, that $F_n$ is not generally a suitable measure to compare with the Liapunov exponent. We define a more appropriate measure $L_n$ as the logarithmic average of the prediction error after $n$ iterations:

$$L_n = \left\langle \log\left|\frac{\tilde{f}^n(x_t)-f^n(x_t)}{\sigma}\right| \right\rangle_{\mathscr{P}_2}, \tag{4}$$

where $\tilde{f}(x_t)$ is the predicted value for $x(t+\tau)$, while $f(x_t)$ equals $x(t+\tau)$. The components of $x_t$ are the time delayed coordinates $x(t)$, $x(t-\tau)$, ..., $x(t-(m-1)\tau)$ supplied by the input units and $\sigma$ is the normalization factor of the root-mean-square prediction error.

For an embedding dimension of $m \geq 1$ we need $m$ iterations of $\tilde{f}$ to construct an entirely predicted vector $x_{t'=t+m\tau}$ as every iteration just gives one component. For good approximations $\tilde{f}$ of $f$ we can now write for $n > m$

$$\begin{pmatrix} \tilde{f}^m(x_t) \\ \vdots \\ \tilde{f}^2(x_t) \\ \tilde{f}^1(x_t) \end{pmatrix} \approx \begin{pmatrix} f^m(x_t) \\ \vdots \\ f^2(x_t) \\ f^1(x_t) \end{pmatrix} + \varepsilon = x_{t+m\tau} + \varepsilon, \tag{5}$$

where $\varepsilon$ is a small correction. Therefore we rewrite eq. (4) as

$$L_n = \left\langle \log\left|\frac{\tilde{f}^{n-m}(x_{t+m\tau}+\varepsilon)-f^{n-m}(x_{t+m\tau})}{\sigma}\right| \right\rangle_t. \tag{6}$$

As the time average is over many times, we may sum over $t'=t+m\tau$ and obtain

$$L_n = \langle \log|\tilde{f}^{n-m}(x_{t'}+\varepsilon)+f^{n-m}(x_{t'})| \rangle_{t'} + \text{const}$$

$$\stackrel{\text{def}}{=} \lambda^*(n-m)\tau + \text{const}, \quad \text{for } n > m. \tag{7}$$

This equation defines a Liapunov exponent $\lambda^*$. Note that the definition of the usual Liapunov exponent $\lambda$ is recovered for $\tilde{f} \equiv f$. For $\tilde{f} \not\equiv f$, the error made by the approximation increases $\lambda^*$, so that $\lambda^* \geq \lambda$. The slope $\lambda^*$ of eq. (7) thus gives a criterion for the best possible error evolution $(\lambda^*=\lambda)$. For multidimensional systems, $\lambda$ represents the largest Liapunov exponent, which dominates the divergence of trajectories in phase space. Recently, Wales [21] has related the Liapunov exponent to the fall of the correlation coefficient. The relation between $L_n$ and $\lambda$ (eq. (7)), however, can be derived in a straightforward way without assuming a particular distribution of the $\{x_i\}$.

Fig. 5, which displays the error evolution for iterative prediction of the logistic map, demonstrates that the optimum error evolution was reached by the hierarchically trained networks. Besides, the root-mean-square prediction error $F_n$ (eq. (3)) is also included in this figure. It is usually believed that its error evolution is given by the Liapunov exponent. An analytic calculation [17] and fig. 5, however, show that this is not the case here and that $\log(F_n)$ grows with a different slope $\frac{3}{2}\lambda = \frac{3}{2}\log 2$. On the other hand, the error measure $L_n$ introduced above has the advantage that its minimum growth is determined by the Liapunov exponent. In addition, the logarithmic average is more stable numerically.

The difference in the slope of $L_n$ and $F_n$ does not arise for the Rössler system where we found that $\log(F_n)$ and $L_n$ grow at the same rate. We have considered the Rössler equations [6] for $a=0.15, b=0.2, c=10.0$ where the attractor has fractal dimension $d=2.01$. The largest Liapunov exponent is $\lambda=0.13$ bits/s and the average circulation time around the attractor is $T_c=6.07$ s. Predictions were made using an embedding dimension $m=4$, a time delay of $\tau=T_c/7$, and a $(4,20,1)$-network that was trained hierarchically based on a learning set of 1000 patterns. As is seen in fig. 6, the optimum error evolution was achieved. The decreasing slope for large $n$ arises as the error approaches 1, where the predicted values are essentially random. Fig. 6 also includes the error evolution of the other prediction methods (taken from ref. [12]) for comparison. The local linear method [10] starts with a very small prediction error, but becomes useless after some iterations. The predictions based on UPOs (unstable periodic orbits) [12] already achieve the optimum error evolution, but the absolute prediction error is reduced substantially by our hierarchical neural network technique.

We want to point out that the performances of most local methods can be improved considerably by increasing the learning set size. We have obtained an optimum error evolution e.g. with a set of 7500 data points for the local linear method. In cases where sufficiently many empirical training values are available, the local methods become superior to global techniques like our neural network approach. The latter becomes too time consuming, as we have to increase both the pattern set and the system size, but is advantageous for learning sets with fewer data points.

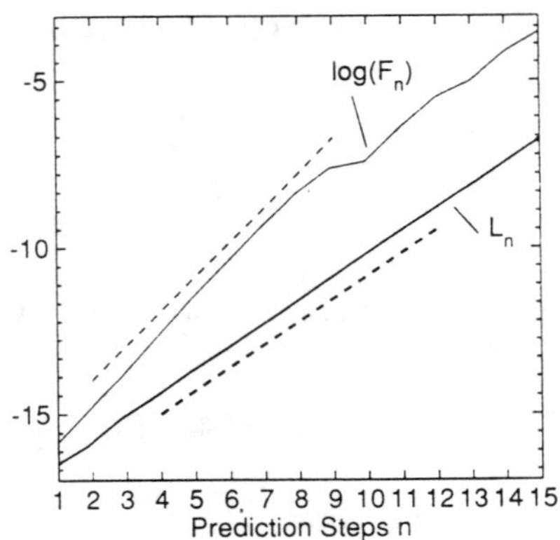

Fig. 5. Iterated prediction of the logistic map. The error growth of the prediction using a hierarchically trained $(1,8,1)$-network (solid lines) is compared to the theoretical optimal error growth (dashed lines). The error $F_n$ (thin line) grows with an exponent $\frac{3}{2}\log 2$ which differs from the Liapunov exponent $\log 2$. The growths of the error $L_n$ (thick line), however, is governed by the Liapunov exponent (thick dashed line and eq. (7)), if the optimum error evolution is achieved as in this case.

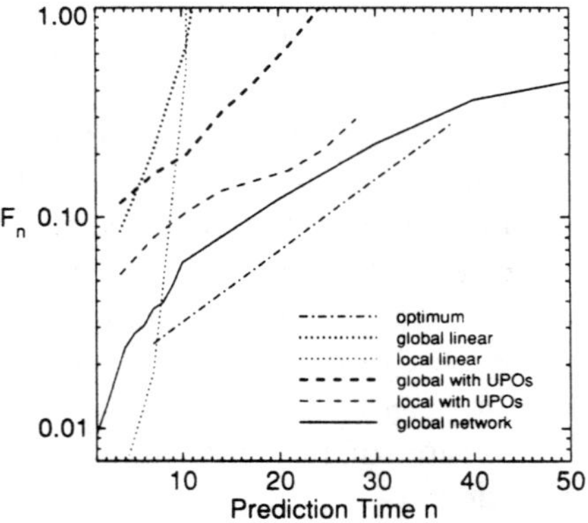

Fig. 6. Error evolution of the Rössler system for iterated predictions obtained by various methods and compared with the theoretical optimum. The prediction steps are in increments of the time delay $\tau=T_c/7$ used for the phase-space reconstruction.

**Acknowledgement**

We acknowledge very useful discussions with K. Pawelzik and financial support by the Deutsche Forschungsgemeinschaft.

**References**

[1] T.J. Sejnowski, NETtalk, Technical Report 86/01, J. Hopkins University (1986).

[2] H.-U. Bauer and T. Geisel, Int. J. Neural Syst. 1 (1989) 187.

[3] W.S. Stornetta, T. Hogg and B.A. Huberman, in Neural information processing systems, ed. D. Anderson (AIP, New York, 1988) p.750.

[4] H.-U. Bauer and T. Geisel, Phys. Rev. A 42 (1990) 2401.

[5] D.E. Rumelhart and J.L. McClelland, Parallel distributed processing, Vol. 1 (MIT Press, Cambridge, 1986) p. 318.

[6] O.E. Rössler, Phys. Lett. A 57 (1976) 397.

[7] N.H. Packard, J.P. Crutchfield, J.D. Farmer and R.S. Shaw, Phys. Rev. Lett. 45 (1980) 712.

[8] H. Froehling, J.P. Crutchfield, J.D. Farmer, N.H. Packard and R.S. Shaw, Physica D 3 (1981) 605.

[9] F. Takens, in: Lecture notes in mathematics, Vol. 898. Dynamical systems and turbulence, eds. D.A. Rand and L.S. Young (Springer, Berlin, 1981) p. 366.

[10] J.D. Farmer and J.J. Sidorowich, Phys. Rev. Lett. 59 (1987) 845.

[11] G. Sugihara and R.M. May, Nature 344 (1990) 734.

[12] K. Pawelzik and H.G. Schuster, Phys. Rev. A 43 (1991) 1808.

[13] A. Lapedes and R. Farber, Technical Report LA-UR 87, Los Alamos National Laboratory (1987).

[14] A.S. Weigend, B.A. Huberman and D.E. Rumelhart, submitted to Int. J. Neural Syst.

[15] J.D. Farmer and J.J. Sidorowich, in: Evolution, learning and cognition, ed. Y.C. Lee (World Scientific, Singapore, 1988) p. 277.

[16] J. Moody, Yale Computer Science Research Report, New Haven (1989).

[17] J. Deppisch, diploma thesis, Universität, Würzburg (1990).

[18] N.Z. Hakim, J.J. Kaufman, G. Cerf and H.E. Meadows, in: Proc. IJCNN'90 San Diego, IEEE Neural Network Council (Edwards, Ann Arbor, 1990) p. 593.

[19] R. Fletcher, Practical methods of optimization, Vol. 1 (Wiley, New York, 1981).

[20] W. Liebert, K. Pawelzik and H.G. Schuster, Europhys. Lett. A 6 (1991) p. 521.

[21] D.J. Wales, Nature 350 (1991) 485.

# Time Series Forecasting with Specialized Architectures

# A Tree-Structured Adaptive Network for Function Approximation in High-Dimensional Spaces

Terence D. Sanger

*Abstract*—Nonlinear function approximation is often solved by finding a set of coefficients for a finite number of fixed nonlinear basis functions. However, if the input data are drawn from a high-dimensional space, the number of required basis functions grows exponentially with dimension, and this has led many authors to suggest the use of adaptive nonlinear basis functions whose parameters can be determined by iterative methods. This paper proposes a different technique, one based on the hope that for most of the data only a few dimensions of the input may be necessary to compute the desired output function. Additional input dimensions are incorporated only where needed. The learning procedure grows a tree whose structure depends upon both the input data and the function to be approximated. This technique has a fast learning algorithm with no local minima once the network shape is fixed, and it can be used to reduce the number of required measurements in situations where there is a cost associated with sensing. Three examples are given: controlling the dynamics of a simulated planar two-joint robot arm, predicting the dynamics of the chaotic Mackey-Glass equation, and predicting pixel values in real images from pixel values above and to the left.

## I. INTRODUCTION

WE can often approximate a desired scalar function $f$ over $d$-dimensional input using a linear combination of basis functions $\sigma_i$ according to

$$f(x_1, \cdots, x_d) \approx \sum_{i=1}^{L} c_i \sigma_i(x_1, \cdots, x_d). \tag{1}$$

Once the basis functions $\sigma_i$ are chosen, the choice of the coefficients $c_i$ is easily solved by standard methods in linear algebra. There are three major techniques for choosing the basis functions: (1) a large fixed basis can be chosen which is used to approximate any desired function $f$, (2) a smaller adaptive basis can be chosen which depends on parameters that are varied to obtain an optimal approximation, or (3) new basis functions can be added as new data points arrive. The first technique has the advantage that the only training is the adaptation of the coefficients $c_i$, which can be done simply using linear techniques. It has the disadvantage that in a space of dimension $d$ the number of required basis functions $L$ grows as $N^d$ for some constant $N$, so that this technique rapidly becomes infeasible for input dimensions greater than 10 or so. The second technique has the advantage of small memory requirements, but the parameters must often be determined using iterative gradient-descent algorithms which can be slow and are not guaranteed to converge

Manuscript received June 29, 1990; revised November 26, 1990. This work describes research done within the laboratory of Dr. E. Bizzi in the Department of Brain and Cognitive Sciences at the Massachusetts Institute of Technology. Support was received from the Division of Health Sciences and Technology and from NIH Grants 5R37AR26710 and 5R01NS09343 to Dr. Bizzi.

The author is with the Massachusetts Institute of Technology, Room E25-534, Cambridge, MA 02139.

IEEE Log Number 9042125.

to an optimal solution. The third technique takes advantage of the possibility that the number of data points does not depend on the dimension of the input space, but it requires large amounts of memory to handle large numbers of sample points or a nonstationary distribution of sample points.

Current examples of all three types of approximation basis exist, and neural network implementations often combine elements from more than one. Backpropagation [1]–[4] is an example of the second technique, while radial basis functions (see [5] for review) can be designed for any of the three techniques. Local approximation algorithms (e.g. [6]–[10]) generally fall into the third category.

A problem common to all three techniques is that all the dimensions of the data must be available, and all the dimensions must be used. For example, if the different dimensions represent different sensor measurements and there is some cost associated with making these measurements, then one might like to reduce the number of measurements to the minimum required to determine the output with reasonable accuracy.

Unlike most existing techniques for nonlinear approximation, the algorithm proposed here takes advantage of the possibility that successful approximation will not always require all the dimensions of the input data. This represents an assumption of a high degree of (nonlinear) dependency between different measurements of a single phenomenon. The algorithm will not be efficient if such dependencies do not occur.

This paper is organized into several sections. In the next section the tree-structured learning algorithm is described, along with the way in which it is implemented in practice. In the following section three examples of applications of the algorithm are given. In the last two sections the significance of the algorithm is discussed, as is its relation to other techniques. Before proceeding, a brief informal description of the algorithm is given.

Pick a single dimension of the input $x_1$ and code it using one-dimensional basis functions $\phi_1(x_1), \cdots, \phi_N(x_1)$. Now compute the best approximation to the desired output function from this basis:

$$f(x_1, \cdots, x_d) \approx \sum_{n=1}^{N} \alpha_n \phi_n(x_1). \tag{2}$$

An iterative method to compute the coefficients $\alpha_n$ is given by the Widrow–Hoff LMS rule [11]:

$$\Delta \alpha_n(t) = \eta \delta(t) \phi_n(x_1(t))$$

where $x_1(t)$ is the value of $x_1$ for the sample data present at time $t$, $\delta(t)$ is the output error at time $t$, $\eta$ is a small rate term, and $\Delta \alpha_n$ is the change in weight. After this algorithm has converged, the average value of $\Delta \alpha_n$ will be zero, so that the weights are not changing (on average). This means that the er-





Reprinted from *IEEE Transactions on Neural Networks*, Vol. 2, No. 2, Mar. 1991, pp. 285-293. Copyright © 1991 by The Institute of Electrical and Electronics Engineers, Inc. All rights reserved.

ror $\delta$ and the input $\phi_n(x_1)$ are uncorrelated, since

$$E[\eta\delta\phi_n(x_1)] = E[\Delta\alpha_n] = 0$$

for all $n$. However, the variance

$$E\left[(\eta\delta\phi_n(x_1))^2\right] = E\left[(\Delta\alpha_n)^2\right]$$

will not in general be zero, representing the fact that sometimes the error would be decreased if the weight $\alpha_n$ were smaller, and sometimes it would be decreased if the weight were larger (although the network has converged to the minimum mean-squared error solution for any fixed value of $\alpha_n$). We can thus improve the performance of the network by training a second network to modify the weights $\alpha_n$ when necessary. Generate a subnetwork below the weight with largest variance, and train this subnetwork to modify that weight in order to reduce the error. The subnetwork will approximate over a different dimension of the data $x_2$ (see Fig. 1). Further subnetworks can be added as needed, thereby growing a tree structure. If a sparse tree is capable of adequate approximation to the desired output function, then this procedure may considerably reduce computation and storage compared with other algorithms.

Although the discussion above implies that it is necessary to order the dimensions, in actual practice one would usually have all input dimensions present at each level of the tree, so that the depth of the tree would correspond to the order of the interactions between different input dimensions. As we will see in the next section, training the weights in such trees is exactly equivalent to training a single-layer network with the LMS algorithm. Thus there are no local minima in the energy surface, and the optimal weights will always be found for any given tree structure. The choice of tree structure, however, is determined by some simple heuristics which are not guaranteed to produce minimal size trees.

## II. Method

We begin by defining the notation to be used. For a tree of degree $N$, label each node by the path to that node from the root. A node at depth $p$ in the tree is labeled $\langle r_1, \cdots, r_p \rangle$, where each $r_i$ is an integer between 1 and $N$ that indicates the branch of the tree taken at depth $i$. An edge from a child node to its parent (which usually represents a weight value) takes the label of the child node. Thus an edge $\alpha$ connecting nodes $\langle r_1, \cdots, r_{p-1} \rangle$ and $\langle r_1, \cdots, r_p \rangle$ is labelled $\alpha_{r_1, \ldots, r_p}$. Note that the number of subscripts of an edge determines the depth of the distal node at that edge.

Now, consider a finite set of scalar one-dimensional basis functions $\phi_n(a)$, where $a$ is a scalar, and $1 \leq n \leq N$. Along any dimension $p$ of the input, the basis is given by $\phi_1(x_p)$, $\cdots$, $\phi_N(x_p)$. To approximate the desired function $f(x_1, \cdots, x_d)$ using only the first dimension of the input, we can compute coefficients $\alpha_n$ so that

$$f(x_1, \cdots, x_d) \approx \hat{f}(x_1) = \sum_{n=1}^{N} \alpha_n\phi_n(x_1).$$

If the input data are stationary and random samples are available, then the Widrow–Hoff LMS learning rule [11] can be used to minimize the mean-squared approximation error. The learning rule (with the argument $t$ removed for clarity) is given by

$$\Delta\alpha_n = \eta\left(f(x_1, \cdots, x_d) - \hat{f}(x_1)\right)\phi_n(x_1) \qquad (3)$$

where $\eta$ is a rate term which should decrease to zero as $1/t$ [12], [13], and $\Delta\alpha_n$ is the change in the weight $\alpha_n$ made in

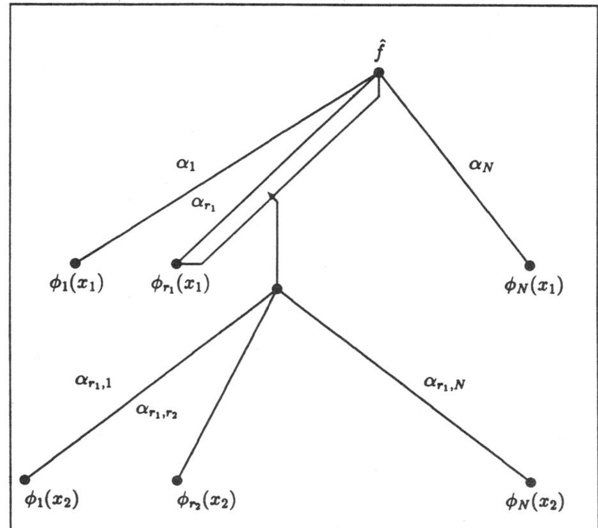



Fig. 1. Network structure with a single subnetwork. See text for explanation.

response to the current value of $x_1$. This algorithm has no local minima in the energy surface, and thus always converges to a value of $\alpha_n$ which minimizes the mean-squared approximation error [11], [12]. After convergence, the expected value of the weight change $\Delta\alpha_n$ will be zero, so that

$$E[\Delta\alpha_n] = E\left[\eta\left(f(x_1, \cdots, x_d) - \hat{f}(x_1)\right)\phi_n(x_1)\right] = 0. \qquad (4)$$

This implies that the residual error $(f - \hat{f})$ is either zero or uncorrelated with the output of the basis functions. No further adjustment in weights $\alpha_n$ will improve the approximation, so $\hat{f}(x_1)$ is the best approximation to $f$ based on linear combinations of $\phi_1(x_1), \cdots, \phi_N(x_1)$.

However, if $x_1$ does not provide sufficient information to approximate $f$, then there will be some nonzero residual error $(f(x_1, \cdots, x_d) - \hat{f}(x_1))$. Although this error is uncorrelated with $\phi_n(x_1)$ for all $n$ so that the mean $E[\Delta\alpha_n] = 0$, there will be considerable variance $E[(\Delta\alpha_n)^2] \neq 0$. The relation between the mean-squared output error and the weight-change variance is given by

$$E\left[(\Delta\alpha_n)^2\right] = E\left[\left(\left(f(x_1, \cdots, x_d) - \hat{f}(x_1)\right)\phi_n(x_1)\right)^2\right]$$

and Holder's inequality implies that this is less than or equal to

$$E\left[\left(f(x_1, \cdots, x_d) - \hat{f}(x_1)\right)^2\right] \cdot E\left[(\phi_n(x_1))^2\right].$$

Since this is true for all $n$, the mean-squared error is lower bounded by

$$E\left[\left(f(x_1, \cdots, x_d) - \hat{f}(x_1)\right)^2\right] \geq \max_n \frac{E\left[(\Delta\alpha_n)^2\right]}{E\left[(\phi_n(x_1))^2\right]}. \qquad (5)$$

To obtain an upper bound, note that

$$\sum_{n=1}^{N} E\left[(\Delta\alpha_n)^2\right] = E\left[\left(f(x_1, \cdots, x_d)\right)\hat{f}(x_1))^2 \sum_{n=1}^{N} \phi_n^2(x_1)\right]$$

$$\geq E\left[(f - \hat{f})^2\right] \min_{x_1} \sum_{n=1}^{N} \phi_n^2(x_1).$$

It is assumed that $\min_{x_1} \sum_{n=1}^{N} \phi_n^2(x_1) = \epsilon > 0$, which represents the assumption that at least one basis function responds for any possible input value. This gives the upper bound on mean-squared error,

$$\frac{1}{\epsilon} \sum_{n=1}^{N} E[(\Delta\alpha_n)^2] \geq E[(f(x_1, \cdots, x_d) - \hat{f}(x_1))^2]. \quad (6)$$

We thus want to minimize $\max_n E[(\Delta\alpha_n)^2]$, since the error will be zero if and only if $E[(\Delta\alpha_n)^2] = 0$ for all $n$. For any particular $n$, $E[(\Delta\alpha_n)^2] = 0$ implies that the output error is zero whenever $\phi_n^2(x_1) \neq 0$. If $\phi_n$ is a local basis function, this statement has the simple interpretation that the output error is zero in the region of the input to which $\phi_n$ responds. The $\phi_n$'s thus partition the $x_1$ dimension into different regions, and a separate approximation can occur within each region.

The weight-change variance $E[(\Delta\alpha_n)^2]$ indicates that there is pressure to increase or decrease weight $\alpha_n$, but the pressure in each direction exactly cancels that in the other, so that the change in expected value $E[\Delta\alpha_n]$ is zero. We can decrease the variance by using another network to modify the weight $\alpha_n$ according to this pressure. The new subnetwork will be based on a different dimension of the input $x_2$. The choice is made to grow a single subnetwork below the weight with largest variance. Let the label of this weight be $r_1$. When computing the output approximation $\hat{f}$, a variable component is then added to weight $\alpha_{r_1}$, which is computed by

$$\sum_{m=1}^{N} \alpha_{r_1, m} \phi_m(x_2)$$

where $\alpha_{r_1, m}$ specifies the second-level weights (see Fig. 1). Since this variable component is a weight, it multiplies $\phi_{r_1}(x_1)$. The network output is now given by

$$\hat{f}(x_1, x_2) = \sum_{n=1}^{N} \alpha_n \phi_n(x_1) + \phi_{r_1}(x_1) \sum_{m=1}^{N} \alpha_{r_1, m} \phi_m(x_2). \quad (7)$$

To learn the weights $\alpha_{r_1, m}$, $\Delta\alpha_{r_1}$ is used as the error term for LMS learning (see below), so that

$$\Delta\alpha_{r_1, m} = \Delta\alpha_{r_1} \phi_m(x_2).$$

The output of the subnetwork will increase whenever $\Delta\alpha_{r_1}$ is positive and decrease when it is negative. The modified weight from $\phi_{r_1}(x_1)$ to the output is given by

$$\alpha_{r_1} + \sum_{m=1}^{N} \alpha_{r_1, m} \phi_m(x_2).$$

This procedure of adding and training new subnetworks can be followed repeatedly until the output error is reduced below some chosen threshold. Periodically, a subnetwork is added below whichever weight $\alpha_{r_1, \ldots, r_p}$ (at any level $p$ of the tree) has the highest variance, and this network is trained according to the recursive rule

$$\Delta\alpha_{r_1, \ldots, r_{p+1}} = \Delta\alpha_{r_1, \ldots, r_p} \phi_{r_{p+1}}(x_{p+1}) \quad (8)$$

where

$$\Delta\alpha_\phi = \eta(f(x_1, \cdots, x_d) - \hat{f})$$

is defined as the learning rule for a constant term $\alpha_\phi$ associated with the root of the tree.

To understand the tree structure, consider a finite scalar basis $\sigma_i(x_1, \cdots, x_d)$ over a $d$-dimensional input space where $1 \leq i \leq L$. Let this basis be separable, so that each function $\sigma_i$ can be written as a product of some combination of the one-dimensional functions $\phi_n(x_p)$. (An example of such a basis is the ra-

dially symmetric Gaussian basis used in several different network algorithms [5], [14]–[17].) We can extend any such basis to include all functions of the form

$$\sigma_i(x_1, \cdots, x_p) = \prod_{q=1}^{p} \phi_{r_q^i}(x_q)$$

where $\phi_{r_q^i}$ specifies the one-dimensional basis function along the $q$th dimension for the $i$th basis $\sigma_i$, and $p \leq d$. Now consider node $\langle r_1, \cdots, r_p \rangle$ in the tree constructed by the above algorithm. When we compute the output of the tree, this node will contribute a term $\alpha_{r_1, \ldots, r_p}(x_p)$ to the weight from node $r_1, \cdots, r_{p-1}$. But since this is a weight term, it will be multiplied by $\phi_{r_{p-1}}(x_{p-1})$ at the next level, so the contribution to the weight from node $r_1, \cdots, r_{p-2}$ will be $\alpha_{r_1, \ldots, r_p} \phi_{r_p}(x_p) \phi_{r_{p-1}}(x_{p-1})$ (see (7)). Continuing this reasoning, it can be seen that the contribution to the output $\hat{f}$ is given by

$$\alpha_{r_1, \ldots, r_p} \prod_{q=1}^{p} \phi_{r_q^i}(x_q) = \alpha_{r_1, \ldots, r_p} \sigma_i(x_1, \cdots, x_p) \quad (9)$$

for some $\sigma_i$. The tree structure thus has exactly equivalent computational power to a single-layer network with the basis $\sigma_1, \cdots, \sigma_L$ (see eq. (1)).

To understand the training algorithm, consider the LMS rule for the net in (1), which is given by

$$\Delta c_i = \eta(f - \hat{f}) \sigma_i(x_1, \cdots, x_p). \quad (10)$$

From (9) we see that $c_i$ is equivalent to $\alpha_{r_1, \ldots, r_p}$. Expanding using (8) gives

$$\Delta c_i = \Delta\alpha_{r_1, \ldots, r_p}$$

$$= \Delta\alpha_{r_1, \ldots, r_{p-1}} \phi_{r_p}(x_p)$$

$$= \Delta\alpha_{r_1, \ldots, r_{p-2}} \phi_{r_{p-1}}(x_{p-1}) \phi_{r_p}(x_p)$$

$$\vdots$$

$$= \Delta\alpha_\phi \prod_{q=1}^{p} \phi_{r_q^i}(x_q)$$

$$= \eta(f - \hat{f}) \sigma_i(x_1, \cdots, x_p)$$

so that the training is exactly equivalent to performing standard LMS learning on a single-layer network with the $\sigma$ basis. Once a tree structure is fixed, all convergence results (such as [12]) for the LMS rule apply directly to the algorithm in (8). The only difference is that here the tree is grown incrementally. Note that the tree growing method is not guaranteed to produce minimal size trees (this is further discussed below). But if the tree is sparse then not all $\sigma_i$'s are computed and weights do not need to be learned to the unnecessary basis functions. The computational advantage of this algorithm rests on the assumption that a sparse tree will allow adequate approximation.

As described so far, the tree structure has imposed an implicit ordering on the dimensions of the input. To incorporate a measurement of $x_p$ it is necessary to build a tree of at least depth $p$. If the desired output function depends only on the last dimension $x_d$, then a complete tree may be built before adequate approximation is possible. In order to avoid this problem, in actual practice all dimensions are made available at each depth in the tree. Instead of providing the one-dimensional basis $\phi_1(x_1), \cdots, \phi_N(x_1)$ to the first level, an augmented one-dimensional basis $\phi_1(x_1), \cdots, \phi_N(x_1), \cdots, \phi_1(x_d), \cdots, \phi_N(x_d)$ is provided, and the same augmented basis is provided at all deeper levels. Thus each level has access to all dimensions of the data. This is not as elegant from a theoretical point of view, since the optimal tree for a given approximation problem is not unique, and the required storage may increase. (A subtle theoretical issue is the existence of products of basis functions along a single dimension, such as $\phi_p(x_1)\,\phi_q(x_1)$.) However, the increase in memory storage for a fixed tree structure is only a factor of $d$, and there may be an advantage to allowing the network to determine the best ordering of dimensions. (Of course, ordering can always be imposed if it is known that certain dimensions are more likely to be useful than others.)

Although the function of the algorithm is best understood with respect to local basis functions such as Gaussians, it is important to remember that arbitrary one-dimensional basis functions can be used. In the simulations shown in the next section, use is made of the Fourier basis consisting of $\sin(nx_p)$, $\cos(nx_p)$ for integer $n$. This basis was chosen because under certain conditions the Fourier basis forms a more compact representation than a local Gaussian basis [18], and because the sin and cos functions can be computed quickly. Other bases are possible and may be chosen to be optimally useful for a particular class of approximation problems, or perhaps to maximize performance for special hardware.

One interesting basis is the linear basis, for which the only one-dimensional basis function is $\phi(x_p) = x_p$. In this case, the network incrementally builds a polynomial approximation. However, there is no maximal depth to the tree, and adequate approximation may require trees of very large depth. This basis points out the relation between the depth of the tree and the approximation "order." A depth $p$ node is able to look at cross products of $p$ dimensions of the input, and thus contributes an order $p$ term to the output approximation (polynomial).

The description above makes it clear that for a given tree structure the approximation ability is equivalent to a single-layer network over a finite basis, and the learning algorithm is equivalent to LMS. Thus all known convergence and optimality results from these techniques can be applied directly. However, these results do not apply to the mechanism used to generate the tree structure. Although it seems intuitive that we should grow subtrees below weights with high "variance," it is important to realize that this is only a heuristic. The reason that it is not necessarily optimal is that the weight variance only gives bounds on the decrease in error if a full subtree is grown which is able to reduce the weight variance to zero. It does not indicate whether a single layer grown beneath that weight will accomplish anything useful. The behavior of this heuristic may be worse for certain classes of basis function. It seems to perform particularly badly for the linear basis $\phi(x_p) = x_p$, probably due to the fact that a potentially infinite subtree (polynomial) may need to be grown in order to provide a reduction in error. This heuristic also performs badly in the presence of noise if there are different noise levels on different basis functions, since the basis functions with the largest noise will always have the highest weight variance, independent of their usefulness to the approximation. Since the computational savings of the tree-structured approach are unrelated to the actual mechanism used to generate the tree, different heuristics can be used if they are known to perform better under certain circumstances.

## III. Examples

In this section three examples of the algorithm are demonstrated. The first two use synthetic data, and the third uses real data. The first example is the control of a simulated two-joint planar robot arm. The second and third examples both involve predictions: the second predicts the evolution of the Mackey-Glass differential delay equation, while the third predicts future pixel values in real images given previous pixels.

In all three cases, the algorithm was implemented with a time-varying rate term which decreased proportional to $1/t$ from a starting value of 0.005. To avoid ordering the dimensions, all dimensions were present at each level, as discussed in the last section. The basis functions used were the Fourier basis. New subtrees were added at fixed intervals. For the first half of each interval, the new subtree was allowed to converge. During the second half, convergence continued, but estimates of the weight variances were accumulated (under the assumption that the weights had stabilized.) At the end of the interval, a single new subtree was added below the leaf node with the highest weight variance.

### A. Two-Joint Arm Dynamics

A two-joint planar arm with inertia but without gravity or friction was simulated. The task was to compute the joint torques necessary to drive the arm along a series of desired trajectories specified in terms of hand position, velocity, and acceleration. During training, the correct torque outputs to the two joints were supplied to the network. The desired trajectories consisted of 1000 time steps, of which the first 500 constituted the movement phase with a raised cosine velocity profile and the last 500 consituted a hold phase at the endpoint position. The network was given three trajectories to learn, and it was tested for generalization to other similar trajectories. A low-gain position and velocity feedback controller operated in parallel with the network.

The network used ten Fourier basis functions ($\sin(nx_p)$, $\cos(nx_p)$ for $n = 1, \cdots, 5$) for each of the six input dimensions. A full network would thus have equivalent approximation ability to $10^6$ basis functions. The network was trained on 3000 sample points drawn from random positions on the three training trajectories. A new subnetwork was added every 200 samples, and variances were accumulated for 100 samples. The final network had a total of 15 subtrees with a maximal depth of 3. Learning required 5 min of elapsed time on a Sun-4 computer.

Fig. 2 shows five trajectories made by the arm when controlled by the trained network. The input was position, velocity, and desired acceleration in joint coordinates for straight trajectories (with endpoint holds) at $35°$, $25°$, $10°$, $0°$, and $-25°$ angles. The training trajectories were at $25°$, $0°$, and $-25°$. The normalized RMS error

$$\text{NMSE} = \frac{E\left[\left(\hat{x}(t) - x(t)\right)^2\right]^{1/2}}{E\left[\left(x(t) - E[x(t)]\right)^2\right]^{1/2}} \tag{11}$$

for joint angle $\theta$ and joint torque $\tau$ are given in Fig. 3 for each trajectory (the values shown are the sum of the NMSE's for the two joints). Although the table shows that the network performed better on the trajectories on which it had been trained, Fig. 2 shows that it was able to interpolate reasonably well to the intermediate trajectory at $10°$, for which most of its error was due to slow drift at the endpoint.

### B. Predicting Chaotic Dynamics

In this section the network is used to attempt to duplicate some results of Farmer and Sidorowich [9], Lapedes and Farber

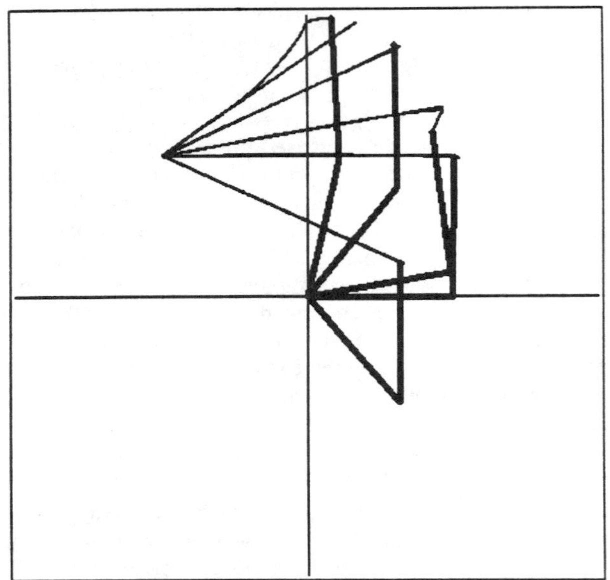

Fig. 2. Five trajectories controlled by the network after training. Thick lines represent the final arm position.

| angle | 35 | 25 | 10 | 0 | -25 |
|---|---|---|---|---|---|
| $\theta$ error | 0.264 | 0.0217 | 0.341 | 0.0422 | 0.0136 |
| $\tau$ error | 0.508 | 0.0718 | 0.297 | 0.0977 | 0.166 |

Fig. 3. Joint angle $\theta$ NMSE error and joint torque $\tau$ NMSE error for each of the five trajectories shown in Fig. 2.

[19], [20], and Moody [17], [21], on predicting future values produced by the chaotic Mackey–Glass differential delay equation [22]:

$$\dot{x}(t) = \frac{0.2x(t - \tau)}{1 + x^{10}(t - \tau)} - 0.1x(t) \qquad (12)$$

(see [19] and [9] for a thorough discussion of the issues involved). This equation is integrated using a fourth-order Runge-Kutta method to provide values of $x$ at discrete time steps. The initial condition was a constant function at $x = 0.8$. The value $\tau = 30$ is chosen and the network is provided with six input values $x(t - 6m)$, $m = 0, \cdots, 5$. The task is to predict $x(t + 6)$. If the network can perform this sufficiently accurately, then it can be used iteratively to make predictions farther into the future. Since iterative prediction will cause small errors to accumulate, we expect that the prediction error will increase the farther into the future we attempt to predict.

The sample inputs to the network were taken from the continually evolving time series $x(t)$. A new subnetwork was added every 400 samples. There were 20 Fourier basis functions per input dimension. Although the six-step prediction error is usually very small after only 20 subtrees have been added, the network was trained for 42 400 samples (giving 106 subtrees) to obtain an indication of how accurate the results could become (this required about 40 min on a Sun 4 Microcomputer). The final network had a maximum depth of 2. Fig. 4 shows the true time series dynamics and the six-step prediction at each point (they are indistinguishable here). It also shows the iterated time series prediction to 600 steps beyond the start of the frame. Fig.

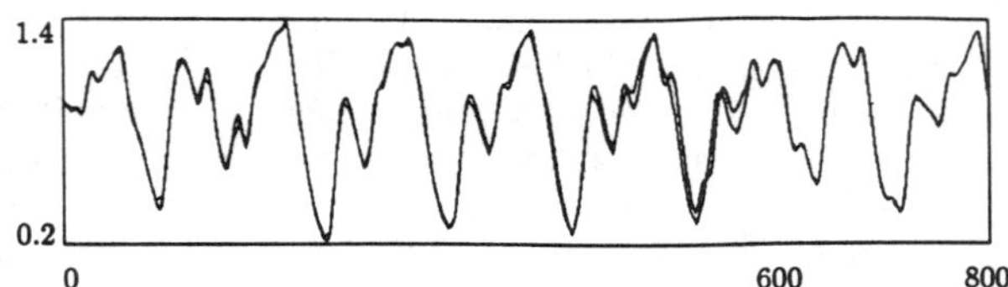

Fig. 4. Mackey–Glass time series, six-step ahead predictions (which are indistinguishable from the time series here), and iterated prediction time series up to 600 time steps into the future. The network has converged for 42 400 samples. (From [44]—courtesy of the MIT Press.)

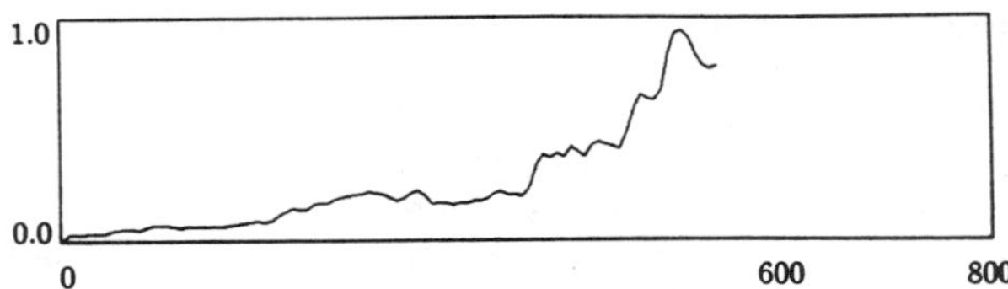

Fig. 5. Iterated prediction error for the Mackey–Glass equation, showing normalized mean-squared error as a function of prediction time up to 600 steps into the future. (From [44]—courtesy of the MIT Press.)

5 shows the increase in normalized RMS error (eq. (11)) with increasing prediction iterations. The six-step NMSE was 0.025. Note that these results are comparable to and perhaps exceed the results in [19] and [20], which required an hour of supercomputer time. The results in [21] and [17] are comparable to those presented here, but iterated prediction errors were not measured. Although their results are difficult to compare, the six-step prediction error in [9] appears to be an order of magnitude better than here (the iterated prediction error and the computation time are not available).

### C. Predicting Real Images

The final example is similar to the time series prediction task in subsection III-B, except that data from real images are used. The task is to predict the pixel in the lower right-hand corner of a $5 \times 5$ region given the values of the other 24 pixels. (The reason for predicting the corner is that the network will form a causal nonlinear two-dimensional filter which can be iterated over the image if desired.) Four $128 \times 128 \times 8$ bit images of human faces under similar lighting conditions were used, since it was assumed that the image statistics would be similar. Two images were used for training, and the other two were used to test generalization.

The network had nine basis functions for each of the 24 input dimensions, consisting of eight Fourier components $\sin(nx_p)$, $\cos(nx_p)$ as well as a linear basis function $\phi_0(x_p) = x_p$. Samples were drawn from randomly chosen $5 \times 5$ blocks of each of two training images. A subtree was added every 2000 samples. Fig. 6(a) shows the two face images used for training, the network approximations, and the errors after 44 000 $5 \times 5$ sample blocks had been presented. Fig. 6(b) shows the results on two different images used to test generalization. The network had 22 subtrees with a maximal depth of 2, and training required about 1 hr of elapsed time on a Sun-4. The RMS errors were 8.66 and 9.02 gray levels (out of 256) on the two training images, and 9.38 and 8.34 on the two test images.

The network could be used as part of a DPCM coding system (see [23], for example) in which only the errors would be transmitted. Ziv–Lempel coding [24] of the errors yields a rate of

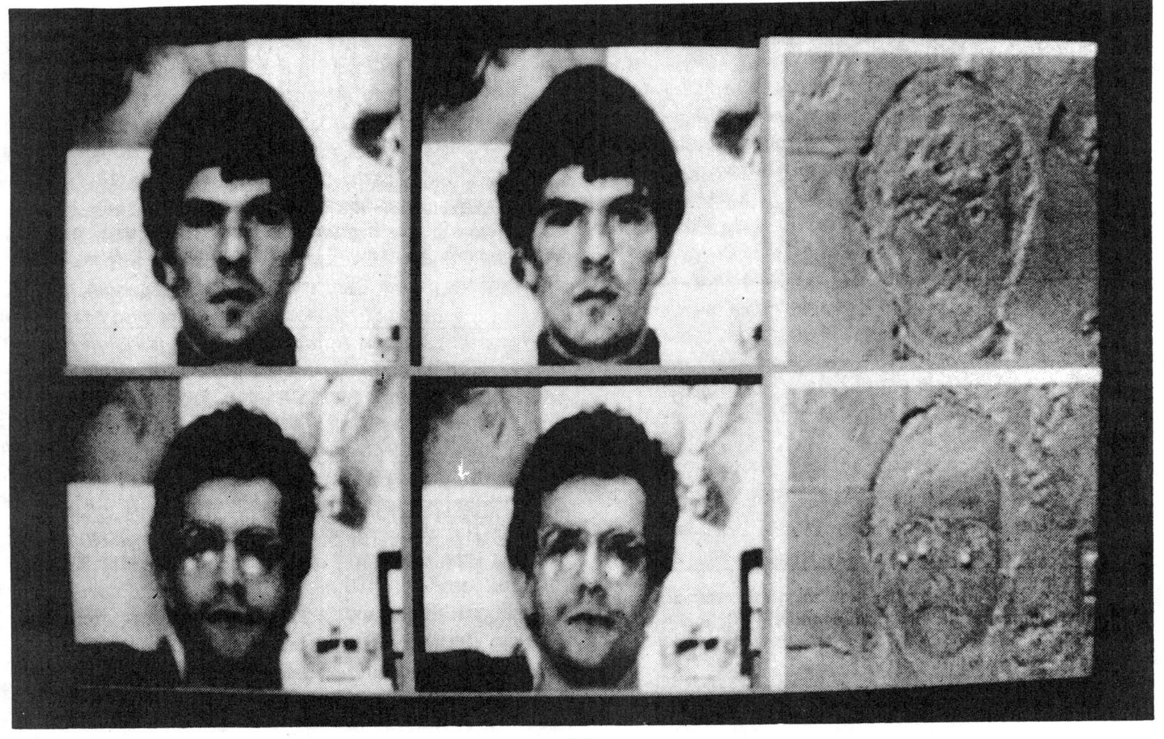

Fig. 6. (a) Training set for the image prediction task. Left: original images. Center: Network approximations. Right: Errors. (b) Test set for image prediction.

approximately 4 bits per pixel for exact reproduction of the (8 bit) images. If the errors are quantized to five values, then the coding rate increases to approximately 2 bits per pixel, but exact reconstruction is not possible. The RMS reconstruction error in this case is usually around 22 gray levels, but the reconstructed images tend to be indistinguishable to human observers.

This task points out some of the properties of the algorithm. The input space is 24-dimensional, so the network has an equivalent computational ability to $9^{24}$ basis functions. More input dimensions (such as $6 \times 6$ or $8 \times 8$ regions) or more basis functions were occasionally used during testing, but were found not to give significant improvement in the quality of the results for this task. The importance of using the algorithm on real data is that its success depends on the assumption that high-dimensional input data for real problems are often redundant. It is possible to construct artificial problems for which the algorithm performs quite poorly. Its usefulness lies in the possibility that in practice it will perform efficiently.

## IV. Discussion

The algorithm presented here can be seen as a method for making basis-function approximation possible for high-dimensional input spaces. Many existing networks which make use of radial (or nonradial) basis functions (see [5] for review) could incorporate features of this algorithm to improve their processing speed or increase their ability to handle large-scale problems. In addition, the motivation behind this algorithm can provide some interesting insights into standard problems in both biology and control theory.

### A. Generalization and Specialization

The network represents a progressive specialization of prediction. Initial predictions apply to large subsets of possible inputs, since most sensor measurements are ignored. As the tree is grown, the output values respond to more dimensions of the input space. If the network is provided with a previously unknown input, it will not necessarily generalize to the closest input it has seen, but will instead compute the output based on dimensions previously found to be useful. It is possible to implement the algorithm in such a way that if a sensor measurement is not available, the best prediction from the remaining sensors can still be made simply by setting the missing sensor's basis values to zero.

Consider the general problem of a multisensor robotic or biological system which must combine measurements from multiple sensors in order to estimate environment parameters. Each sensor's measurement may be available in a distributed representation over a finite basis, yet there will be no representation of the "cross terms" which would tell about coincidences of response values from different sensors. The algorithm presented here suggests that a central processor should make the best estimate it can from the sensory data without cross terms. If this estimate is insufficient, then it should compute second-order cross terms only for those sensor measurements with the highest weight variance. Higher order cross terms can be added as needed. This provides a simple and general way to combine measurements from different sensors while maintaining fast learning and efficient use of memory.

It is important to note that the network does not construct "features" for subsequent processing, and that it does not have a hierarchical processing structure. The outputs of subnetworks do not provide inputs to higher networks, but instead change the weights. All inputs are present in a single "level," and are occasionally multiplied with each other. The outputs of the sub-

networks do not have any simple interpretation in terms of the input; they are computing weight correction terms.

### B. Nonlinear Control

Consider the problem of a robot which can measure its current state $x$ and must combine this with a command input $c$ to produce correct motor commands $u$. It will try to approximate the function $u = g(x, c)$ which describes this mapping. Suppose that $x$ and $c$ are coarse coded using a local basis. If the algorithm presented here is used to approximate $g(x, c)$, then the resulting network can be constructed two ways. If the first layer approximates using $x$, the network attempts to compute $u \approx \hat{g}(x)$ and then corrects the weights using $c$. This corresponds to an adjustable-gain servo controller, where $c$ adjusts the feedback gains from $x$ to $u$. If instead the first layer approximates using $c$, then the network computes $u \approx \hat{g}(c)$ and then modifies the weights using $x$. This corresponds to a feedforward controller whose parameters are adjusted by state measurements. Note that the ability to approximate $g$ is the same in both cases. The first type of network will be smaller if most modes of the feedback loop are fixed and only a few need to be adjusted. The second type will be smaller if many of the control input effects are independent of the state.

A slight variation of this problem is the use of a network to forward model a nonlinear system $\dot{x} = f(x, u)$. Again, the network can be thought of in two ways. If it first approximates $\dot{x} \approx \hat{f}(x)$ and corrects using $u$, then $u$ can be thought of as selecting between parallel systems $f_u(x)$. If the network approximates $\dot{x} \approx \hat{f}(u)$ and corrects using $x$, then the current state $x$ is used to modify the direction in which the input $u$ moves the system.

There is a close relation to bilinear system theory [25]. Consider $u$ and $x$ to be $N$-vectors of basis function outputs. A full network which incorporates all cross terms $x_i u_j$ will approximate

$$\dot{x}_k \approx \sum_i a_{ik} x_i + \sum_{i,j} b_{ijk} x_i u_j + \sum_j c_{jk} u_j$$

which can be written $\dot{x} \approx Ax + u^T Bx + Cu$, where $B$ is a three-dimensional tensor. Brockett [26] describes a system of this form which uses a polynomial basis in the state $x$. He claims that such systems are good for approximating arbitrary nonlinear dynamical systems since a model can be chosen which approximates any Volterra series description arbitrarily well. It is more difficult to prove such results for bases other than the polynomial basis, and it is unknown whether local bases or the Fourier basis provide similar properties.

### C. Relation to Other Algorithms

There are several network algorithms which are closely related to the one proposed here. Basis function approximation is a well-known technique in statistics, as is approximation by polynomials of increasing order [27]–[29]. The perceptron algorithm [30] and backpropagation [1]–[4] are related since they are both variants of the LMS rule [11]. There are several algorithms which grow similar tree structures [31]–[36], although most (except [36]) are intended for classification tasks rather than approximation. There also exist algorithms for which the output of one network controls the behavior of another [37], [38]. The relationship to these algorithms will now be discussed in more detail.

As mentioned in Section II, the algorithm proposed here is exactly equivalent to LMS learning [11]. The tree structure provides a convenient mechanism for forward propagation and weight modification, and the tree growing heuristic determines how to add additional basis functions. It is not a multilayer network in the sense of networks trained with backpropagation [1]–[4]. The structure of the network changes dynamically during learning and is determined by the data distribution and the output function to be approximated. For a given structure, the learning algorithm has no local minima and is guaranteed to converge to the minimum mean-squared error solution. Note that additional approximation power is created by increasing the network downward, rather than upward as for backpropagation networks. The network has no ''hidden nodes'' and does not learn any features; the tree structure simply allows for the weights from higher nodes to change dynamically in response to the input.

Approximation by polynomials of increasing order is a well-known technique. It was proposed in [27], where fixed sets of monomials were chosen and coefficients were adjusted to obtain good predictions of the data. The GMDH algorithm [28], [29] builds a network upwards using increasing orders of polynomials by multiplying pairs of featues at each level. GMDH builds an adaptive network using entirely different heuristics from those proposed here, and the resulting structure works by combining intermediate features rather than modifying weights. The performance of GMDH in relation to the method proposed here will most likely depend on the specific heuristics used to generate the networks and the data sets used for testing.

There are several examples of networks which construct new ''features'' as needed [32], [34]–[36]. Note that such approaches are different from the one proposed here, in which weights are modified and the only ''features'' are cross products of the one-dimensional basis functions. In additive regression [39] a set of spline functions is chosen along each dimension, and a model is generated which is equivalent to a single-layer tree of the type proposed here when basis functions from all dimensions are present at each layer. There are also a few networks in which weights are controlled by other networks. One example is found in [37], in which one network controls the selection of a subnetwork by modifying a single output weight. Another example is found in [38], where a distributed representation can modify the connection between two other representations depending on the context.

There exist several tree-structured algorithms for classification which locally select input dimensions. k-d trees [33] partition the data into regions with similar numbers of data points within each region. The partition will be finest near high concentrations of data points. The CART algorithm [31], [32] partitions the data according to an information measure intended to reduce misclassification error. In practice, a full tree is usually grown and then less useful subtrees are pruned out to yield an efficient structure. Other related algorithms are found in [40], [41], [32] and [34]. The main difference with the algorithm proposed here is that k-d trees and CART have sharp partition boundaries and assign a single output value to each region, leading to piecewise constant approximations. The algorithm here generalizes the k-d tree and CART by allowing arbitrary basis functions which may be overlapping, coefficients are trained by regression, and new dimensions are selected for splitting based on the weight variance as described in Section II. This leads to smooth approximations which minimize mean-squared error.

The most closely related algorithm is MARS [42], which uses a generalized spline basis along each dimension. Coefficients are trained by least-squares fitting to the complete data set, and new subtrees are grown by testing all possible subtrees and choosing the one which minimizes a ''lack-of-fit'' criterion based on cross-validation arguments. Each new subtree has two

basis functions, but these can be added to intermediate nodes in the existing tree. As in CART, the tree is grown larger than necessary and then pruned back. Since the knot points of the splines are fixed at data points, the basis set depends on the data and is not fixed as in the method proposed here. It is difficult to compare the performance of MARS with this algorithm, since standard benchmarks are not easily available. For the two-joint arm problem described above, this algorithm required 5 min of learning time on a Sun-4, while MARS was unable to control the arm at all after 12 hr of computation on the same data set. This observation should be interpreted with caution, however, since there may be other problems in which MARS is able to perform significantly better.

MARS can be seen as a special case of the algorithm proposed here with a different tree-growing heuristic and in which the basis functions are truncated polynomials up to third order. Similarly, CART can also be seen as a special case with the basis functions being step functions placed at each data point. However, both CART and MARS make use of the complete data set to learn coefficients and grow new subtrees, and they cannot be easily adapted to continuously arriving or nonstationary data. The computations in CART and MARS are not performed locally within nodes of the tree, which makes a ''neural'' interpretation difficult. But in certain cases their tree-growing heuristics may have greater statistical validity than the weight variance techniques, and may thus grow smaller or even ''optimal'' trees. The algorithm proposed here sacrifices optimality in the tree-growing algorithm in favor of a simpler and local implementation with significantly faster learning.

## V. Conclusion

The method proposed here provides a fast general technique for function approximation over high-dimensional input spaces. It relies on the assumption that most of the input dimensions are redundant. Its main advantage is that it is simple to implement, and it can be easily added to existing networks which use LMS approximation on multidimensional input. There are no local minima in the training algorithm (for a fixed tree structure), so convergence is fast and could be increased further with a parallel hardware implementation. If there is a cost associated with making measurements, the algorithm may be able to reduce the number of different measurements needed to make a good approximation.

The major problem with the algorithm as it stands concerns the tree-growing heuristic. Although the learning algorithm will always converge for a given tree structure, there is no way to guarantee that a particular tree structure is optimal. The bounds in (5) and (6) provide partial justification for this choice of heuristic, but it is not difficult to construct situations and basis functions for which it will perform quite poorly. Further study is needed to understand what classes of basis function work well with this heuristic, how to use pruning techniques to reduce the size of the final tree, and whether there exist different tree-growing rules which perform better under certain circumstances.

## Acknowledgment

Thanks are due to M. Turk for providing the face images, C. Atkeson for the arm simulator, and the many people at Snowbird and elsewhere who gave me comments and suggestions. This work was inspired by a course at MIT taught by C. Atkeson, M. Jordan, and M. Raibert. The image approximation task was first suggested to me by T. Adelson. Parts of this work will appear in [43] and [44].

## REFERENCES

[1] P. J. Werbos, "Beyond regression: New tools for prediction and analysis in the behavioral sciences," Ph.D. thesis, Harvard Univ., 1974.

[2] Y. Le Cun, "A learning scheme for asymmetric threshold networks," in *Proc. Cognitiva*, vol. 85 (Paris, France), 1985, pp. 599–604.

[3] D. B. Parker, "Learning-logic," Tech. Report TR-47, Sloan School of Management, MIT, 1985.

[4] D. E. Rumelhart, G. E. Hinton, and R. J. Williams, "Learning internal representations by error propagation," in *Parallel Distributed Processing*. Cambridge, MA: MIT Press, 1986, ch. 8, pp. 318–362.

[5] T. Poggio and F. Girosi, "Regularization algorithms for learning that are equivalent to multilayer networks," *Science*, vol. 247, pp. 978–982, 1990.

[6] M. H. Raibert, "A model for sensorimotor control and learning," *Biol. Cyber.*, vol. 29, pp. 29–36, 1978.

[7] W. S. Cleveland and S. J. Devlin, "Locally weighted regression: An approach to regression analysis by local fitting," *J. Amer. Statist. Ass.*, vol. 83, pp. 596–610, Sept. 1988.

[8] W. S. Cleveland, S. J. Devlin, and E. Grosse, "Regression by local fitting," *J. Econometrics*, vol. 37, pp. 87–114, 1988.

[9] J. D. Farmer and J. J. Sidorowich, "Predicting chaotic dynamics," in *Dynamic Patterns in Complex Systems*, J. A. S. Kelso, A. J. Mandell, and M. F. Shlesinger, Eds. World Scientific, 1989, pp. 265–292.

[10] C. Atkeson, "Comparison of memory-based motor learning with other neural network approaches," in *Abstr. Neural Networks for Computing Conf.*, (Snowbird, UT), Apr. 1990.

[11] B. Widrow and M. E. Hoff, "Adaptive switching circuits," in *IRE WESCON Conv. Record*, part 4, 1960, pp. 96–104.

[12] B. Widrow, J. M. McCool, M. G. Larimore, and C. R. Johnson, "Stationary and nonstationary learning characteristics of the LMS adaptive filter," *Proc. IEEE*, vol. 64, no. 8, pp. 1151–1162, 1976.

[13] L. Ljung, "Analysis of recursive stochastic algorithms," *IEEE Trans. Automat. Contr.*, vol. AC-22, pp. 551–575, Aug. 1977.

[14] R. W. Klopfenstein and R. Sverdlove, "Approximation by uniformly spaced Gaussian functions," in *Approximation Theory IV*, C. K. Chui, L. L. Schumaker, and J. D. Ward, Eds. New York: Academic Press, 1983, pp. 575–580.

[15] M. J. D. Powell, "Radial basis functions for multivariable interpolation: A review," in *Algorithms for Approximation*, J. C. Mason and M. G. Cox, Eds. Oxford: Clarendon Press, 1987, pp. 143–167.

[16] D. S. Broomhead and D. Lowe, "Multivariable functional interpolation and adaptive networks," *Complex Syst.*, vol. 2, pp. 321–355, 1988.

[17] J. Moody and C. Darken, "Fast learning in networks of locally-tuned processing units," *Neural Computation*, vol. 1, pp. 281–294, 1989.

[18] T. D. Sanger, "Learning nonlinear features using eigenvectors of radial basis functions," submitted to *IEEE Trans. Neural Networks*.

[19] A. Lapedes and R. Farber, "Nonlinear signal processing using neural networks," Los Alamos National Laboratory LA-UR-87-2662, 1987 (submitted to *Proc. IEEE*).

[20] A. Lapedes and R. Farber, "How neural nets work," in *Neural Information Processing Systems*, D. Z. Anderson, Ed. New York: Am. Inst. Physics, 1988, pp. 442–456.

[21] J. Moody, "Fast learning in multi-resolution hierarchies," in *Advances in Neural Information Processing Systems 1*, D. S. Touretzky, Ed. San Mateo, CA: Morgan Kaufmann, 1989, pp. 29–39.

[22] M. C. Mackey and L. Glass, "Oscillation and chaos in physiological control systems," *Science*, vol. 197, pp. 287–289, July 1977.

[23] J. S. Lim, *Two-Dimensional Signal and Image Processing*. Englewood Cliffs, NJ: Prentice Hall, 1990.

[24] J. Ziv and A. Lempel, "Compression of individual sequences via variable-rate coding," *IEEE Trans. Inform. Theory*, vol. IT-24, no. 5, pp. 530–536, 1978.

[25] P. D'Alessandro, A. Isidori, and A. Ruberti, "Realization and structure theory of bilinear dynamical systems," *SIAM J. Contr.*, vol. 12, no. 3, pp. 517–535, 1974.

[26] R. W. Brockett, "On the algebraic structure of bilinear systems," in *Theory and Applications of Variable Structure Systems*. New York: Academic Press, 1972, pp. 153–168.

[27] D. Gabor, "A universal nonlinear filter, predictor, and simulator which optimizes itself by a learning process," *Proc. Inst. Elec. Eng.*, vol. 108B, pp. 422–438, 1961.

[28] A. G. Ivakhnenko, "Polynomial theory of complex systems," *IEEE Trans. Syst., Man. Cybern.*, vol. SMC-1, pp. 364–378, Oct. 1971.

[29] S. Ikeda, M. Ochiai, and Y. Sawaragi, "Sequential GMDH algorithm and its application to river flow prediction," *IEEE Trans. Syst., Man, Cybern.*, vol. SMC-6, pp. 473–479, July 1976.

[30] F. Rosenblatt, *Principles of Neurodynamics*. New York: Spartan Books, 1962.

[31] L. Breiman, J. Friedman, R. Olshen, and C. J. Stone, *Classification and Regression Trees*. California: Wadsworth Belmont, 1984.

[32] G. Z. Sun, Y. C. Lee, and H. H. Chen, "A novel net that learns sequential decision process," in *Neural Information Processing Systems*, D. Z. Anderson, Ed. New York: American Institute of Physics, 1988, pp. 760–766.

[33] J. H. Bentley, "Multidimensional binary search trees used for associated searching," *Commun. Ass. Comput. Mach.*, vol. 18, no. 9, pp. 509–517, 1975.

[34] S. Knerr, L. Personnaz, and G. Dreyfus, "Single-layer learning revisited: A stepwise procedure for building and training a neural network," to be published.

[35] M. F. Tenorio and W.-T. Lee, "Self organizing neural network for optimum supervised learning," Tech. Rep. TR-EE 89-30, Purdue Univ. School of Elec. Eng., June 1989.

[36] S. E. Fahlman and C. Lebiere, "The cascade-correlation learning architecture," Tech. Rep. CMU-CS-90-100, Carnegie Mellon School of Computer Science, Pittsburgh, 1990.

[37] R. A. Jacobs, M. I. Jordan, and A. G. Barto, "Task decomposition through competition in a modular connectionist architecture: The what and where vision tasks," Tech. Rep. COINS TR 90-27, U. Mass., Amherst, Mar. 1990.

[38] G. E. Hinton, J. L. McClelland, and D. E. Rumelhart, "Distributed representations," in *Parallel Distributed Processing*, J. L. McClelland, D. E. Rumelhart, and The PDP Research Group, Eds. Cambridge, MA: MIT Press, 1986, pp. 77–109.

[39] C. J. Stone, "Additive regression and other nonparametric models," *Ann. Statis.*, vol. 13, no. 2, pp. 689–705, 1985.

[40] J. N. Morgan and J. A. Sonquist, "Problems in the analysis of survey data, and a proposal," *J. Amer. Statist. Ass.*, vol. 58, pp. 415–434, 1963.

[41] J. A. Sonquist, E. L. Baker and J. N. Morgan, "Searching for structure," Inst. Social Research, Univ. Michigan, Ann Arbor, 1971.

[42] J. H. Friedman, "Multivariate adaptive regression splines," Tech. Rep. 102, Stanford Univ. Lab for Computational Statistics, 1988.

[43] T. D. Sanger, "Basis-function trees for approximation in high-dimensional spaces," in *Proc. 1990 Connectionist Models Summer School*.

[44] T. D. Sanger, "A tree-structured algorithm for reducing computation in networks with separable basis functions," *Neural Computation*, vol. 3, no. 2, 1991.

*

**Terence D. Sanger** received the B.S. (1985) and S.M. (1986) degrees in applied mathematics from Harvard University, Cambridge, MA, and the M.S. (1989) degree in electrical engineering and computer science from the Massachusetts Institute of Technology, Cambridge, MA. He is currently in the combined M.D./Ph.D. program of Harvard Medical School and M.I.T.

Since 1989 he has been working in the laboratory of Emilio Bizzi studying neural network models of motor learning. From 1986 to 1989 he worked with Tomaso Poggio at the M.I.T. Artificial Intelligence Laboratory and developed an unsupervised neural network learning algorithm which could be used for image coding, texture analysis, feature extraction, and stereo. From 1984 to 1986 he worked in the Harvard Robotics Laboratory under Roger Brockett studying a stereo algorithm based on biological receptive fields.

# A Modified Probabilistic Neural Network (PNN) for Nonlinear Time Series Analysis.


Anthony Zaknich, Member IEEE, Associate Member AES

Christopher J. S. deSilva

Yianni Attikiouzel, Senior Member IEEE, Fellow IEE

**Department of Electrical and Electronic Engineering**

**The University of Western Australia**

**Nedlands 6009,Western Australia**



## Abstract

Donald Specht introduced a one-pass learning algorithm called the Probabilistic Neural Network (PNN) for classification, mapping and associative memory. A modified PNN is proposed that can be used for nonlinear time series analysis without loss of the advantages offered by Specht's PNN architecture. It is shown how the Gaussian Radial Basis Function, expressed as a Parzen like probability density function (pdf) estimator, can be used to estimate and implement nonlinear mappings applied to time series data. The performance of this modified PNN is demonstrated by showing its effectiveness in smoothing a sinusoidal signal which has been compressed in amplitude and then corrupted with wideband non-gaussian noise. The network is also compared with the multi-pass learning Backpropagation Network (BPN), and relative merits of the proposed modified PNN are discussed.


## Introduction

The main purpose of this paper is to show how the Probabilistic Neural Network (PNN) architecture proposed by Specht can be easily adapted for nonlinear time series analysis. This is done by exploiting the links between the PNN architecture and Gaussian Radial Basis Functions. A short summary of the PNN classifier is given, as the modified PNN for time series analysis shares its features. This is followed by a theoretical development which is the basis for the modified network. Experimental results are reported and analysed for a nonlinear noisy time series filtering problem using the modified PNN and a BPN for comparison.

## PNN Classifier

Specht's PNN [1,2] classifier is a three-layer, feed-forward, one-pass, learning network that uses sums of Gaussian distributions to estimate the class probability density functions as learned from training vector sets. Consequently, the PNN is able to make a classification decision in accordance with the Bayes strategy for decision rules and to provide probability and reliability measures for each classification. Learning involves choosing a single suitable smoothing factor which is the common standard deviation for all the Gaussians). The PNN uses one of a class of probability density function estimators which asymptotically approach the underlying parent density provided that it is smooth and continuous [3]. The network is tolerant of erroneous training vectors and sparse data samples can be adequate for optimal performance. It is both easy to use and fast for moderately sized data bases. The major disadvantage of the PNN is that all training vectors must be stored and used to classify new vectors, thus requiring large memories for many practical problems. This is not a severe disadvantage if the PNN is implemented in a parallel hardware structure where memory is relatively inexpensive.

## Theory: Parzen pdf Estimators and Gaussian Radial Basis Functions

The process of learning a linear or nonlinear input-output mapping from a set of examples can be seen as developing an approximation for a multivariate function. When dealing with pattern classification problems methods such as Parzen, pdf estimators [3] are commonly used, whereas for continuous mappings regularization techniques (which are closely related to the interpolation technique of Radial Basis Functions) can be used [4]. These two methods are closely related to each other as well to some neural networks including the BPN and PNN. The following development shows this relationship and leads to the modified PNN for nonlinear time series analysis. The equation for a Parzen like pdf


Reprinted from *Proceedings of the International Joint Conference on Neural Networks*, 1991, pp. 1530-1535. Copyright © 1991 by The Institute of Electrical and Electronics Engineers, Inc. All rights reserved.

estimator which can be used in Specht's PNN classifier is:

$$f_i(\mathbf{x}) = (1/((2\Pi)^{p/2}\, s^p\, M_i)) \sum_{j=1}^{M_i} \exp(-(((\mathbf{x}-\mathbf{x}_{ij})^T (\mathbf{x}-\mathbf{x}_{ij}))/(2\, s^2))) \qquad (1)$$

where:

T indicates the transpose.
i indicates the class number.
j indicates the pattern number.
$\mathbf{x}_{ij}$ is the $j^{th}$ training vector from class i.
$M_i$ is the number of training vectors in class i.
p is the dimension of vector $\mathbf{x}$.
s is the smoothing factor, standard deviation.
$f_i(\mathbf{x}) =$ sum of multivariate Gaussians centred at each of the vectors $\mathbf{x}_{ij}$, for the $i^{th}$ class pdf estimate.

The Bayes decision $d(\mathbf{x}) = C_i$ is made (i.e. multi-dimensional vector $\mathbf{x}$ belongs to class i) if $l_i.h_i.f_i(\mathbf{x}) > l_k.h_k.f_k(\mathbf{x})$ for all k not equal to i. The $l_i$ are the losses associated with making an incorrect decision for each class i. In many cases the losses can be considered equal so they may be cancelled from the equation. The $h_i$ are the a priori probabilities of occurrence of class i vectors.

Poggio and Girosi [4] have developed a theoretical framework for a class of three-layer regularization networks which includes the Radial Basis Function methods as a special case. Schoenberg's theorem [5] on positive definite functions shows the radial basis function expansion to be:

$$O(X) = \sum_{i=1}^{NS} c_i.g(||X-X_i||) \qquad (2)$$

The unknown coefficients $c_i$ are determined by solving $O(\mathbf{x}_i) = O_i (i=1,...NS)$ where the $O_i$ are the known or desired values of the multivariate function at specific inputs $\mathbf{x}_i$ and NS is the total number of known function values. Michelli [6] has justified the use of a number of basis functions $g(r)$ for practical data interpolation problems. One of these, is the Gaussian function: $g(r) = \exp(-(r/a)^2)$ (3) If equations (2) and (3) are combined and $2.s^2$ is equated to $a^2$ this results in equation (4) as follows:

$$O(\mathbf{x}) = \sum_{i=1}^{NS} c_i \exp(-(((\mathbf{x}-\mathbf{x}_i)^T (\mathbf{x}-\mathbf{x}_i))/(2\, s^2))) \qquad (4)$$

The function $O(\mathbf{x})$ can be used to find estimates of interpolation values at $\mathbf{x}$ for a partially known function. However, we need to solve a slightly different problem. We do wish to solve for interpolation but in our case the known input vectors $\mathbf{x}_i$ form clusters of points with specific probability density distributions and these map into the desired values $O_i$ with their own a priori probabilities of occurrence. Our function $O(\mathbf{x})$ must in some way use the known samples $O_i$ to form a best fit for not only the known samples but also for all subsequent samples which will be generated by the parent process. To show one way this can be achieved we shall develop equation (4) a little further and eventually draw out of it the required pdf estimator as represented in equation (1). If we let:

$$c_i = O_i / [ \sum_{k=1}^{NS} \exp(-(((\mathbf{x}-\mathbf{x}_k)^T (\mathbf{x}-\mathbf{x}_k))/(2\, s^2)))] \qquad (5)$$

then, as s approaches zero, $O(\mathbf{x})$ approaches the training values $O_i$ exactly with no interpolation. This occurs because the Gaussian basis functions approach delta functions centred at the $O_i$ values. However, as s increases we find that interpolation occurs at the expense of being true to the original $O_i$ fit. Thus, equations (4) and (5) can be used to learn a nonlinear time series mapping by taking a training set of data $\{\mathbf{x}_i --> O_i | i=1,...NS\}$ and finding an s value which minimises the mean squared error, (mse) between $O(\mathbf{x}_j)$ and the desired output $O_j$ for all the points of another independent testing set. We have discovered that if the data sets have sufficiently representative samples of the parent process then the function $O(\mathbf{x})$ at the optimal s will perform a satisfactory mapping.

So far we have taken each $\{\mathbf{x_i}\text{-->}O_i\}$ pair as a separate and independent process sample without regard for any clustering or relationship amongst sets of samples. In actual fact, putting a radial basis function at the centre of each sample automatically builds up a multivariate function which is proportional to the pdf estimates of the natural clusters of samples. We can show this for a discretely sampled time series by assuming that for each possible digital quantization level $y_i$ we can build up an $i^{th}$ class pdf estimate in accordance with equation (1). If we now say that the estimate of the multivariate function $O(\mathbf{x})$ is denoted by $Y(n)$ it can be shown that equations (1), (4) and (5) can be merged to form equation (7). This is done by taking $M_i$ groupings of equal $O_k$ values and their associated input vectors $\mathbf{x_{ij}}$ and giving them all the same value $y_i = O_k$ for each class i. Equation (6) in conjunction with the fact that $h_i$, the a priori of occurrence of $y_i$, is directly proportional to $M_i$, the number of vectors in class i, provides the required bridge between equations (1), (4) and (5) and equation (7).

$$\sum_{i=1}^{NS} O_i.\exp(-(((\mathbf{x}\text{-}\mathbf{x_i})^T (\mathbf{x}\text{-}\mathbf{x_i}))/(2 s^2))) = \sum_{i=1}^{N} \sum_{j=1}^{M_i} y_i.\exp(-(((\mathbf{x}\text{-}\mathbf{x_{ij}})^T (\mathbf{x}\text{-}\mathbf{x_{ij}}))/(2 s^2))) \qquad (6)$$

In this present study all time series samples $O_k$ with equal values and on positive slopes were classed together, while those of the same value but on negative slopes were taken together into a separate class. For simple time series signals, like sinusoids, this kind of grouping is adequate but for other signals where there may be a number of different slopes associated with the same $O_k$ value, a different grouping rule and a slight modification to equation (7) is needed to maintain good performance. This, however, is not the subject of this present work but will be reported in a future publication. It is sufficient to say that the desired groupings must be chosen properly before the modified PNN can perform its function adequately.

$$Y(n) = [\sum_{i=1}^{N} y_i\, h_i\, f_i(\mathbf{x})] / [\sum_{k=1}^{N} h_k\, f_k(\mathbf{x})] \qquad (7)$$

where for our chosen filter experiment:

$\mathbf{x} =$ [X(n-5),X(n-4),X(n-3),X(n-2),X(n-1),X(n),X(n+1),X(n+2),X(n+3),X(n+4),X(n+5)], vector.
$N$ is the number of classes.
$y_i$ is the desired output for training vectors in class i.
$h_i$ is the a priori probability of occurrence of class i vectors.
$NS = \sum_{i=1}^{N} M_i$, which is the total number of training samples.

Equation (7) is the basis of our modified PNN shown in Figure 3. Although in the equation, N represents all the possible classes, it is possible to achieve minor improvements in performance by choosing a lower value of N and using only the N highest $f_i(\mathbf{x})$ estimates for each input vector $\mathbf{x}$ in turn. It is possible to look at equation (7) as a weighted sum of all $y_i$ multiplied by the relative probabilities that vector $\mathbf{x}$ belongs to each class i. The estimate $Y(n)$ is weighted more by classes which are closest to $\mathbf{x}$ but since all classes contribute to it this performs an interpolation with a beneficial smoothing effect.

## Experimental Results

To test the modified PNN for nonlinear time series analysis a system was built according to the block diagram shown in Figure 1. Inspiration for the test set up was gained from the works of Uncini et al [7] and Hoyt et al [8]. The system was driven by a continuous sinusoidal signal S(t) at a constant frequency of 1.000 KHz. The sinusoid was amplified, then compressed (by an approximate exponential compressor made up of back-to-back signal diodes) Z(t) and finally corrupted with three levels of wideband non-gaussian noise N(t), resulting in signal X(t). Example plots of the three noise levels (a) low, (b) medium and (c) high and the compressed signal Z(n) are shown in Figure 4. All three levels of noise had approximate zero means and skews of -0.36. The three signal to noise ratios represented are (a) 12.2 dB, (b) 3.7 dB and (c) -0.4 dB.The S(t) and X(t) continuous signals were both digitised with an 8 bit analog to digital converter (ADC) at a sample rate of 30.1 KHz. The ADC level of 128 represented a signal voltage of zero volts,with 255 being the most positive voltage and 0 the most negative voltage.

Three independent data sets of digitised sequences of S(t) and X(t), denoted as S(n) and X(n) respectively, were then used to train, test and evaluate both the modified PNN and a four layer BPN. The three data sets are referred to as the Training, Testing and Evaluation sets. Figures 5 and 6 show the results of passing the same Testing signal sequence X(n) through the PNN and BPN filters each trained with the Training data set. Figure 5 shows the output from the PNN filter for N=129. Figure 6 shows the best output of the BPN filter trained over 8 million iterations with a gain factor of 0.1 and momentum factor of 0.01. The Training set was composed of 504 discrete samples and both the Testing and Evaluation sets were composed of 501 samples each. The Evaluation set was used to verify the performances of both filters after training and testing. The neural network filters in both cases were configured as smoothing filters as shown in Figure 2. Each discrete output sample Y(n) maps from an eleven coefficient input vector **x** made up of the five discrete time series samples immediately prior to and following the current discrete sample X(n) of the digitised nonlinear system output. The resulting smoothed signals Y(n), may be compared with each other and the original source signal S(n). The mean squared errors of the source signal S(n) compared with each of the filtered outputs Y(n) for each network filter are given in the tables below. Quoted times are the running times of software implementations written in C and executed on an 80386 AT compatible PC with a clock frequency of 33 MHz. The N referred to in the modified PNN FILTER table indicates the number of highest class pdf estimates used for each filtered vector, where, 129 indicates all the classes formed from the 504 training samples and 1 indicates only the single highest class. Initially all the pdfs are calculated for each input vector **x**, according to equation (7), but then only the highest N are used in the equation.

**Modified PNN FILTER** (The Training set is used for the PNN weights $x_{ij}$, Input Layer=11 nodes)

| Data Set | MSE | N | Best s | Training Time | Vector Execution Time |
|---|---|---|---|---|---|
| Testing | 0.000274 | 129 | 0.21-0.22 | 60.70 secs | 0.121 secs per vector |
| Evaluation | 0.000153 | 129 | 0.16-0.17 | 60.70 secs | 0.121 secs per vector |
| Testing | 0.000273 | 64 | 0.21 | 67.28 secs | 0.134 secs per vector |
| Evaluation | 0.000153 | 64 | 0.16-0.17 | 67.23 secs | 0.134 secs per vector |
| Testing | 0.000271 | 32 | 0.21-0.22 | 67.01 secs | 0.134 secs per vector |
| Evaluation | 0.000153 | 32 | 0.16-0.17 | 67.01 secs | 0.134 secs per vector |
| Testing | 0.000277 | 16 | 0.22 | 66.96 secs | 0.134 secs per vector |
| Evaluation | 0.000149 | 16 | 0.17-0.18 | 66.96 secs | 0.134 secs per vector |
| Testing | 0.000293 | 8 | 0.20 | 66.90 secs | 0.133 secs per vector |
| Evaluation | 0.000161 | 8 | 0.17 | 66.85 secs | 0.133 secs per vector |
| Testing | 0.000362 | 4 | 0.21 | 66.90 secs | 0.134 secs per vector |
| Evaluation | 0.000204 | 4 | 0.17 | 66.85 secs | 0.133 secs per vector |
| Testing | 0.000482 | 2 | 0.24 | 66.85 secs | 0.133 secs per vector |
| Evaluation | 0.000279 | 2 | 0.20 | 66.79 secs | 0.133 secs per vector |
| Testing | 0.000658 | 1 | 0.21 | 60.31 secs | 0.120 secs per vector |
| Evaluation | 0.000413 | 1 | 0.19 | 60.37 secs | 0.121 secs per vector |

**BPN FILTER** (1st Layer=11 nodes, 2nd=21 nodes, 3rd=11 nodes, Last=1 node)

| Data Set | MSE | Iterations | Training Time | Vector Execution Time |
|---|---|---|---|---|
| Training | 0.000169 | $2 \times 10^6$ | 877.71 mins | |
| Testing | 0.000210 | | | 0.014 secs per vector |
| Evaluation | 0.000198 | | | 0.014 secs per vector |
| Training | 0.000153 | $4 \times 10^6$ | 1755.42 mins | |
| Testing | 0.000198 | | | 0.014 secs per vector |
| Evaluation | 0.000192 | | | 0.014 secs per vector |
| Training | 0.000154 | $8 \times 10^6$ | 3510.84 mins | |
| Testing | 0.000177 | | | 0.014 secs per vector |
| Evaluation | 0.000164 | | | 0.014 secs per vector |

To compare the generalised performance of the filters another test signal which was of a similar type but different to the training signal having a similar amplitude and with a linear frequency sweep (chirp) from

650-1550 Hz plus a high noise level (S/N = 0 dB) was sampled. Figures 7 and 8 show the results of filtering this test set of 502 samples through the PNN and BPN filters respectively. The modified PNN filter produced a filtered output Y(n) with a mse=0.001632 at s=0.23 while the best BPN filter produced a mse=0.001071. It is interesting to note that although the modified PNN appeared to give a better overall source signal amplitude recovery the BPN filter achieved a lower mse. Another test involved filtering a compressed signal with no noise added. Although neither network filter had been trained with no noise they both achieved excellent source signal recovery. The modified PNN filter achieved a mse=0.000125 for an s=0.11-0.12 and the best BPN filter achieved a mse= 0.000127.

## Network Comparisons and Discussion

Our work has shown that it is possible to perform effective nonlinear time series analysis with a modified PNN classifier architecture. All the usual advantages and characteristics of the PNN are evident. The mse variation with changing s showed  fairly smooth but distinct minima around the optimum s values. As the number of allowable quantization levels $y_i$, were gradually reduced the performance of the modified PNN degraded slowly and gracefully. The same occurred when the number of training samples were reduced, showing that the modified PNN was able to generalise the filtering very well. Comparing the results of the modified PNN for N=1 and N= 2 to N=129 shows that interpolation and smoothing is occurring for N>1. For N=1 the network works as a normal PNN classifier, choosing the most likely $y_i$ as the filter output. The experimental results have shown that the modified PNN and BPN filters achieve reasonably similar performance with the BPN giving an overall lower mean squared error. However, for the software implementations of the filters, the modified PNN required approximately three orders of magnitude less training time but only one order of magnitude more signal filtering time for 504 training samples. One of the major advantages of the modified PNN over the BPN is that it can follow changing or nonstationary waveform statistics quickly and simply by either adding to or replacing old training data with new data as it becomes available.

The present study has shown that equation (7) has valuable application to nonlinear time series analysis, however, a more complete investigation needs to be made to establish its full capabilities and limitations. A better understanding of $y_i$ class grouping rules for various types of nonlinear signals needs to be developed. It is suspected that for more complex signals the class grouping may need to be further sub-divided into sub-groups with similar features. In this case it would first be necessary to choose the best sub-group for each new vector **x** and then only use the classes in that sub-grouping for equation (7) rather than including all the possible trained classes.

## References:

[1]   Specht, D. F., "Probabilistic Neural Networks For Classification, Mapping, or Associative Memory", IEEE Conference on Neural Networks, Vol. I, San Diego, July 1988, pp. 525-532.

[2]   Specht, D. F., "Probabilistic Neural Networks and Polynomial Adaline as Complementary Techniques for Classification", IEEE Transactions on Neural Networks, Vol. I, No 1, March 1990, pp. 111-121.

[3]   Parzen, E., "On estimation of a probability density function and mode," Ann. Math. Stat., Vol. 33, September 1962, pp. 1065-1076.

[4]   Poggio, Tomaso and Girosi, Federico, "Networks for Approximation and Learning", Proceedings of the IEEE, Vol. 78, No. 9, September 1990, pp. 1481-1497.

[5]   Schoenberg, I. J., "Metric spaces and positive definite function," Ann. of Math, Vol. 44, 1938, pp. 522-536.

[6]   Michelli,C. A., "Interpolation of scattered data: Distance matrices and conditionally positive definite functions," Constr. Approx., Vol. 2, 1986, pp. 11-22.

[7]   Uncini, A.,Marchesi, M., Orlandi, G. and Piazza, F., "Improved Evoked Potential Estimation Using Neural Network", IEEE Conference on Neural Networks, Vol. I, San Diego, June 1990, pp.143-148.

[8]   Hoyt, John D. and Wechsler, Harry, "An Examination of the Application of Multi-Layer Neural Networks to Audio Signal Processing", IEEE Conference on Neural Networks, Vol. II, San Diego, June 1990, pp. 305-310.

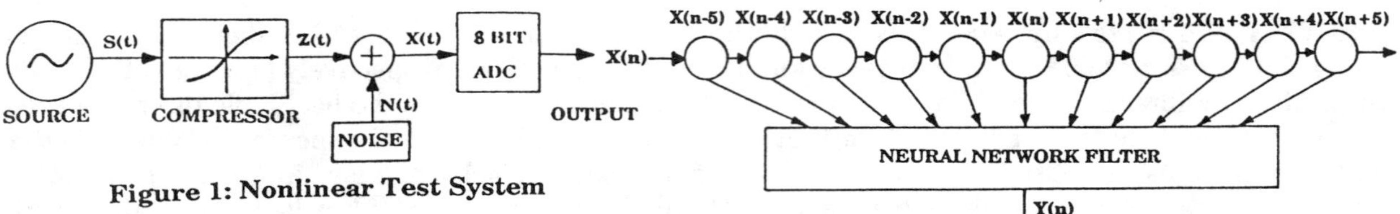

**Figure 1: Nonlinear Test System**

**Figure 2: Neural Network Smoother**

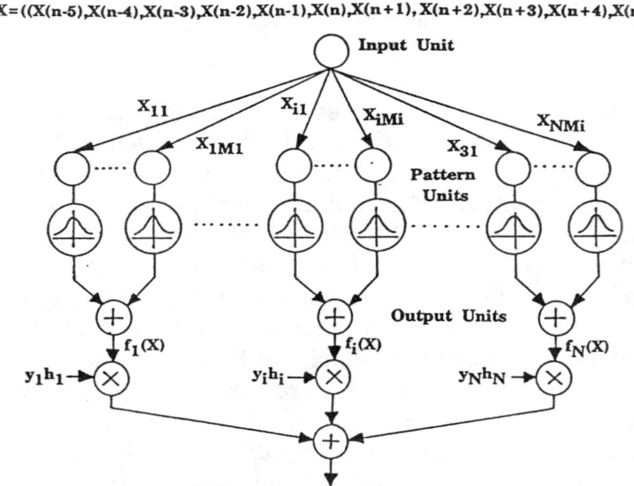

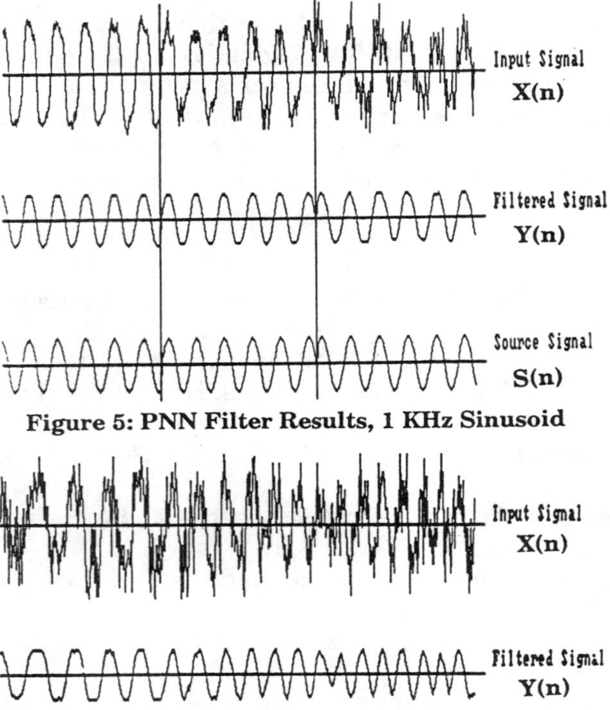

**Figure 3: Probabilistic Neural Network (PNN)**

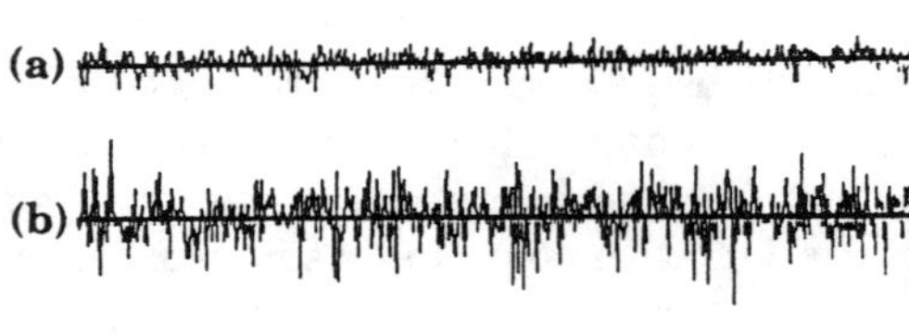

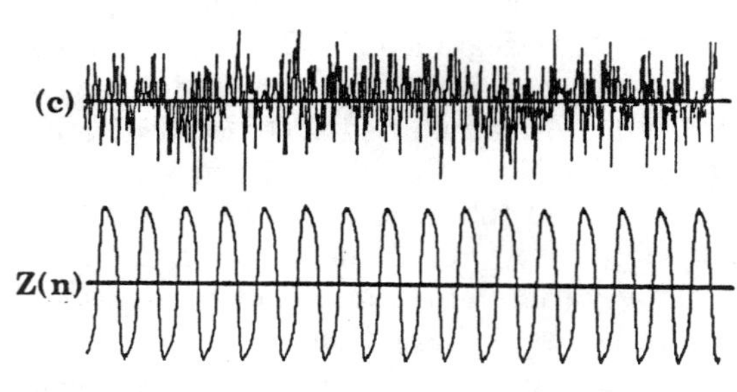

**Figure 4: Noise N(n) & Compressed Signal Z(n)**

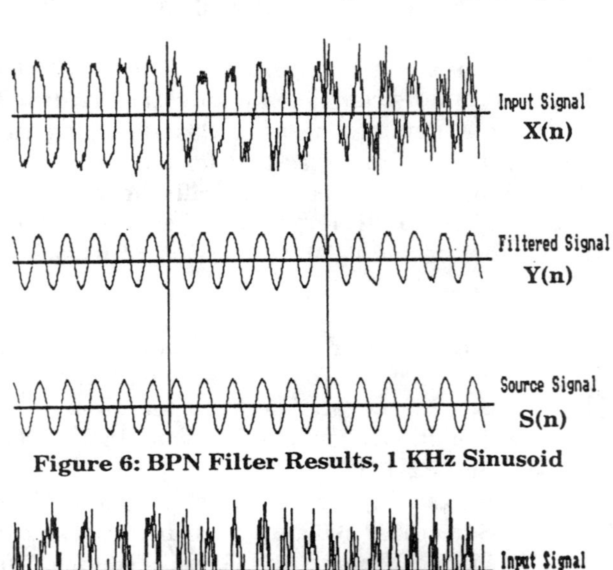

**Figure 5: PNN Filter Results, 1 KHz Sinusoid**

**Figure 6: BPN Filter Results, 1 KHz Sinusoid**

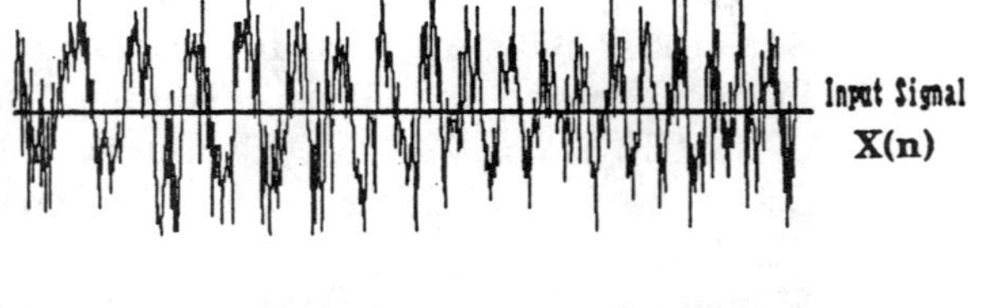

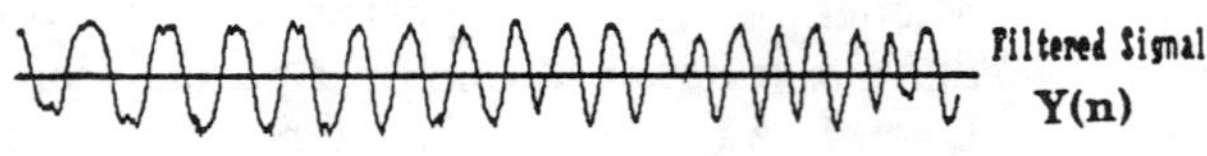

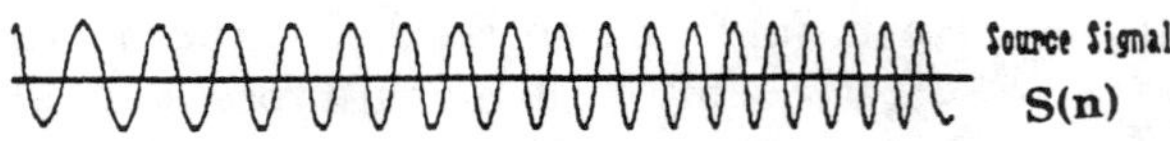

**Figure 7: PNN Filter Results, 650-1550 Hz Chirp**

**Figure 8: BPN Filter Results, 650-1550 Hz Chirp**

# Using CNLS-Net to Predict the Mackey-Glass Chaotic Time Series

W. C. Mead[a,b], R. D. Jones[a,b], Y. C. Lee,[b,c] C. W. Barnes[a,b]
G. W. Flake[a,b,d], L. A. Lee[a,b], and M. K. O'Rourke[a,b]

[a]*Applied Theoretical Physics Division*
[b]*Center for Nonlinear Studies*
*University of California*
*Los Alamos National Laboratory, Los Alamos, NM 87545*

[c]*Department of Physics and Astronomy*
[d]*Department of Computer Science*
*University of Maryland, College Park, MD 20740*

January 21, 1991

## ABSTRACT

We use the Connectionist Normalized Local Spline (CNLS) network to learn the dynamics of the Mackey-Glass time-delay differential equation, for the case $\tau = 30$. We show the optimum network operating mode and determine the accuracy and robustness of predictions. We obtain predictions of varying accuracy using some $2-120$ minutes of execution time on a **Sun SPARC-1** workstation. CNLS-net is capable of very good performance in predicting the Mackey-Glass time series.

## Introduction

The Connectionist Normalized Local Spline (CNLS) network[1] combines a number of appealing features to yield a capable, versatile adaptive-computing network. The net features normalized radial basis functions, a linear gradient term, and simple, rapid solution of the training algorithm, plus a variety of optional capabilities including Kalman Noise Filtering.[2] The CNLS network has been successfully applied to a number of fitting, prediction, and control test examples, including a preliminary test of the net's ability to predict the Mackey-Glass equation.[2]

The Mackey-Glass (M-G) equation[3] is a time-delay ordinary differential equation that displays well-understood chaotic behavior with dimensionality dependent upon the chosen value of the delay parameter.[4] The time series generated by the M-G equation has been used as a test bed for a number of new adaptive computing techniques: a local linear (or quadratic) approximation method,[5] a back-propagation neural network,[6] and at least two radial basis function approaches.[7,8] In this work, we have performed extensive studies on the use of the CNLS-net to model and predict the Mackey-Glass time series.

## The CNLS-Network Architecture

The Connectionist Nonlinear Local Spline Network (CNLS-net) was developed as an extension of previous adaptive network experience.[6,7,9,10] A natural evolution is to modify radial basis function (RBF) nets in a manner that improves interpolation and reduces the amount of training necessary for accurate learning.[1,11] CNLS-net architecture has a single hidden layer and starts from the identity

$$g(\vec{x}) = \frac{\Sigma_{j=1}^{N} g(\vec{x})\rho_j(\vec{x})}{\Sigma_j \rho_j(\vec{x})}. \tag{1}$$

Here, as in the RBF network, $\rho_j(\vec{x})$ is a localized function of $\vec{x}$ about some $\vec{x}_j$. Hence, $g(\vec{x})$ on the right of Eq. 1 can be approximated by its Taylor expansion about $\vec{x}_j$. We have then,

$$\phi(\vec{x}) = \Sigma_{j=1}^{N}[f_j + (\vec{x} - \vec{x}_j) \cdot \vec{d}_j]\frac{\rho_j(\vec{x})}{\Sigma_j \rho_j(\vec{x})} \tag{2}$$

Reprinted from *Proceedings of the International Joint Conference on Neural Networks*, Vol. II, 1991, pp. 485-490. Copyright © 1991 by The Institute of Electrical and Electronics Engineers, Inc. All rights reserved.

for an approximation to $g(\vec{x})$. This net differs from the RBF net in two ways: (1) the use of basis-function normalization and (2) the addition of a linear term, $(\vec{x} - \vec{x}_j) \cdot \vec{d}_j$. The use of a normalization term was suggested but not pursued by Moody and Darken.[7] The addition of these two terms is responsible for the reduction in the amount of training data needed to obtain reasonable approximations. As in the case with radial basis functions, the training of $f_j$ and $\vec{d}_j$ is linear and hence very fast.

## The Mackey-Glass Equation

The Mackey-Glass (M-G) equation was first advanced as a model of white blood cell production.[3] It is a time-delay differential equation, namely

$$\frac{dx}{dt} = \frac{ax(t-\tau)}{[1 + x^c(t-\tau)]} - bx(t), \tag{3}$$

where the constants are often (and in this work) taken to be $a = 0.2, b = 0.1$, and $c = 10$. The behavior of the M-G equation as a function of the delay parameter $\tau$ has been studied extensively and is reported by J. D. Farmer in Ref. 4. At $\tau = 30$, the value used for all of the studies reported here, the M-G equation's attractor has an information dimension of 3.6.[4] Figure 1 shows a plot of the M-G equation with $\tau = 30$, slightly renormalized to limit its range approximately to the interval $(0, 1)$. The standard deviation of the function so normalized is 0.24. In the results presented below, we use as a performance indicator, the "Error Index," defined as the root mean squared fitting or prediction error (RMSE) divided by the standard deviation. With this definition of the Error Index, a constant fit through the mean value of the function leads to a value of 1.0.

## Initial Choices for Embedding, Data sets, and Architecture

The starting place for this work was determined in large measure by the desire to compare CNLS-net's performance with that of the back propagation net used by Lapedes.[4] Thus, we initially chose the embedding used in previous works[5-7]: the training and test patterns were composed of 6 inputs, spaced at time intervals of 6 time units each, plus a test output, the point 6 time units after the last entry of the input sequence. Later, we found that embedding is a very sensitive matter, and performed more detailed studies of the issue.

The training and test files consisted of $1000 - 5000$ points at fixed time spacing (usually, $\Delta t_{dat} = 1$). The training and test files were non-overlapping time sequences, with the test file usually continuing the series begun in the training file. Except where noted, we used 500 training patterns, and we always used 500 test patterns, as did Lapedes.[6] The training patterns were selected at random and the test patterns sequentially. Also, the selected training patterns were held fixed for the entire training period, but were usually "tumbled," *i.e.*, presented in random, varying sequences for successive training epochs.

The CNLS-net architecture chosen initially used 6 input nodes, 28 hidden nodes (having 7 adjustable weights each), and one output node. This yields about 200 weights, fewer than Lapedes' reported back-propagation net calculation: he used two hidden layers of 14 nodes each, giving about 540 weights, total.[6] Our initial architecture yielded a network that could be trained in about $2 - 6$ minutes and tested in about 1 minute (at 21 iterations into the future), which made multiparameter optimization feasible.

## Optimizing CNLS-Net's Parameters

We performed an extensive optimization of the adjustable parameters of CNLS-net: the learning rate, the width of the basis functions, and the discreet parameters governing embedding and network size. We also devised two specific tests of versatility and robustness.

CNLS-net has two continuously-adjustable parameters. The learning rate shows a broad optimum, and learning behavior showed some regions of instability. We found a broad range of acceptable performance. Generally, higher learning rates led to faster training, with increased susceptability to instability. The width of the basis functions showed a broad optimum, as well. The optimum width appears to be related to the characteristic structures of the function being fit, under the chosen embedding.

The embedding structure is determined by the number of inputs to the network and the time-separation between each input. Results of the two-dimensional embedding study show that there is a lot of "structure." Small changes in the embedding integers lead to prediction errors that differ by a factor of $2\times$ or more. This is an important issue that needs to be understood better. We can summarize the embedding results by noting that most of the "successful" embeddings have $\Delta t_{samp}$ in the range of $30-45$. We suspect this is related to the choice of $\tau = 30$ as the Mackey-Glass delay parameter. The parameter $\tau$ sets a "coherence timescale," and embeddings for which $\Delta t_{samp}$ differs greatly from this time interval are either supplying the network with too little or too much information.

An example of the M-G time series and CNLS-net's fit is shown in Fig. 1. The plot of Fig. 2 shows the net's training and prediction accuracy as a function of training epoch. The net's prediction accuracy shows a broad optimum, but the net can be either over- of under-trained. We also found that trainability and prediction accuracy were influenced by the random initial choice of the basis function centers. Some of this sensitivity may be exacerbated by marginal stability of the learning algorithm, while some of the variation is due to the small numbers of basis functions used and the statistical effects of redistributing them.

## Best Results

Our best results are compared with Lapedes' successful prediction in Fig. 3. The plot shows three sets of CNLS-net predictions, made with hidden layer sizes of $28, 56$, and $112$ nodes.

The Mackey-Glass, $\tau = 30$ calculation of Lapedes and Farber[6] was trained for about 60 minutes on a **Cray XMP** with vectorized coding. Our calculations were performed using **CNLSTOOL**, written in the C language, and executed on a **Sun SPARC-1** workstation. We estimate, without detailed, specific code measurements, that a speed conversion factor of about $40\times$ is probably about right between the two computers. Thus, our longest run, with predictive accuracy exceeding that of Lapedes' back propagation network, and with its training time of 2 hours, represents about a factor of $20\times$ improvement in computing resource requirement. Our faster runs, which of course are considerably less accurate in longer-time predictions, showed an additional factor of $20-60\times$ speedup, thus requiring fairly modest computing resources.

## Versatility and Robustness

General concepts of versatility and robustness for numerical algorithms exist. For the purposes of this section, we qualitatively define "versatility" as the extent of the domain over which the network achieves "near-optimum" accuracy. We define "robustness" as the level of performance fluctuations, *e.g.*, fluctuations in prediction accuracy. We devised two ways of testing the versatility and robustness of the network: (1) changing the sampling time interval in the training and test files and (2) changing the time delay parameter in the Mackey-Glass equation. These tests can be made more or less sensitive by adjusting the continuous parameter excursions to match the versatility of the network being tested.

Here, we discuss the first test, varying the time spacing of data points in the training and test files. This test provides a continuous handle on the matching of effective feature size or "wavelength" of the function to be fit and the network basis functions. Figure 4 shows the results for three different network sizes. For a fixed set of network parameters, but retraining the net for each $\Delta t_{dat}$, we find that variations of order 10% in point spacing significantly affect the ability of the network to obtain predictive fits. Increasing the network size gradually improves the net's versatility and robustness, both on this test and in our other, related calculations.

## Conclusions

CNLS-net has proven able to accurately predict the behavior of the Mackey-Glass equation. We have obtained predictions that match the accuracy of previous work,[5,6] while requiring about $20\times$ lower computational effort.[6] Data requirements are comparable with those of a back propagation network[6] and much less than those of unnormalized radial basis function nets.[7] Overall, CNLS-net's use of normalized, localized basis functions with linearized correction terms appears to be a successful approach. Qualitatively, in this low-dimensional space, CNLS-net behaves in ways that are roughly intermediate between typical back propagation (BP) networks and radial basis function (RBF) nets. CNLS-net learns much faster than a BP net, but becomes more readily confused in cases of high dimensionality or with excess data to analyze. CNLS-net requires less training data than RBF nets. Accuracy generally improves with larger networks, larger training sets, and greater training times. Versatility and robustness of the net improve somewhat with network size.

## ACKNOWLEDGEMENTS

The authors appreciate the support of the Center for Nonlinear Studies, the Inertial Fusion and Plasma Theory Group (X-1), the Applied Theoretical Physics Division (X), and Los Alamos National Laboratory. This work was supported in part by the U.S.D.O.E.

## REFERENCES

[1] R. D. Jones, Y. C. Lee, C. W. Barnes, G. W. Flake, *et al.*, "Function Approximation and Time Series Prediction with Neural Networks," Los Alamos National Laboratory Rpt. No. LA-UR-90-21 (1990).

[2] R. D. Jones, Y. C. Lee, S. Qian, C. W. Barnes, *et al.*, "Nonlinear Adaptive Networks: a Little Theory, a Few Applications," in preparation (1990).

[3] M. C. Mackey and L. Glass, Science **197**, 287 (1977).

[4] J. D. Farmer, Physica **4D**, 366 (1982).

[5] J. D. Farmer and J. J. Sidorowich, *Phys. Rev. Lett.* **59**, 845 (1987).

[6] A. Lapedes and R. Farber, Los Alamos National Laboratory Rpt. No. LA-UR-87-2662 (1987).

[7] J. Moody and C. J. Darken, Neural Comp. **1**, 281 (1989).

[8] M. Casdagli, Physica D **35**, 335 (1989).

[9] D. E. Rumelhart, G. E. Hinton, and R. J. Williams, "Learning internal representations by error propagation," in **Parallel Distributed Processing, Vol. 1**, eds. D. E. Rumelhart and J. L. McClelland (MIT, Cambridge, 1986), pp. 318-362.

[10] P. D. Wasserman, **Neural Computing: Theory and Practice** (Van Nostrand Reinhold, NY, 1989), pp. 56-58.

[11] Y. C. Lee, "Neural networks with memory for intelligent computations," in **Proceedings of the 13$^{th}$ Conference on the Numerical Simulation of Plasmas**, Santa Fe, New Mexico, September 17-20, 1989; J. A. Howell, C. W. Barnes, S. K. Brown, G. W. Flake, R. D. Jones, Y. C. Lee, S. Qian, and R. M. Wright, "Control of a negative-ion accelerator source using neural networks," to be published in **Proceedings of the International Conference on Accelerator and Large Experimental Physics Control Systems**, Vancouver, B.C., Canada, October 30-November 3, 1989 and Los Alamos National Laboratory Rpt. No. LA-UR-89-3597 (1989).

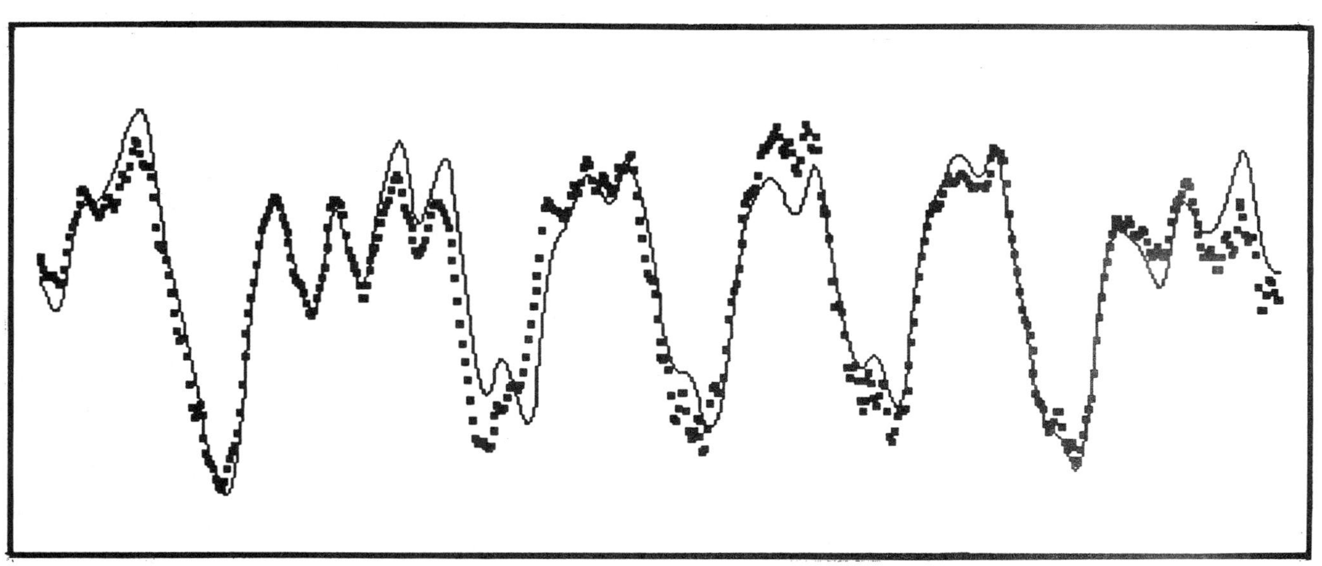

Fig. 1. The Mackey-Glass time series (solid line) and the predictions (points) of CNLS-net with 28 hidden nodes, for 500 test points. The net was trained for 40 epochs and tested at 21 iterations or $\Delta t_{pred} = 126$.

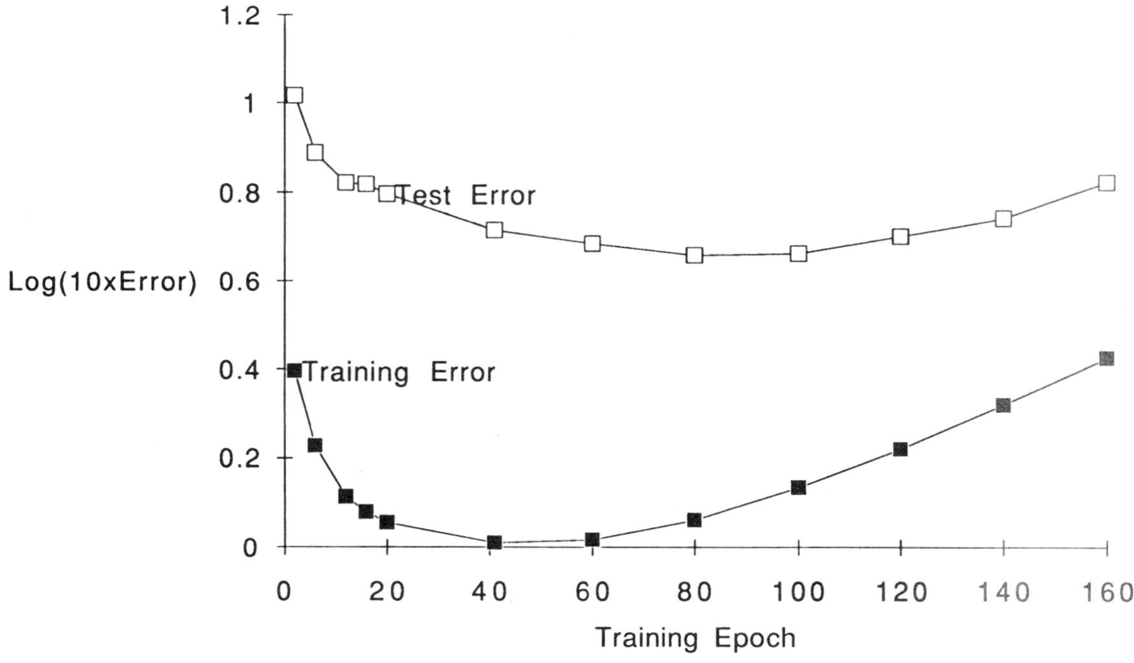


Fig. 2. Training and test error as a function of training epoch, for CNLS-net with 15 hidden nodes.

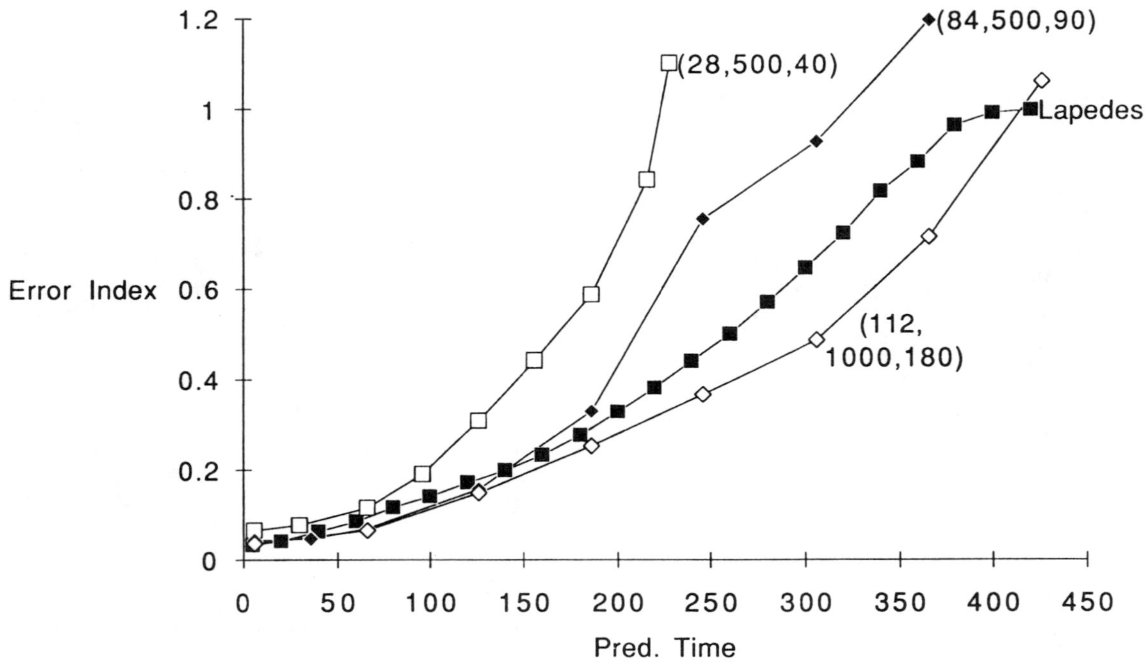


Fig. 3. Prediction error *vs.* prediction time for three CNLS-net configurations. Each CNLS-net curve is labelled by the number of hidden nodes, the number of training sets, and the number of training epochs. Curve labelled "Lapedes" is from Ref. 6.

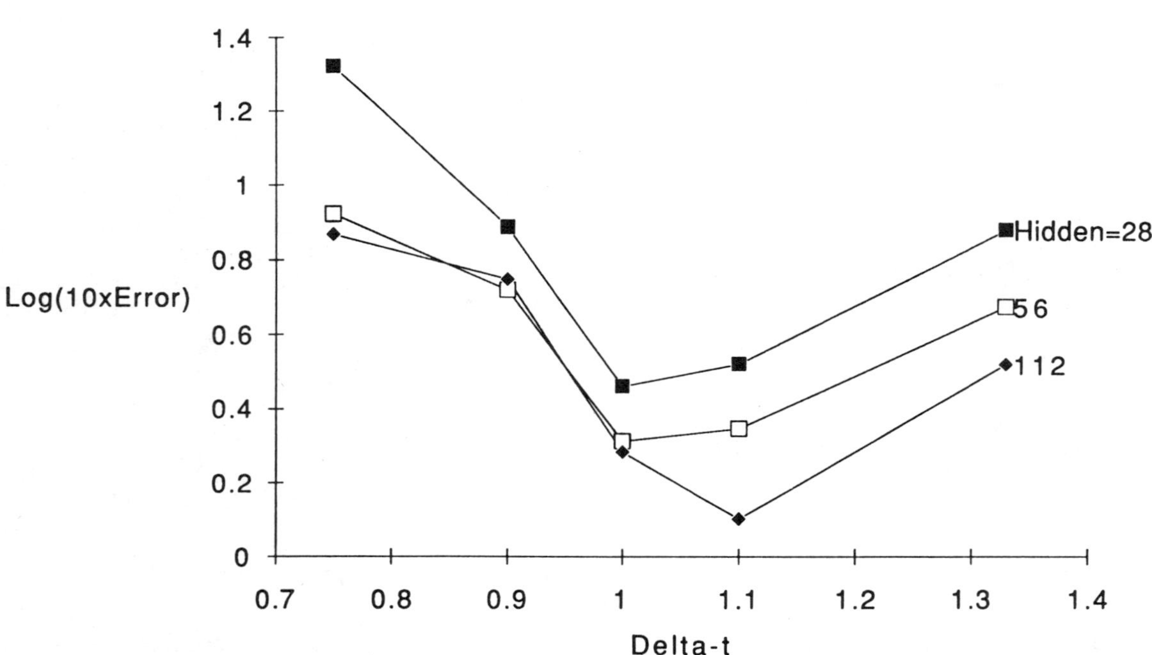


Fig. 4. Prediction error as the data files' $\Delta t_{dat}$ is varied shows versatility of CNLS-net. Net parameters were held fixed and net was retrained for each value of $\Delta t_{dat}$.

*SIMULATION* 58:5,333-339
© 1992, Simulation Councils, Inc.
ISSN 0037-5497/92 $3.00 + .10
Printed in the United States of America

# Extrapolation of Mackey-Glass data using Cascade Correlation

**David Ensley**
200 Broun Hall
**Department of Electrical Engineering**
*Auburn University*
Auburn, Alabama 36849

**Dale E. Nelson**
WL/AAAT-1
*Wright Laboratory*
Wright-Patterson AFB  OH  45433-6543

*Attempting to find near-optimal architectures, ontogenic neural networks develop their own architectures as they train. As part of a project entitled "Ontogenic Neural Networks for the Prediction of Chaotic Time Series," this paper presents findings of a ten-week research period on using the Cascade Correlation ontogenic neural network to extrapolate (predict) a chaotic time series generated from the Mackey-Glass equation. During training the neural network forms a model of the Mackey-Glass equation by observing its behavior. Then the neural network is used to simulate the function in order to extrapolate it, that is, to predict its behavior beyond the space observed by the neural network. Truer, more informative measures of extrapolation accuracy than currently popular measures are presented. The effects of some network parameters on extrapolation accuracy were investigated. Sinusoidal activation functions turned out to be best for our data set. The best range for sigmoidal activation functions was [-1, +1]. Though surprisingly good extrapolations have been obtained, there remain pitfalls. These pitfalls are discussed along with possible methods for avoiding them.*

**Keywords:** ontogenic neural networks, Mackey-Glass data, sinusoidal activation, sigmoidal activation

## Introduction

The project entitled "Ontogenic Neural Networks for the Prediction of Chaotic Time Series," of which this work is a part, has two primary motivations. One is to explore and expand the relatively new genre of neural networks called ontogenic neural networks. The name ontogenic comes from the biological term ontogenesis, which The American College Dictionary [Barnhart, 1970] defines as "the development of an individual organism." Thus, ontogenic neural networks develop their architectures as they learn instead of requiring the user to specify an architecture before training.

Traditionally neural network developers have had to find the optimum architecture for their networks by trial and error. In the last three years or so, researchers have made progress in developing networks that attempt to determine the optimum architecture automatically. Alpaydin recently published a taxonomy of such networks he calls incremental learning [1]. His two classes of incremental learning are networks that start with many nodes, pruning themselves as they train, and networks that start with a minimum number of nodes, adding more as they train. It is this latter category that we refer to as ontogenic neural networks.

The other primary motivation for the project is to explore the application of neural networks, ontogenic neural networks in particular, to extrapolating, especially predicting the future behavior of a chaotic system given its past behavior. Chaos is defined as "the complicated behavior of simple deterministic equations" [8]. In order to simulate a system, the network must first form an accurate model of the system's behavior. This is done by presenting exemplars of known system behavior to the neural network inputs. Network weights are adjusted to force the network outputs to match the desired outputs given by the exemplars. The trained network can then be used to produce outputs for a system state not given by the training exemplars. A properly trained network can interpolate between the training exemplars or extrapolate beyond the training exemplars.

## Problem Discussion

The goal of this study is to discover how to accurately extrapolate a chaotic time series using the Cascade Correlation ontogenic neural network. Our hypothesis is that some of Cascade Correlation's network parameters affect the extrapolation accuracy. We designed experiments to find out which pa rameters affect training accuracy, how, and to what extent.

## Cascade Correlation: An Ontogenic Neural Network

Cascade Correlation [4] begins with only input and output layers. Weights are trained using any learning algorithm that applies to such a topology. Examples are the Widrow-Hoff delta rule, the Perceptron learning algorithm, backpropagation, and the quickprop learning algorithm descri bed in [3]. We used quickprop for this study.

When it is determined that further training is not constructive, a pool of candidate nodes for a new hidden layer are trained to capture the remaining network error. The criterion used to select the best candidate is the correlation (hence the second part of the name) between each candidate's output and the remaining network error. When it is determined that further training of the candidates is not constructive, the candidate with the highest correlation score is installed in its own new hidden layer, with inputs from all input nodes and all previously installed hidden nodes. Because each hidden unit is in its own layer, a cascade of single-node hidden layers is formed (hence the first part of the name). Once installed, hidden nodes are never modified. Thus, they become permanent feature detectors.

After installing a new hidden node, the weights of the output nodes are retrained as described above. If the conditions for successful training have not been met, a new candidate pool is trained and the output weights are retrained. This process is repeated until the conditions for successful training have been met. The condition for successful training used in all of the experiments presented in this paper was that the error for each training exemplar must be less than one percent.

The network parameters we believe may affect extrapolation accuracy include the number of nodes in the input and output layers, the number of training exemplars, the number and nature of the nodes in the candidate pool, the criteria used to determine when further training is not constructive, and parameters which determine the rate of change of the weights over the weight space. This last set of parameters is determined by the weight-update learning algorithm chosen.

## The Mackey-Glass Equation: A Chaotic Time Series

Two chaotic time series generated by the Mackey-Glass equation were used by Lapedes and Farber in their pioneering work on neural network extrapolation [Lapedes, 1987]. We chose to use one of these chaotic time series for comparability with prior works and availability of data. The Mackey-Glass equation is a nonlinear differential delay equation:

$$\frac{dx(t)}{dt} = \frac{ax(t - \tau)}{1 + x^{10}(t - \tau)} - bx(t)$$

The parameter t is the time variable, x is a function of t, and a, b, and $\tau$ (tau ) are constants. We used a = 0.2 and b = 0.1. Different values of $\tau$ produce various degrees of chaos. We used $\tau$ = 17, which is just beyond the onset of chaos. Solving the Mackey-Glass equation (for solution details see [7] yields the time series x(t). The data set used in our experiments consists of values of x(t) spaced at equal time intervals $\Delta$t. A portion of this data set is shown in Figure 1.

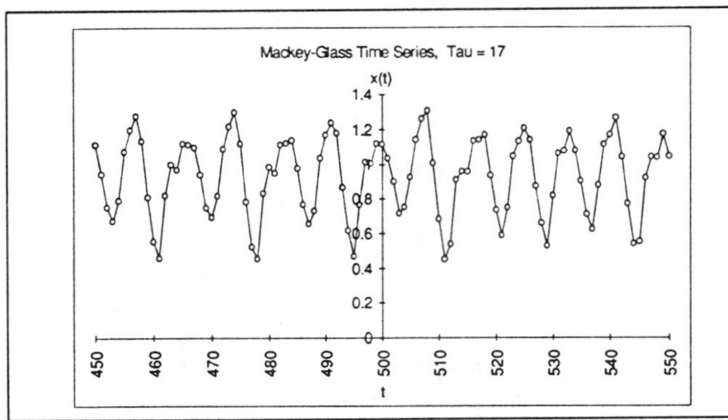


**Figure 1**: Time series generated using Mackey-Glass equation

When observing the behavior of a chaotic system, it appears that the underlying mathematics are quite complex. However, as the Mackey-Glass equation illustrates, a seemingly random, ill-behaved system can be described by a relatively simple deterministic equation. With $\tau$ = 17 the Mackey-Glass time series exhibits a chaotic quasi-periodicity.

As Lapedes and Farber [6] showed, such a non-polynomial chaotic series is difficult, if not impossible, to extrapolate using conventional polynomial extrapolation methods, but can be successfully extrapolated for a short time using neural networks. Theiler points out that, "The hallmark of a chaotic system is the sensitivity of the system's individual trajectories to their initial conditions."[8] For extrapolation of a chaotic time series, this means that if the initial extrapolations are not extremely accurate, the following extrapolations will stray exponentially from the correct values. Herein lies the difficulty in extrapolation when chaos is present.

## Mechanics of Extrapolation

To understand how extrapolation is accomplished using a neural network, it is first necessary to understand how an extrapolation network is trained. For an n input, m output network, a training exemplar is formed by taking n + m consecutive values from the data series to be extrapolated. Starting at an arbitrary value $x_i$, the first n values $(x_i,...,x_{n+i})$ are presented to the network inputs, and the next m values $(x_{n+i},..., x_{n+m+i-1})$ are compared to the network outputs for the calculation of training error. Thus a general training exemplar for an n input, m output network can be represented as $(x_i,..., x_{n+i-1}, x_{n+i},..., x_{n+m+i-1})$. Each successive exemplar is formed by starting one value beyond the previous starting value. We name the last known value in the data series $x_k$. Thus $x'_{k+1}$ is the first value to be extrapolated. We use a prime ( ´ ) to distinguish the extrapolated value from the un-primed actual value. For fair comparisons we always used k=500 so that the first value extrapolated was always $x'_{501}$ (see Table 1).

Table 1: Examples of training exemplars and extrapolations for n = 4, m = 1, k = 500

| Network Inputs | Network Outputs |
|---|---|
| : | : |
| $x494, x495, x496, x497$ | $x498$ |
| $x495, x496, x497, x498$ | $x499$ |
| $x496, x497, x498, x499$ | $x500$ (Last training exemplar) |
| $x497, x498, x499, x500$ | $x'501$ (First extrapolation) |
| $x498, x499, x500, x'501$ | $x'502$ (Second extrapolation obtained using first extrapolation) |
| : | : |

After the extrapolation network is trained, the first extrapolation $x'_{k+1}$ is made by presenting the last n values in the data series $(x_{k-n+1},...,x_k)$ to the network inputs. Thus for $x'_{k+1}$, all inputs are known data values. The second extrapolation $x'_{k+2}$ is made by presenting $(x_{k-n+2},...,x'_{k+1})$ to the network inputs. The successive input exemplars are likewise shifted by one. For $x'_{k+2}$ one input is an extrapolated value, for $x'_{k+3}$ two inputs are extrapolated values, etc. Eventually all extrapolations are made based upon previously extrapolated data.

## Evaluation of Extrapolation Accuracy

After the first few experiments were run and examined, it became clear that determining which extrapolations are best is not a simple problem. Some extrapolations were very good for a short period only; others were not very close but did not stray far. Which of these is best may depend on the application. Therefore, we need ways of evaluating extrapolation accuracy which will allow us to select the best network for a particular application.

One common method for examining extrapolation results is to plot the extrapolation curve along with the correct curve. For a quasi-periodic function such as the Mackey-Glass equation, it seems logical to describe this plot in terms of four measurements of periodic functions: offset, amplitude, phase, and frequency.

Offset error was only noticed in our earliest experiments when the training criteria were not very strict (e.g., only trained to ten percent error for each exemplar). The extrapolation curve followed the actual curve, but at a different height. We call this problem offset error because it resembles the adjustment of the dc offset of a waveform as viewed on an oscilloscope. To get rid of offset error, train further or retrain with stricter training criteria.

Amplitude errors almost always accompanied offset errors. We encountered three types of amplitude errors: permanent, temporary, and growing (exploding). As with offset errors, permanent errors in amplitude only occurred with slack training criteria. Interestingly enough, when these errors occurred, the shape of the extrapolation curve otherwise matched the shape of the actual curve; the network had begun to learn the underlying mathematical model. To get rid of permanent amplitude error, train further or retrain with stricter training criteria. Sometimes the amplitude of the extrapolation curve would get temporarily larger or smaller than that of the actual curve. This may be due to the fact that the chaotic data of the Mackey-Glass equation has temporary changes in amplitude. If this is true, then the network learned of these changes and was simply predicting these changes in the wrong places. The worst possible extrapolation error is the growing amplitude error. It comes in three varieties: the extrapolation increases exponentially to positive infinity, the extrapolation decreases exponentially to negative infinity, or the extrapolation is a quasi-sinusoid with exponentially growing amplitude. We refer to this type of error as an exploding extrapolation.

Most of the phase errors we found were lagging phase errors; the extrapolation curve lagged the actual curve. In a small number of cases the phase error was leading. Some phase errors are due to frequency errors. This produces an interesting result. If the frequency of the extrapolation curve is lower than that of the actual curve, the extrapolation lags at first with growing phase error. After being totally out of phase the extrapolation will lead. Eventually the extrapolation will temporarily get back on track.

Another useful plot describing individual extrapolation errors is the extrapolation error curve, a plot of the extrapolated values minus actual values. When the extrapolation error curve is positive, the extrapolation is greater than the actual; when the extrapolation error curve is negative, the extrapolation is less than the actual. This plot gives a truer, more informative, and more easily read graph of individual extrapolation errors than does the plot of the extrapolation along with the actual, which can be misleading. An example of how the extrapolation vs. actual curve can be misleading is shown in Figures 2 and 3. Notice that though the extrapolation curve appears to closely trace the actual curve for the first 45 extrapolations, individual extrapolation errors are large. Compare with the extrapolation error curve, which quickly identifies the poor extrapolation.

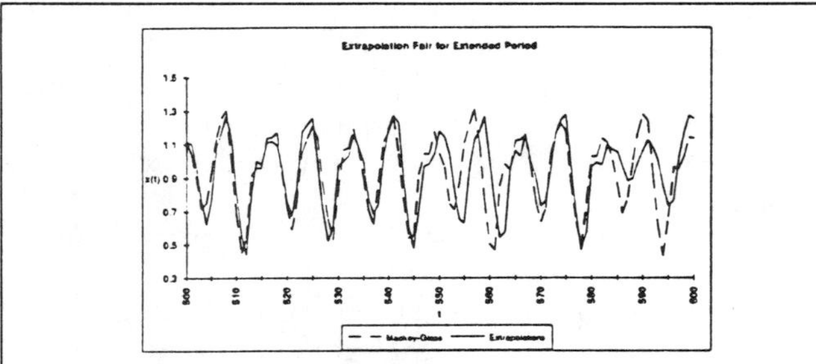

**Figure 2:** Misleading representation of extrapolation errors.

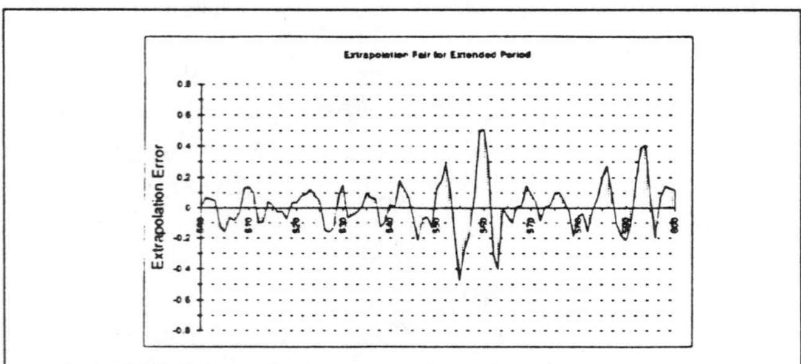

**Figure 3:** Truer representation of extrapolation errors

## Calculating the RMS Error for a Given Range of Extrapolations

The RMS error is a popular error measure. It is effective for comparing extrapolations of different networks over a particular range. It offers the advantage of a single value for measuring extrapolation accuracy, but at the expense of information. This requires that one use caution when using the RMS error for comparing different networks. Whereas one network may have the lowest RMS error over one range, a different network may have the lowest RMS error over another range. The desired criteria of extrapolation accuracy will help determine the proper range to use for the RMS error.

Caution must still be used, for networks with similar RMS errors over one range may rank differently if the range is changed even slightly .

## Plotting the Cumulative Extrapolation Error Curve

The *cumulative extrapolation error curve* overcomes this disadvantage of RMS error calculations while allowing easier comparison of different networks than the other plots discussed in this paper. At each point the cumulative extrapolation error curve displays the total of the absolute values of all extrapolation errors up to and including that particular point. The absolute value is used so that high and low extrapolations do not cancel each other's effect on this error curve. This plot will help identify the points at which changes in rank (by extrapolation accuracy) occur. Notice in Figure 4 that Net 2 has better extrapolation accuracy only if the number of extrapolations needed by an application is between 16 and 32.

The cumulative extrapolation error curve also provides a good check of the validity of RMS error comparisons. In Figure 5 notice that Net 3 has the smallest error for 100 extra polations. If only the RMS error was investigated, Net 3 would be incorrectly chosen as the best network. Actually, Net 3 provided the poorest extrapolation accuracy, while Nets 1 and 2 were quite good for a short period.

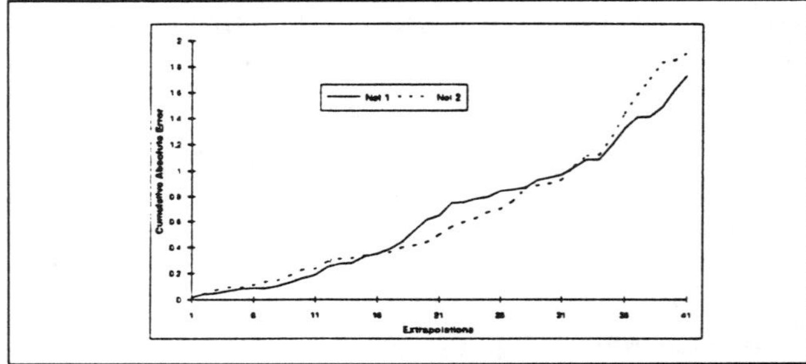

**Figure 4:** Cumulative extrapolation error curves show best extrapolations for any range.

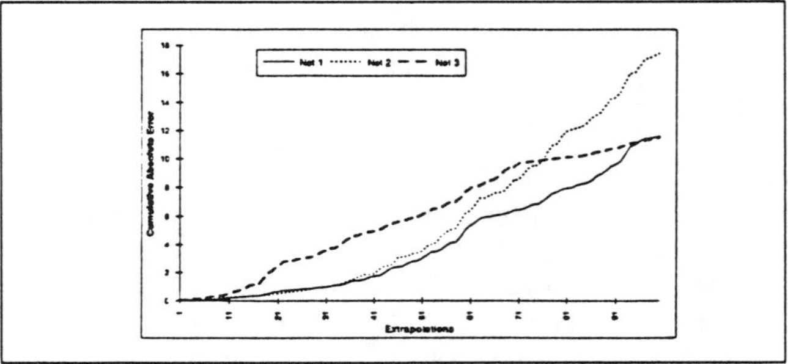

**Figure 5:** Cumulative extrapolation error curves show where RMS error is misleading.

## Experiments

We feel that most of the keys to accurate extrapolation lie in understanding how network parameters affect extrapolation accuracy.Early experiments yielded some insight into how the nature of candidate nodes affects extrapolation accuracy. Another experiment investigates how the numbers of inputs and outputs affect extrapolation accuracy.

## Activation Functions

The source code we used for the Cascade Correlation algorithm was provided by Dr. Scott Fahlman and Scott Crowder of Carnegie Mellon University. It included the Gaussian, logistic sigmoid, and symmetric logistic sigmoid activation functions. We added several activation functions to the Cascade Correlation algorithm (see Tables 2 through 4). We then modified the algorithm to allow more than one activation function in the candidate pool. This meant that nodes with different activation functions could compete simultaneously. Cascade Correlation automatically selects the best candidate, and thus helped us determine which activation functions are best for our data.

When given a choice among the activation functions in Tables 2 through 4 , Cascade Correlation chose sines and cosines almost exclusively and in nearly equal quantities. Of networks trained with only one activation function, sines and cosines outperformed all others in extrapolating. This is not surprising considering the quasi-sinusoidal data set (refer to Figure 1).

Of the Gaussian types, the negative Gaussian performed best on our data set. The Gaussian also performed satisfactorily. Compare the Gaussian with the hyperbolic secant. The latter approaches zero more slowly. Surprisingly, there was a marked difference between the two in training; for our data set, the hyperbolic secant was the worst of all activation functions we tried.

For our data set, sigmoids in the range [-1, +1] had more success in training than those of other ranges. The sigmoid most often chosen by Cascade Correlation was the double symmetric logistic sigmoid. The hyperbolic tangent also performed satisfactorily.

The authors developed the equations for the sigmoids with square terms. We believe the flat spot around the origin will help eliminate noise; small weight perturbations during training would be dampened. With standard sigmoids, oscillations are introduced due the steep slope of the sigmoid at zero. With this new function, training should be accelerated and oscillations reduced by the "flat spot" at zero. However, caution must be exercised because there is a zero derivitive, inflection point, at zero which must not be used in the weight update formula. Though these functions' performance on our data set was only fair, we plan to try these functions on different data sets to test this hypothesis.

**Table 2.** Sinusoidal hidden activation functions.

| Activation Function | Formula | Graph | Range |
|---|---|---|---|
| Sine | $f(x) = \sin(x)$ | | [-1,+1] |
| Cosine | $f(x) = \cos(x)$ | | [-1,+1] |

**Table 3.** Gaussian and similar hidden activation functions.

| Activation Function | Formula | Graph | Range |
|---|---|---|---|
| Gaussian | $f(x) = e^{-(x^2/2)}$ | | [0,1] |
| Negative Gaussian | $f(x) = -e^{-(x^2/2)}$ | | [-1,0] |
| Hyperbolic Secant | $f(x) = \mathrm{sech}(x)$ | | [0,1] |

**Table 4.** Sigmoidal hidden activation functions.
* Invented by Dale Nelson and David Ensley.

| Activation Function | Formula | Graph | Range |
|---|---|---|---|
| Logistic Sigmoid | $f(x) = \dfrac{1}{1+e^{-x}}$ | | [0,1] |
| Symmetric Logistic Sigmoid | $f(x) = \dfrac{1}{1+e^{-x}} - 0.5$ | | [-0.5,+0.5] |
| Double Symmetric Logistic Sigmoid | $f(x) = \dfrac{2}{1+e^{-x}} - 1$ | | [-1,+1] |
| Symmetric Logistic Sigmoid with Square* | $f(x) = \dfrac{1}{1+e^{-x^2}} - 0.5$ | | [-0.5,+0.5] |
| Double Symmetric Logistic Sigmoid with Square* | $f(x) = \dfrac{2}{1+e^{-x^2}} - 1$ | | [-1,+1] |
| Hyperbolic Tangent | $f(x) = \tanh(x)$ | | [-1,+1] |

## Numbers of inputs and outputs

Takens' theorem tells us that the number of inputs n to an extrapolating neural network should be greater than d and less than 2d + 1, where d is the fractal dimension (a measure of the degree of chaos [5]) of the data set [6]:

$$d <\_ n <\_ 2d + 1$$

The fractal dimension of the time series generated by the Mackey-Glass equation with $\tau = 17$ is approximately 2.1 [6;7]. Thus Takens' theorem tells us that we need 3, 4, or 5 inputs for accurate extrapolation.

Following the example of [6] and [7], all of our early experiments used 4 inputs and 1 output. To investigate the effect of the number of inputs and outputs on extrapolation accuracy, we chose one network whose extrapolations were worse than average in accuracy but not exploding. Keeping all other parameters unchanged (including the seed for the random number generator), we retrained this network with every combination of 2 through 10 inputs and 1 through 3 outputs. (Unfortunately, time restraints allowed us only one run for each case.) The two-output case forces the network to learn the first derivative (slope) of the actual curve along with future points. The three-output case forces the network to additionally learn the second derivative (curvature). The second and third outputs are used for training purposes only and are ignored during extrapolation.

The resulting RMS errors for the first 100 extrapolations are shown in Figure 6 . The absence of a column indicates that the extrapolation exploded with an RMS error greater than 2. For each number of outputs, data from the best results appear in Table 5. The best results were all in the range of inputs predicted by Takens' theorem. More precisely, the best range of inputs for this experiment was between d and 2d. With only one run for each combination of inputs and outputs, we cannot say conclusively that Takens' range was too broad. Using more outputs seems to produce fewer exploding errors at the cost of overall extrapolation accuracy. Again, we need more data to be sure.

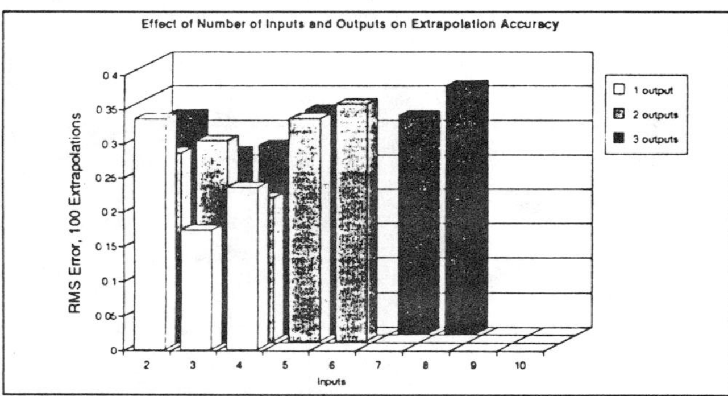


**Figure 6.** Inputs/outputs experiment results.

**Table 5.** Best results from inputs/outputs experiment for 1, 2, and 3 outputs.

| # Inputs | # Outputs | # Training Epochs | # Hidden Nodes | RMS |
|---|---|---|---|---|
| 3 | 1 | 9626 | 42 | 0.172 |
| 4 | 2 | 15021 | 62 | 0.208 |
| 3 | 3 | 13549 | 69 | 0.265 |

## Conclusions

One of the major concerns in developing a neural network for extrapolation is the possibility of exploding extrapolation errors. Several trained networks that perform well on the training exemplars can have very different extrapolations. A few well-trained networks may have exploding extrapolation errors. At this time we do not know how to tell in advance if a well-trained network's extrapolations will explode or not. Neither can we tell in advance how accurate the extrapolations will be if they do not explode. For most applications the existence of exploding extrapolations can be easily tested; this is not the case for applications requiring real-time learning. More research is needed to determine how to prevent both inaccurate and exploding extrapolations. As mentioned earlier, we have found ways of preventing two types of extrapolation error, namely offset and permanent amplitude errors.

Cascade Correlation can help select the best hidden layer activation functions for a particular data set by using a mixture of activation functions in the candidate pool. Proper selection of the activation function, the number of training exemplars, the numbers of inputs and outputs, and possibly other network parameters provides greater extrapolation accuracy. We are beginning to discover how to properly select these parameters.

We have shown that when judging networks on extrapolation accuracy, plotting the extrapolation curve vs. the actual curve and using the RMS error over extrapolations can both be misleading. The extrapolation error curve and cumulative extrapolation error curve, respectively, are useful for checking these measurements. In addition, the extrapolation error curve is much easier to read, and the cumulative extrapolation error curve quickly identifies the best networks for the extrapolation ranges of interest.

## Acknowledgement

The authors extend thanks to Dr. Scott Fahlman and Scott Crowder of Carnegie Mellon University for the source code for Cascade Correlation and for their assistance and recommendations .

## References

1. Alpaydin, E., "GAL: Networks That Grow When They Learn and Shrink When They Forget," Technical Report TR 91-032, International Computer Science Institute, Berkeley, CA, May 1991.

2. Barnhart, C. L., Editor in Chief, *The American College Dictionary*, Random House, New York, 1970.

3. Fahlman, S. E., "An Empirical Study of Learning Speed in Back-Propagation Networks," Technical Report CMU-CS-88-162, Carnegie Mellon University, Pittsburgh, PA, September 1988.

4. Fahlman, S. E. and C. Lebiere, "The Cascade-Correlation Learning Architecture," Technical Report CMU-CS-90-100, Carnegie Mellon University, Pittsburgh, PA, February 1990.

5. Gearhart, T. K., "Correlation Dimension of Chaotic Attractors," Technical Report , Avionics Directorate, Wright-Patterson Air Force Base, Dayton, OH, July 1991.

6. Lapedes, A. and R. Farber, "Nonlinear Signal Processing Using Neural Networks: Prediction and System Modelling," Technical Report LA-UR-87-2662, Los Alamos National Laboratory, Los Alamos, NM, June 1987.

7. Stright, J. R., "A Neural Network Implementation of Chaotic Time Series Prediction," Thesis, Air Force Institute of Technology, December 1988.

8. Theiler, J., "Estimating the Fractal Dimension of Chaotic Time Series," *The Lincoln Laboratory Journal*, Vol. 3, No. 1, pp. 63-85 (1990)

DAVID ENSLEY received the Bachelor of Electrical Engineering degree from Auburn University in 1989. He is currently working on the M.S. degree in electrical engineering at Auburn University. His research interests are in the development of ontogenic neural network algorithms and their application.

DALE NELSON received his B.S. degree in Aerospace Engineering from Tri-State University in 1969 and his M.S. degree in Computer Science from Wright State University in 1981. He is currently completing his dissertation for the PhD in Computer Engineering at the Air Force Institute of Technology. He has been employed by the Air Force since 1972 where he is currently Chief of the Advanced Systems Research Group at the Avionics Directorate of Wright Laboratory. He is the Avionics Directorate focal point for machine intelligence and an Air Force representative to the Tri-Service Neural Networks Working Group. He is the author of papers dealing with structural fatigue of aircraft, combat battle damage evaluation, and automated structural design of aircraft. His current research interests are in neural networks and machine intelligence, with special emphasis on ontogenic neural networks.

# How to Get Started with ANN Research

The explosive growth in artificial neural network (ANN) research has resulted in demands for textbooks, reprint collections, journals, conferences, workshops, and electronic mailboxes, as well as hardware systems and software simulators. Most of these demands are being met adequately. This chapter is an attempt to help the novice access some of these resources.

The Annotated Bibliography at the end of this book is a succinct guide to the literature in the general areas of time series, chaos and neural nets. What follows below is a brief summary of available computational tools. The list is not complete and does not indicate the authors' preferences. There is no suggestion that either the prices or the capabilities indicated here are current. They are given purely for guidance. Well over seventy software simulators are available in the market place. The June 1992 issue of *AI Expert* listed about fifty of these, along with addresses and telephone numbers of sources.

Most of the neural network tools fall into two broad categories: simulations to assist biological research in natural neural networks and simulations to assist computational scientists in artificial neural networks.

Building simulators that support biological research (such as BIOSIM, developed at the Royal Institute of Technology in Sweden; GENESIS, developed at California Institute of Technology, Pasadena; and a version of CAJAL under development at the University of Southern California) is a complex process involving compartmental models and differential equations such as the Hodgkin-Huxley equations. Because the scope of this chapter is limited to efforts aimed at studying artificial neural nets, no attempt is made to survey simulation activities in natural neural nets.

Work in the area of hardware and software tools to simulate ANNs is taking place in three broad directions: teaching and research, design and development, and end use. Demand in these areas can be met in three different ways: Software simulation, board-level emulation, and true neurocomputers. It appears to us that all these tools are useful mostly during the learning phase; researchers tend to write their own code to suit their specialized needs.

In the teaching and research sphere, by far the most widely used software simulators use a conventional digital computer as a host to process programs (typically written in C, Basic, or Fortran). Simulators that are aimed at the personal computer market are often slow and inflexible; they are mostly useful as tutorial introductions. Simulators that run on workstations are a little faster and more expensive. In both cases, the user typically does not have access to the source code. The public-domain software simulators, such as University of California at San Diego's SunNet, University of Rochester's RCS (Rochester's connectionist simulator); and University of California at Los Angeles's SFINX are free, usually elaborate, and almost always very flexible. However, they are not maintained and supported by an organization dedicated to that task.

There are two possible approaches to the board-level emulation route:

1. to use conventional processors to emulate virtual neurons or processing elements
2. to build special-purpose coprocessor boards or accelerator boards dedicated to the processing of neurocomputer simulation; these boards can be inserted into a microcomputer or minicomputer host

Finally, one can fabricate application-specific integrated circuits (ASICs), using VLSI technology, to perform the neuronal and synaptic functions. As yet, no neurocomputer, in its true sense, exists. Many research facilities are working on various versions using ultraparallel architectures that permit dynamically programmable synaptic weights. Among the important players are Japan's Hitachi, Fujitsu, and Mitsubishi. Indeed, Hitachi is developing a wafer scale integrated neurocomputer, with 8 wafers and 144 neurons per wafer, for predicting 10-day stock fluctuations and for verification of signatures on checks. Fujitsu is developing a computer customized for ANN simulation that can purportedly deliver an average speed of 180 MCUPS (million connection updates per second) and a peak of 587 MCUPS. This machine uses available components and technology (Texas Instrument's TMS 320C30 digital signal processing chips in a ring architecture) and relegates the learning algorithm to the software.

One who is interested in acquiring one of these systems should keep the following evaluation questions in mind.

a. How good is the user interface? Is it easy to learn? Is it easy to use? How many different modes of data entry does it support? Can data be entered from a database? From a spreadsheet? Is it menu-driven? What sort of output options are there? Is there a graphics output? Color? Is there a need for a special PC board to support color graphics?
b. How diverse is the tool? How many paradigms can it support?
c. How flexible is the tool? Does it allow user-generated code to interface easily with the existing features?
d. What is the maximum size of a network it can support? Are there any restrictions on the number of layers? The number of neurons per layer? Total number of synapses?
e. How fast does the system run with and without an accelerator board? The speed of neurocomputers is often measured in terms of the connections per second (CPS) and connections updated per second (CUPS).

## Public-domain software simulators

These programs are available at practically no cost except possibly some handling charges. The source code can be compiled and used on most computers.

- The PDP simulator: This is listed in this category in spite of the $35 one has to pay to get a copy of the book and the disk because the disk contains nonproprietary source code. The book *Explorations in Parallel Distributed Processing* by J.L. McClelland and D.E. Rumelhart, published by MIT Press, is widely known as the "explorations book," and its companions, volumes 1 and 2 of *Parallel Distributed Processing* by the same authors, are known as the "PDP books." For someone who is a newcomer to this field, these are a good investment.

The PDP book discusses the theoretical concepts and the "explorations book" discusses the software implementations. When ordering *Explorations*, one can choose between IBM PC-compatible disks or Apple Macintosh disks. The hardware requirements for the Apple version include a Mac Plus, Mac SE, or Mac II. For the IBM PC-compatible programs the hardware requirements include an IBM PC or compatible with a 256K RAM, MS-DOS version 2.0 or higher, standard 24 line by 80 character display, and a text editor. The IBM PC-compatible version comes with two 360 KB disks that contain several C language programs and executable files to help simulate some of the problems discussed in Volume I of the PDP book. In addition, the disks contain a "make" file for porting the software to the Unix environment. There should be no difficulty in compiling this code using the standard Unix "cc" compiler.

The disks contain programs to simulate seven different kinds of neural network models. The interactive activation and competition (IAC) model allows one to produce networks such as those studied by Grossberg. The interactive activation (IA) model allows one to model word perception experiments. The constraint satisfaction (CS) program permits the implementation of the harmony theory model, discussed in Chapter 6 of the PDP book, the Boltzmann machine, discussed in Chapter 7, and the schema model, discussed in Chapter 14. The autoassociator (AA) program allows one to simulate Kohonen-type networks, discussed in Chapter 17 (Vol. 2) of the PDP book. Other models are the competitive learning (CL) program, the back-propagation (BP) program, and the pattern associator (PA) program. Within each model, the user is allowed to specify the network topology, weights, and output layout.

- University of Rochester's Rochester connectionist simulator (principal contributors: Feldman, Fanty, Goddard, and Ballard): RCS, Version 4.2, is a computational tool for simulating networks of highly interconnected information processing units. The new version also runs on X Windows. RCS, written in C, is designed to operate in a Unix environment. This package consists of a number of pieces and options that can be combined in various ways to suit different needs. Although RCS can be used without knowledge of the C language, knowledge of C is advantageous because the user interface is in C; the user must specify everything using C language statements. The designers made every effort to make this tool flexible by giving the user the ability to add new paradigms, new data structures, and new code.

The software is available at no cost by "anonymous FTP" via the Internet from the host "cayuga.cs. rochester.edu" in the directory "simulator". Do not forget to use "type binary" to retrieve compressed files. Official bug patches are also included in this directory. The source code takes about 10 Mbytes before compilation and about 12 Mbytes after compilation. Permanent installation of the binary code takes about 2 Mbytes. If a graphics capability is needed, X-libraries and an X-include directory should be installed. Further information can be obtained from the Department of Computer Science, University of Rochester, Rochester, NY 14627.

- UCLA's SFINX (principal contributors: Paik, Gungner, and Skrzypek): The SFINX (structure and function in neural connections) is similar to RCS; it is written in C for the Unix environment. This software package, written with machine vision applications in mind, contains a library of functions and a graphics interface and has been used by the designers for image segmentation, texture analysis, and shape recognition. In SFINX, a neural network architecture is specified in a high-level language. After compilation and linking, the object module is loaded into the SFINX simulator for interactive execution. The network specifications are represented by virtual processing elements, each comprising a functional pointer, output register, and a vector of associated interconnection-weight registers. Further information can be obtained from UCLA Software Office, UCLA, Los Angeles, CA 90024.

- UCSD/AT\&T's SunNet (principal contributor: Yoshiro Miyata): The SunNet is a computational tool for simulating connectionist networks of highly interconnected structures. SunNet allows the user to deal with a network at a high level of conceptualization and to construct a variety of networks of virtually arbitrary structure and size. SunNet was written for use with Sun graphics workstation, but it can run on any Unix machine. There are several variations in the software. For example, whereas the original SunNet runs on any Sun workstation, SkyNet is meant for Sun stations equipped with the accelerator board called Skyboard. StarNet runs on any Unix machine with no graphics capability, and PlaNet runs any Unix machine and sends the graphics output to Solar program, which runs on Sun. Finally, AllieNet runs on the Alliant minisuper computer and sends the graphics to Solar.

A problem can be defined on this network using a high-level interactive interface program. The user can examine the internal network status any time through a graphics display. Further information can be obtained from "miyata@soma.colorado.edu" or from the Institute for Cognitive Sciences, University of California at San Diego, La Jolla, CA 92093.

- Aspirin/MIGRAINES: The Mitre Corporation has developed a neural network simulator with a graphical user interface called Aspirin/MIGRAINES. One can obtain a copy of this code by anonymous ftp to "ps.cs.cmu.edu." Log in as "anonymous" with your user name as password. Then change directories with 'cd /afs/cs/project/connect/code'. Type 'binary' and then type 'get am6.tar.Z'.

## Neural net simulators from commercial vendors

Almost all the ANN simulation vendors supply their software products packaged to meet different price ranges. They typically fall into personal computer-oriented simulators and workstation-oriented simulators. The following list is but a minute sample of what is available. A more exhaustive, but not complete, list appears in the June 1992 issue of *AI Expert.*

- Ward Systems is marketing three products: NeuroShell, NeuroWindows, and an accelerator board, called NeuroBoard. NeuroShell ($200), specializing in classification and categorization, can run on an IBM PC with 256K bytes of RAM and DOS 2.0 or higher. A math coprocessor is recommended. Both binary and continuous versions of neural networks can be simulated. NeuroShell uses back-propagation and lets the user pick either a main menu or an advanced options menu. NeuroShell does not include graphics, but it lets the user see the options selected. NeuroWindows ($400) is a little more powerful than NeuroShell (that is, more types of nets and more neurons) and is capable of combining supervised and unsupervised training methods into one scheme.

- California Scientific Software's BrainMaker is priced at $100, runs on the IBM PC (MS-DOS), and can support five types of nodes and make up to 500,000 connections per second. The BrainMaker Professional ($800) has more features. This company also sells accelerator boards to go along with the above two systems. With an additional investment one can get the capability to build neural networks and download the programs to Intel's N64 (see below).

- NeuralWare puts out NeuralWorks Explorer and Professional II. The entry-level Explorer for MS-DOS is priced at about $300 and the top-of-the-line Professional II is priced at about $1,500 for MS-DOS and Macintosh versions and $3,000 for Sun-3, Sun-4, and Intel 386i versions. Professional II is a software tool. NeuralWorks does not produce any hardware system to support this product. Professional II has more graphics orientation than ExploreNet and supports three types of representations on the screen. In the network representation, every neuron along with its connections is displayed. In the activation representation, only the neurons are displayed, but not the connections. In the so-called Hinton representation, only the matrix of connection weights is displayed. In the network and activation representations, the size of the blip representing the node indicates the activation level. This tool permits the simulation of fairly large networks with a limit of 50 on the number of layers, 1000 on the neurons per layer, 20,000 on the total number of neurons, and 1.5 million on the total number of synaptic weights.

Professional II's interface is flexible enough to let the user build arbitrary networks and add or delete arbitrary connections. Professional II can be linked to user-produced C programs with the help of a software package, Designer Pack. Designer Pack essentially translates a network built with the aid of Professional II into a C language program. NeuralWorks, in partnership with ParaSoft, has plans of producing Professional II that can be ported to the NCube supercomputer with a hypercube architecture.

- Cognitive Software's Cognitron 1.2 is available in three versions: an MS-DOS Windows version, a Macintosh version, and a transputer version, with prices ranging from $300 to $1800. The Cognitron has a good graphics interface. In addition to the graphics representation in the modeling window, the network is represented as a program text in the creator/editor window. The Cognitron allows the user to create an arbitrary number of processing units. These units can be connected in any fashion, and the user has complete control over both activation and weight settings. The Cognitron has a nice user interface with a wide choice in input and output operations. For example, one can choose from a wide set of standardized input and output formats or write one's own programs using Cognitron's Common Lisp. A network saved in Lisp format can easily be transported to other computers.

- HNC offers the ANZA family of neurocomputing coprocessors and the associated software, called Neurosoft. However, if one buys the software alone, it is called ExploreNet. This runs on either Sun- or IBM PC-compatible systems. At the time of this writing, the MS-DOS version of this software simulator costs about $1,000 and the Sun version at about $4,000.

ExploreNet provides two different interfaces: a menu driven interface, called NetSet, and a library of C routines, called the User Interface Subroutine Library (UISL). NetSet is easy to learn: the user essentially fills in the blanks on a window menu. Although ExploreNet supports a large number of paradigms, the NetSet interface supports only two paradigms: back-propagation with up to four layers and counter propagation. The user has to write C language programs for anything outside the scope of these canned programs.

- TRW's Mark II is a software simulator designed to run on the VAX family of computers. The series numbering started with II presumably because Rosenblatt called his perceptron Mark I.

- SAIC markets two products: ANSim, which runs only under Microsoft's Windows, is a menu-based, graphics-oriented tool for creating thirteen of the more popular paradigms, including back-propagation, Hopfield net, and adaptive resonance theory. ANSpec, on the other hand, is a compiler for user-created networks. These software packages run on PC/AT-compatible machines or machines augmented with SAIC's Delta floating point processor. ANSim has been designed only as a stand-alone tool; it does not support integration with other software. ANSpec is a network specification language and compiler for that language.

- Nestor's NDS (Nestor Development System) is written entirely in C and can be used with the IBM PC as well as Sun and Apollo workstations. The N1000, priced from $19,000, is a collection of neural network development tools for signal and image processing applications. A recent announcement of this company included NestorReader and NestorWriter for recognizing machine-printed and handwritten characters.

- IBM's Computational Network Environment (CONE) is a programming environment comprising of a high-level general network specification language (GNL), a general intermediate network specification system (NETSPEC), and an interactive execution program (IXP). Neural network architectures are specified in GNL and compiled into machine-independent NETSPEC. Then an assembler translates the NETSPEC into a network IXL for execution on a specific neurocomputer simulator or emulator. The Network Interactive Execution Program (NET IXP) runs on a PC connected to the Network Emulation Processor (NEP). It is not clear whether this is a product available in the open market or is simply an in-house development tool. However, there is an IBM product, called Neural Network Utility, (NNU) that includes five learning models in an interactive environment: back-propagation, adaptive resonance theory (ART), feature maps, self-organizing routing net, and a constraint satisfaction net.

- Most of the hardware simulators of neural networks have been based on first producing a digital simulation and then accelerating them with high-speed arithmetic units. In contrast, Intel's N64 provides an analog model of a neural network. Intel claims that their chip can achieve speeds of up to $5 \times 10^9$ interconnections per second. The N64 has three layers, each with 64 processing elements. Separating the layers are sets of 4,096 *EE*PROMs (electronically erasable, programmable read-only memories) to store the synaptic weights. The N64 also incorporates analog adders and multipliers to produce the weighted sum. Recently Intel announced the 80170NX, the electrically trainable analog neural network (ETANN), and an associated set of development tools.

## Board-level implementations of neural networks

There are many hardware implementations, including some from Japan.

- TRW's Mark III, IV, and V series of machines are hardware counterparts to its Mark II, mentioned earlier. All the models of the Mark series are based on the concept of a virtual processing element. A virtual PE is a fictitious PE whose state is expressed as a stored value. Similarly, all the interconnections are described in software. This lends flexibility in the description of the PEs and the interconnection structure. Robert Hecht-Nielsen and Todd Gutschow first implemented this idea in TRW's Mark III. All the Mark series models share a common design environment, called the Artificial Neural System Environment (ANSE), which supports the user in the areas of network definition, network editing, network storage, and so on.

TRW's Mark III is a parallel processing system that uses virtual PEs and interconnection structure. The physical processors used are Motorola 68020 microprocessors (up to 15 may be used) that are in turn supported by M68881 floating-point coprocessors. One of these is used as a master and the rest are used as slave processors. This parallel processing system is connected to a VAX computer that acts as a host processor and provides I/O services. Mark III can support up to 65,000 PEs with over 1,000,000 trainable interconnections and can process 450,000 interconnections per second.

Mark IV is a single high-speed pipelined processor that can support up to 256,000 virtual PE's with over 5,500,000 trainable interconnections and is capable of processing five million interconnections per second.

Mark V is an MIMD (multiple-instruction stream, multiple-data stream) machine. The first model, V.1, contains 16 Motorola MC68020 processors, each with a 4-Mbyte local memory and a Wytek 32-bit floating-point coprocessor. This system can be hosted either by a VAX-family computer running the VMS operating system or by a Sun workstation. Preliminary specification claimed that this system can handle 650,000 PEs, 8,000,000 trainable connections, and 9,000,000 nontrainable connections.

- HNC's Anza and Anza Plus are PC-AT compatible coprocessors priced at $7,000 and $12,500 respectively. These boards are based on a Motorola 68020 plus an M68881 floating-point coprocessor. A Sun workstation version, called Anza Plus/VME, costs $24,950. Axon, priced at $1,950 is a neural network description language. The manufacturer claims that the Anza Plus coprocessor board, for example, can implement 2.5 million PEs and interconnections and update 1.5 million interconnections per second while using the back-propagation method. Anza Plus also comes with a software package, called Neurosoft, that gives the user a wide range of neural architectures that integrate into existing C programs.

- SAIC's Delta-1 is a board designed for use as an attached processor for a PC host. The hardware along with the firm's AnsKit modeling software, a mouse, and Microsoft Windows software sells for about $14,950. The Delta-2 is a full floating-point processor board.

## Other sources

There are electronic bulletin boards and other electronic newsletter services available to meet the needs of neural nets researchers.

- Neuron Digest is an electronic newsletter managed by volunteers. You can get on the distribution list by sending an e-mail message to "neuron-request@cattell.psych.upenn.edu."

- You can also get copies of preprints of papers from the preprint bulletin board, which can be accessed via anonymous FTP using the ftp archive.cis.ohio-state.edu with "anonymous" as user name and "neuron" as password, and then the command cd pub/neuroprose. Consult README file for posting and retrieval instructions.

## Reference

"Neural Network Resource Guide," *AI Expert,* June 1992, pp 50-56

# Annotated Bibliography

This partially annotated bibliography contains additional references relevant to time series forecasting. The papers are grouped by topic, and a short description of each topic is given. This bibliography is by no means exhaustive, but represents additional key publications that we were unable to include in this volume.

This first group of references contains introductory material on artificial neural networks. The book by Vemuri is the first volume in the Computer Society Press technology series on artificial neural networks, and is an excellent introduction to the field. The article by Lippmann is a concise review of basic neural network function and training. There are three books by Rumelhart and McClelland. The first two are commonly referred to as the "PDP books" and give a very complete description of neural network research, including different ANN architectures, training techniques, applications, and theoretical considerations. The third book, known as the "explorations book," includes neural network simulation software, examples, and exercises. The books by Zurada and by Hertz et al. are recent textbooks on ANNs.


J. Hertz, A. Krogh, and R. Palmer, *Introduction to the Theory of Neural Computation,* Addison-Wesley, Redwood City, Calif., 1991.

R.P. Lippmann, "An Introduction to Computing with Neural Nets," *IEEE ASSP Magazine,* Apr. 1987, pp. 4-22.

J.L. McClelland and D.E. Rumelhart, *Explorations in Parallel Distributed Processing: A Handbook of Models, Programs and Exercises,* MIT Press, Cambridge, Mass., 1988.

D.E. Rumelhart and J.L. McClelland (eds.), *Parallel Distributed Processing,* Vols. I & II, MIT Press, Cambridge, Mass., 1986.

V. Vemuri, *Artificial Neural Networks: Theoretical Concepts,* IEEE CS Press, Los Alamitos, Calif., 1988.

J. Zurada, *Introduction to Artificial Neural Systems,* West Publishing Company, New York, N.Y., 1992.


The following references contain information on forecasting time series in general, both with ANNs and with classical methods. The seminal text on time series forecasting by Box and Jenkins is included here, as well as important early contributions to the field of ANN prediction of time series by Lapedes and Farber and by Moody and Darken.


G.E.P. Box and G. M. Jenkins, *Time Series Analysis: Forecasting and Control,* Holden-Day, Oakland, Calif., 1976.

D.Y.C. Chan and D. Prager, "Analysis of Time Series by Neural Networks," *Proc. IJCNN,* IEEE Service Center, Piscataway, N.J., 1991, pp. 355-360.

J.P. Coughlin and R. Baran, "Time Series Prediction with Linear and Nonlinear Adaptive Networks," *Proc. IJCNN,* IEEE Service Center, Piscataway, N.J., 1991, pp. 379-384.

R.D. Jones et al., "Function Approximation and Time Series Prediction with Neural Networks," Technical Report LA-UR 90-21, Los Alamos National Laboratory, 1989.

M.J. Korenberg and L.D. Paarmann, "Orthogonal Approaches to Time-Series Analysis and System Identification," *IEEE ASSP Magazine,* July 1991, pp. 29-43.

A. Lapedes and R. Farber, "Nonlinear Signal Processing Using Artificial Neural Networks: Prediction and System Modeling," Technical Report LA-UR 87-2662, Los Alamos National Laboratory, 1987.

J. Moody and C.J. Darken, "Fast Learning in Networks of Locally Tuned Processing Units," *Neural Computation,* Vol. 1, No. 2, Summer 1989, pp. 281-294.

R. Sharda and R.B. Patil, "Neural Networks as Forecasting Experts: An Empirical Test," *Proc. IJCNN,* IEEE Service Center, Piscataway, N.J., 1990, pp. II-490-II-494.

A.S. Weigend, B.A. Huberman, and D.E. Rumelhart, "Predicting the Future: A Connectionist Approach," *Int'l J. Neural Systems,* Vol. 1, No. 3, 1990, pp. 193-209.

Papers in the following group describe individual implementations of time series forecasting by ANNs. Several of these papers discuss the use of other neural networks other than the feedforward network, such as cascade correlation and CNLS-Net, for time series forecasting. The other papers here give applications of ANNs to specific time series, including predictions of the price of a stock and the EEG time series.


K.J. Blinowska and M. Malinowski, "Non-Linear and Linear Forecasting of the EEG Time Series," *Biological Cybernetics,* Vol. 66, 1991, pp. 159-165.

D. Ensley and D.E. Nelson, "Extrapolation of Mackey-Glass Data Using Cascade Correlation," *Simulation,* Vol. 58, May 1992, pp. 333-339.

H. Lee et al., "Nonlinear System Identification Using Recurrent Networks," *Proc. IJCNN,* IEEE Service Center, Piscataway, N.J., 1991, pp. 2410-2415.

K.-C. Lee, J.-S. Yang, and S.-J. Park, "Neural Network-Based Time Series Modeling: ARMA Model Identification via ESACF Approach," *Proc. IJCNN,* IEEE Service Center, Piscataway, N.J., 1991, pp. 232-236.

X.Q. Liu, B.W. Ang, and T.N. Goh, "Forecasting of Electricity Consumption: A Comparison Between an Econometric Model and a Neural Network Model," *Proc. IJCNN,* IEEE Service Center, Piscataway, N.J., 1991, pp. 1254-1259.

I. Matsuba, "Application of Neural Sequential Associator to Long-Term Stock Price Prediction," *Proc. IJCNN,* IEEE Service Center, Piscataway, N.J., 1991, pp. 1196-1201.

T.M. Peng, N.F. Hubele and G.G. Karady, "Advancement in the Application of Neural Networks for Short-Term Load Forecasting," *IEEE Trans. Power Systems,* Vol. 7, Feb. 1992, pp. 250-257.

D. Whitley, T. Starkweather and C. Bogart, "Genetic Algorithms and Neural Networks: Optimizing Connections and Connectivity," *Parallel Computing,* Vol. 14, 1990, pp. 347-361.


These papers focus on chaotic time series. Work here includes theoretical results on chaotic systems and methods for predicting their time series. Both ANN and classical techniques are represented here.


M. Casdagli, "Nonlinear Prediction of Chaotic Time Series," *Physica D*, Vol. 35, No. 3, May 1989, pp. 335-356.

M.R. Guevara et al. "Chaos in Neurobiology," *IEEE Trans. Systems, Man and Cybernetics,* Vol. 13, Sept./Oct. 1983, pp. 790-798.

J. Jimenez, J.A. Moreno, and G.J. Ruggeri, "Forecasting Chaotic Time Series: A Local Optimal Linear-Reconstruction Method," *Physical Rev. A,* Vol. 45, Mar. 1992, pp. 3553-3558.

J.J. Sidorowich, "Modeling of Chaotic Time Series for Prediction, Interpolation, and Smoothing," *Proc. ICASSP,* 1992, pp. IV-121-IV-124.


These last two papers discuss the pruning of network weights and the training of artificial neural networks with genetic algorithms, respectively.


Y. LeCun, J.S. Denker, and S.A. Solla, "Optimal Brain Damage," in *Advances in Neural Information Processing Systems,* Vol. 2, D. Touretzky, ed., Morgan Kaufmann, San Mateo, Calif., 1990, pp. 598-605.

D. Whitley, T. Starkweather, and C. Bogart, "Genetic Algorithms and Neural Networks: Optimizing Connections and Connectivity," *Parallel Computing,* Vol. 14, 1990, pp. 347-361.

# About the Authors

V. Rao Vemuri is a professor in the Department of Applied Science at the University of California, Davis. He holds memberships in the Graduate Group in Computer Science and the Graduate Group in Biomedical Engineering. In addition, he holds a joint appointment with the Engineering Research Division of the Lawrence Livermore National Laboratory, Livermore, California. Prior to obtaining his current position, he taught in the Computer Science Department at the State University of New York at Binghamton, New York, and in the Department of Aeronautics and Astronautics at Purdue University, West Lafayette, Indiana.

His industrial experience includes five years at TRW, Redondo Beach, California, where he participated in and managed several software development projects. He also worked at RCA's Home Instruments Division.

He is the author of four books and well over 60 technical papers in a variety of fields, including modeling, simulation, resource management, numerical methods, and artificial neural networks. He is a senior member of IEEE and actively participates in many IEEE Computer Society activities. His most recent assignment was as Editor-in-Chief of the IEEE Computer Society Press.

Robert D. Rogers is a postdoctoral research fellow at the Lawrence Livermore National Laboratory's Institute of Geophysics and Planetary Physics. His research interests in the field of artificial neural networks include time series forecasting, financial analysis, and the development of pattern recognition software for testing astronomical instrumentation and analyzing images. He received his BA degree in physics in 1987 from the University of California, Berkeley, and his PhD degree in physics in 1991 from Harvard University.

# *Other titles from*
# *IEEE Computer Society Press*

## Simulation Validation:
## A Confidence Assessment Methodology
*by Peter L. Knepell and Deborah C. Arangno*

A systematic, procedural, and practical guide of applications for a variety of simulations. It is divided into three areas: concepts, methodologies, and special topics. The text differentiates between the assessment of a simulation tool and the verification and validation of general software products. It also discusses ways to tailor the methodology for particular situations and objectives and provides numerous assessment aids.

Sections: Introduction, Foundations, Assessment Activities, A Guide to Formal Assessments, A Guide to Limited and Maintenance Assessment, Man-In-The-Loop Model, Hardware-In-The-Loop Model, Assessment Aids, Glossary, References.

*160 pages. 1993. Hardcover. ISBN 0-8186-3512-6. Catalog # 3512-04 — $40.00  Members $30.00*

## Artificial Neural Networks:
## Concepts and Control Applications
*edited by V. Rao Vemuri*

Presents the essential concepts of neural networks and explores their applications to the control of dynamical systems. Each chapter of the book begins with an introductory commentary followed by a collection of papers that discuss the key concepts and introduce the applications for implementing these concepts.

Sections: Artificial Neural Networks: An Overview, Artificial Neural Networks: Architectures and Learning, Hopfield Nets and Applications, Back-Propagation and its Applications, Approximation and Learning, Adaptation and Self-Organization, Applications to Control Problems.

*520 pages. 1992. Hardcover. ISBN 0-8186-9069-0. Catalog # 2069-01 — $60.00  Members $45.00*

## Artificial Neural Networks:
## Concepts and Theory
*edited by Pankaj Mehra and Benjamin W. Wah*

Introduces terminology and classifications, contains recent key research papers, and provides pointers for further reading. In addition, the tutorial focuses on basic concepts, algorithms, and theoretical results emphasizing the complex interplay between abstract theoretical and practical design issues. All the techniques and concepts presented in the text reflect the current trends and directions for ANN research.

Sections: Introduction, Connectionist Primitives, Knowledge Representation, Learning Algorithms, Computational Learning Theory, Stability and Convergence, Empirical Studies.

*680 pages. 1992. Hardcover. ISBN 0-8186-8997-8. Catalog # 1997-01 — $70.00  Members $55.00*

## Knowledge-Based Systems:
## Fundamentals and Tools
*edited by Oscar N. Garcia and Yi-Tzuu Chien*

Details the characteristics of knowledge-based systems in 35 papers that explore rapid prototyping, knowledge engineering, representation paradigms, logical foundations, inferencing modes, verification and validation of knowledge bases, and languages, shells, and tools.

Sections: The Role of Knowledge Engineering; Knowledge — Its Symbolic Representation, Manipulation, and Inferencing; Logic, Logic Programming, and Prolog; Rule-Based Systems; Dealing with Uncertainty; Introduction to Learning and the Connectionist Approach; Knowledge Validation, Verification, and Utilization; Languages, Shells, and Tools; An Overview of Applications.

*512 pages. 1992. Softcover. ISBN 0-8186-1924-4. Catalog # 1924-01 — $56.00  Members $45.00*

 **IEEE COMPUTER SOCIETY**

▼  **To order call toll-free: 1-800-CS-BOOKS**  ▼

▼  **Fax: (714) 821–4641**  ▼

**10662 Los Vaqueros Circle**        **Los Alamitos, CA  90720-1264**        **Phone: (714) 821–8380**